Leading Tomorrow

Leading Tomorrow

How Effective Leaders Change Paradigms, Build Responsible Brands, and Transform Employees

Raj Aseervatham

Routledge
Taylor & Francis Group

A PRODUCTIVITY PRESS BOOK

Cover art concept courtesy of The Groundworks Lab: using repeating symbols reminiscent of early indigenous peoples' art forms, the cover shows a connected societal ecosystem made up of carbon-atom hexagonal shapes that permeate life on Earth. It shows the varying types of connectedness of people to organizations - customers, investors, employees, communities - and your presence as a leader with heart in that societal ecosystem.

First published 2021
by Routledge
600 Broken Sound Parkway #300, Boca Raton FL, 33487

and by Routledge
2 Park Square, Milton Park, Abingdon, Oxon, OX14 4RN

Routledge is an imprint of the Taylor & Francis Group, an informa business

ISBN: 9780367367596 (hbk)
ISBN: 9780367366230 (pbk)
ISBN: 9780429351259 (ebk)

Typeset in Minion
by Deanta Global Publishing Services, Chennai, India

For my darling Rayleigh
At the centre, always

Contents

Preface

When I graduated from university, I entered the business world right in the middle of an era of stunning corporate excess. It was the 1980s. Cinematic slogans like 'Greed is Good' captured a contemporary view of the ethics of big organizations. There was strong organizational lobbying against heeding warnings of climate change. Child labour was used by clothing and sports apparel manufacturers to reduce cost and increase throughput. The Exxon Valdez oil spill was yet to occur. Discrimination was a cultural norm in businesses, diversity was yet to be coined as a term and gender biases were tolerated and even celebrated. Complying with laws was preferable, but you got away with what you could to maximize profits. The internet was yet to become a household feature, and corporate secrets – even the open ones – were more easily kept.

Globalization was the name of the game, and the planet was our chessboard. Our businesses, our economies, roared ahead like V12 cars on a wide, flat straight, and we competed aggressively against all comers in a race to dominate. We measured success in terms of growth, profits, growth in profits and not much else.

We were offered no other world view of business success. Any misgivings I had about this perspective were easily swept away by the heady narcotic of shareholder returns and ballooning bonuses. Leaders used the term 'business is business' to create a broad exemption from societal expectations.

Early in my career, I was a project engineer for one of the largest mining corporations in the world. I saw with dismay (and was a part of) a normalized culture that tread a murky area between legality and ethics. Often, competitive advantages lay in these grey margins, and competitive disadvantages plagued the companies that would not navigate these margins. I knew this was not just in the big corporations. It was endemic across private and public organizations, large and small.

I was fortunate to learn, early in my career, that this norm was not sustainable in our society. I was privileged enough to watch an ethical scandal unfold around me as a large organization purposefully made decisions in securing a mining concession and contracts that, while meeting the laws of the time, would not – and could not – pass a hindsight test of right and wrong, of acceptable and unacceptable. Leaders far above my station – people I had looked up to with awe and had aspired to be like one day – were called to sit that test, and they failed. They failed in the eyes of their customers, their investors, and they failed in the eyes of employees like me. I do not know what happened to those leaders. They did not go to jail, for no legal wrong was committed. But they disappeared from my view, and – at least in that organization – efforts were made to expunge their legacy. They vanished from my aspirations.

Since then, for over three decades, I have worked for large, listed corporations in the stock exchanges of London, New York, Hong Kong, Johannesburg and Sydney, half of this time as an employee and executive, and the other half as a consultant. I have spent that time asking, and answering, a basic question. How should business organizations conduct themselves in society? The answer broadly lies with the ability of leaders to responsibly navigate an increasingly stakeholder-centric world in which those stakeholders care about much more than profits, growth and growth in profits.

For most of my career, I have followed a pattern of working for some time in a corporation, followed by some time as an external consultant, rinse and repeat. It has helped me chart a generation of change. It is a change that I believe will inevitably both grow and accelerate.

Through this time, I have watched, counselled or been a part of, many organizational leadership styles relating to this challenge for change. There have been the cynics of the need for change at all, the cynics of the practicality of achieving change, the leaders who want to look good but not necessarily lead genuine change, the leaders who want to make meaningful change but don't know how and the leaders that are taking courageous strides.

I have watched a one-way trend of accountability unfold. I have watched ethics and sensibilities shift. I have watched the primacy of shareholders gradually become overshadowed by the wider interests of a much broader representation of society. I have watched old paradigms of organizational leadership grapple with new and evolving wisdoms, winning some rounds and losing some, but relentlessly drifting in One compelling direction: greater responsibility and accountability.

Why does it seem to drift reluctantly and not stride purposefully? The pace of change in our society is frenetic. Our successful businesses and corporations generally pride themselves on being responsive – and even proactive – to change. And there is no doubt there are new demands every day for thoughtfulness, inclusivity and ethics in businesses, in corporations and in all types of organizations. They are applied to a very wide realm of issues such as climate change, anti-discrimination, human rights, governance and environmental stewardship. So what inertia exists that would sustain apathy or unclear leadership in these fields? What is responsible for not unlocking the wave of change that we sense is building behind a wall of historically implacable organizational conservatism?

I believe the key is within today's outgoing and tomorrow's incoming business leaders who can and will find themselves in a position to incite change. It is their ability to think more broadly, to empathize more widely and to find the courage to act on both, that is as yet unleashed. It is this personal ability, harnessed and multiplied across the tens or hundreds of millions of current and future business leaders, that has yet to come together to transform the way businesses, corporations and organizations work in society.

As a professional board director, I see many of our current and aspiring leaders. Often I witness them striving gamely but with insufficient guidance to drive and support an emerging culture of societal responsibility. It is for them that I wrote this book. If they are inspired to invoke change with their leadership, I believe our world will follow. I believe it is the leadership we need for tomorrow.

About the Author

Dr. Raj Aseervatham has more than 30 years of experience in government, private industry and consulting. He has worked across a broad range of sectors in North America, South America, Europe, Asia, the Pacific Region and Africa. His qualifications include a PhD in engineering and an MBA majoring in international projects. He has established multinational consulting sectors for one of the world's largest consulting firms, started and grown successful consulting enterprises, and provided strategic direction and governance on the boards of various organizations.

1

The Business Ecosystem

As every leader knows, the genius of true leadership lies in the navigation of change. It lies in the ability to anticipate what is ahead, even when it is foggy. It is the ability to marshal our people towards that destination that marks the virtues of a good leader. But what lies ahead changes all the time. The horizon does not remain fixed; it shifts and tilts every day. With nearly eight billion people on the planet, growing their own knowledge and insights against a backdrop of newly discovered challenges at an exponential rate, how can the horizon not change continually? How can we not re-anticipate our destinations, re-invent our strategies and re-form our plans iteratively as a result?

As we enter the third decade of this century, the magnitude of change seems, once again, unprecedented. There are changes precipitated by the future – for example, the threat of climate change, the growth of artificial intelligence and our continual extensions of the thresholds of space travel. There are changes precipitated by the past and present – for example, a pandemic, a reckoning of race and equality, and a broad realization that yesterday's models of being, and of leadership, may not work tomorrow.

While the change that affects us individually can alter the world within us, the amplified magnitude of change (when it affects us as a collective) has the potential to transform the world around us. A leader chooses, whether by being appointed to the leader's station or by volunteering through leadership action, to guide and support others through this everyday change. It is not a trivial task. It is neither one to engage in via autopilot, nor for the use of an outdated manual. It is not for the lazy or apathetic. The role of leadership is a purposeful, pivotal one.

Leadership, by definition, does not end with isolated personal action. It energizes a greater movement and a higher momentum. The impacts of good leadership and poor leadership spread like ripples on water. They spread through those that follow leaders. They spread through our communities, and they spread forward through time. In our world today, those impacts are increasingly evident when we look at organizations. Organizations dominate our ecosystem; they touch upon almost everything in our lives. Few individuals on Earth can claim total disconnection from an organization of some kind. There are, for example, businesses and corporations, who operate in our markets to fulfil the unmet needs of our communities; governmental organizations, charged with the management and regulation of business, corporations and the functioning of our communities; and intergovernmental organizations, which take on the task of aligning variances between the above parties and marshalling to the extent possible some common pathways to common horizons. The leaders of these organizations hold great responsibility because the impacts they initiate extend much further than their own employees, families and friends, and persist much longer than today and next year.

This book is about such organizations. Specifically, it is about the organizations that fuel our socio-economic prosperity. They are the businesses of the world, the organizations that bring us the products and services that we need, and the ones that we want. They are rewarded for this industrious endeavour because we the customers are willing to pay, directly or indirectly, for the utility that they bring to our lives. We are willing to pay for not just what it costs to bring the product or service to us but its actual value to us. We readily afford a benefit, profit or dividend to these organizations if the value of the utility meets with our approval. In our everyday economy, we will willingly pay various premiums for meeting our needs and our wants. We will seek competitive offerings from others who can bring these products and services. As consumers, we exercise our choices in a free market. Correspondingly, the organizations that cater to our needs and wants jostle for our attention. They are omnipresent because the products and services that we seek fill numerous large and small niches in our everyday lives, whether we are awake or sleeping. Business organizations have grown and prospered around meeting an evolving society's demands. They are, and have always been, a product of our expectations.

This book is about those organizations which, in aggregate and as a result of these demands, are deeply prevalent in our society. Every day, as humans, we connect directly or indirectly with a great number of these providers of products and services. We connect with them because the utility that they bring benefits us. Sometimes we connect with them knowingly, even mindfully. The communications providers we use, the supermarkets we shop at or the coffee that we buy are all consciously selected. Much more often, we connect without knowing or registering those connections. Think of the asphalt on the road that you travel on, the axles on the train, the swipe card you use or the electricity you turn on. We intersect with businesses every day. For some of us, the intersections are too many to count.

This book is about how deeply embedded those organizations are into the fabric of our society. It is about how decisions made in these organizations can cause ripple effects across a great many of the nearly eight billion people on this planet. Some are discernible as waves in our world, others are slight but have the potential to compound with other ripples to form these waves and a few create a staggering tsunami of effect. All of these organizations create ripples, just as all individuals do, albeit often at much larger scales. Some of the ripples are good, and some of the ripples are bad. Some of the ripples manifest immediately, while others take time to metastasize.

This book is about how important these organizations are to the future of society. It is about how their threads, woven deep into our human fabric, are integral to our societal prosperity in ways that far exceed the utility of the products or services they bring. It is about navigating an axis of change in how we recognize this power and this responsibility, and how we act upon it in a way that consistently privileges the good of our society and progressively suppresses the bad.

This book is about leading these organizations tomorrow. The leaders of these organizations, individually and collectively, will set cultures and make decisions that will shape those ripples that continue to fan out into society. As our world populates and interconnects, as its resources are asked to perform more with less to sustain humanity, those ripples have the potential to become larger, compound more readily and manifest in increasingly profound ways.

This book looks to tomorrow because there is ample evidence in society that the future leadership of our organizations can become better. It can be a greater good in our society than it has ever been in our history. There is plenty of room to surpass the past and present leadership of these organizations. We have not had a perfect record, far from it, in fact. But it is in our nature, as human beings, to improve. We learn from others in our past, we learn from those around us, and we learn from ourselves. We learn from our own mistakes, the mistakes of those around us and the mistakes of others in the past. We learn, too, from our successes, the successes of those around us and from those in our past. In the deepest parts of our psyche, we are interested not in regressing or treading water but in moving forward, evolving and improving. Striving for tomorrow is in our DNA.

If consumers are knitted inescapably into the fabric of business organizations, the reverse is also true. It is an obvious fact that a business cannot survive in a vacuum; it must coexist in society. The relationship is, through a complex matrix of direct and indirect overlaps, deeply co-dependent at its full scale. Businesses exist in a societal ecosystem. Yet it is an often glossed-over fact, or one that is sometimes taken for granted, like an aspect acknowledged so often and so automatically that it warrants little further thought. The ecosystem is real and multi-faceted. It is a fact that any business needs connectivity to a set of vital factors that can support, or erode, its success. Notably, at its core, it needs connectivity to markets, finance, resources and labour – four elements without which a successful business organization is difficult to conceive. It needs many other things too, such as inclusion in a communications network, technology, trade connections in the supply chain, logistics such as transport and storage among others, and, of course, a certain amount of goodwill.

Most business organizations catering to, and deriving their revenues from, business or retail consumers identify customers at the very centre of their existence. This is a logical perspective because without the buyer of the goods or services being provided, there is no nexus – the one represented by the transaction interface of buyer and seller – for a business to create its sustained energy from. Service-oriented terminology that has become commonplace in business wisdom – such as *the customer always comes first* – rings true because of that nexus. But there is a one-dimensionality to that well-aged saying. Society is not just made up of customers, although each one of us is a customer of some kind to someone. For every million customers of a business organization, there are hundreds of millions, and billions, of non-customers who share the same societal matrix. Even the largest multinational organizations cater to a customer population that is a humbling small fraction of society's population count.

For modern leaders, the trap of one-dimensionality – the myopia, unwillingness or inability to witness the complexity of a business organization's place in society – brings with it the loss of a broader perspective of the business ecosystem. In addition to business risks that this loss creates, there is a largely untapped value in both understanding and formulating strategies around this complex ecosystem. While there is beauty in simplicity, oversimplification, as every leader knows, is a dangerous practice to adopt. One-dimensional thinking can lead to losing what we have and not accessing what we could gain. Between these two failures of leadership, business organizations have much to lose, including their legitimacy in society, by not adopting an effective multidimensional view of the societal ecosystem in which they exist. Simple is good, but ignoring complexity is folly.

Many old-school leadership paradigms argue for focusing with a high degree of exclusivity on the essentials and in doing so keeping things simple. This would be a sustainable point of view if the world around us was also maintaining a level of relative simplicity and if the essentials were remaining constant. Neither is true. As this narrative will explore, the societal ecosystem around business organizations is getting more complex at a much higher rate than the products and services that are demanded by society. And that is really saying something because as we can see for ourselves with very little analysis, society's demands move at a staggering pace. Each year, and each decade, the number of essentials that society defines for itself increases. In our everyday lives we, as individuals, must consider and balance more aspiration, more abilities and more variables. We must navigate more complexity. And we know that this is not merely an outcome of our individual ageing and maturity; it is more fundamentally related to the pace and tangents of our societal evolution. It is no different for business organizations, except that the compounding and aggregating nature of these complexities increases both the challenge of the task and the stakes that it represents.

If there is a broad view that business organizational leaders are lagging behind this complexity and its pace of change, it is not without foundation. Failures of business leaders in our media are plentiful. We typically witness countless many in just one financial year. The rate of failure that is apparent to us is prolific. Further, we either know or suspect that there are many more invisible failures that do not make, or have not yet made, the media. Society points its finger accusingly at a litany of sins that are visible – bribery, corruption, environmental damage, social failures, tax evasion and many others. Every year there is a louder clamour for greater accountability and greater regulation around more and more of these issues. There is an escalation in negative sentiment; it is not lowering, nor is it staying constant. Little wonder that there are strong emerging views that business organization leaders are out of tune with a broader societal expectation. Trust in business organizations has endured a steady, and sometimes precipitous, decline for many decades. Worse, those views are prone to morphing into darker undercurrents; perspectives that leaders of our business organizations are, deliberately or through lack of care, shadowy enemies of society. How much lower can trust descend before the majority of people say 'enough'?

While conspiracy theories about the business world and its leaders might persist in broader society, the reality is not that dark. We have not had a systemic selection of business leaders on the basis of anti-societal traits, as some would accuse. Instead, we, as a society, have simply not paid sufficient attention to the role of business organizations (and its leaders) in the healthy evolution of humanity. This has played out in a low-level apathy towards creating an environment that strongly encourages positive contributions by the business sector to our world. It has fed a deep-seated reluctance across much of the business organizational landscape to do more than is absolutely needed to stay in the game. From a dearth of content in our educational systems teaching a more holistic style of leadership, to the handing down of corporate torches that burn with the flame of maximized profits and dividends, to the propensity for government and governance to step up in the later, rather than the pre-emptive, stages of the crisis, we have allowed our slide to proceed largely unchecked.

However, we are still learning, in the early stages of digitally advanced industrialization and connected consumerism, about the holistic skills of a business leader that are needed for tomorrow. We are still evolving. It may not be ideal, but it is nevertheless understandable that we are still not in tune with an appropriately broader perspective of leadership. We will presumably evolve for a long while yet as business leaders. And so the question is not so much *are we there yet?* as it is *where are we going?* How do we energize collective wills to check our slide and support the recovery of business leadership as a trusted actor in our search for a brighter future in a better world? While there is altruism to this question, there is also a pragmatic side to it. It is unlikely that a continuous slide of public opinion and trust in our business institutions can continue indefinitely. It is conceivable, perhaps even inevitable, that the population of our increasingly educated and increasingly aware world will, at some point, take profoundly better-organized action. That action may be customers exercising choices, society demanding more accountability and governments regulating with increasing force, or some combination of these. These are broadly undesirable interventions, particularly from the point of view of business organizations and their leaders. They represent a world of increasing constraints rather than a universe of increasing autonomy.

While customers may sit at the centre of the ecosystem for a leader who focuses heavily on the transactional nexus of supply and demand (of the goods or services), there is a much larger universe to consider. It is entirely possible to become myopically focused on the customer, and for the awareness of the broader ecosystem to fade into the peripheral vision of a business. It would be an enormous business risk for a business leader to relegate the customer to the periphery, and that is not the suggestion here. But it is also true to say that this inability to access an ecosystem view plays out as a true business risk no matter how customer-focused you are.

The scope and impact of this risk gathers momentum with each passing year because the ecosystem as we know it is becoming more interconnected. The speed with which information is transferred, linked and transformed to insights around the ecosystem is increasing. There are resonances between parts of the ecosystem that were once distanced from each other. We can readily imagine that there are future resonances which are, as yet, barely felt as connections. There are connections between parts of the business ecosystem that have rapidly strengthened, and continue to strengthen, in the digital age. This fluid interplay between the parts of today's and tomorrow's business ecosystems places greater emphasis on evolved leadership. It is a leadership that grasps, connects, responds to and strategizes around both the parts and the evolving sum of the parts of the business ecosystem.

2

New Leaders

It has been a while – perhaps some decades – since the first, and somewhat constrained, concept of a good business became limited and obsolete. That basic concept was first made a cornerstone of business theory by the renowned economist Milton Friedman, who famously held the view that a business's sole responsibility (after abiding by the law) is to generate profits for its shareholders. Friedman, who received a Nobel Prize in 1976 for his economic theories, grounded as they were in the architecture of a free capitalist market, nevertheless created an unspoken and potentially unhelpful paradigm for the sustainability of business wisdom. Its emphasis on a near-solitary focus on profitability helped defined a purpose that still lives today in the critical discourses around the nature of modern businesses. Barbecue conversations today continue to be peppered with common views that (bad) businesses only want to make profits. Indeed, even without labelling a business as 'bad', there is an underlying narrative in society that businesses are unhealthily thirsty for profits, to the extent that profitability becomes the primary purpose and overshadows others. Even if, as common sense would dictate, elevating profitability to a sole purpose is too narrowly focused and other purposes should be integrated, this deeply embedded theory of business has the effect of placing profitability at the top of the business hierarchy of outcomes. All too often it plays out in the prevailing discourse in for-profit organizations (why *are* they called that?) and, even when deliberately played down in open conversation for fear of appearing too margin-hungry, is palpable in their cultures.

An alternative perspective, and one that has been around for nearly as long in a less celebrated way, is that if a business's purpose is to fulfil a societal need, and it does so satisfactorily, it will more likely than not be profitable. Clearly, this perspective requires a leader to identify what creates the foundations for business success and to believe that these foundations are highly likely to drive profitability. Schools of thinking have long since pivoted to this alternative perspective, but the supremacy of profitability lives on in business DNA, glimpsed through the key performance indicators and remuneration drivers of our time. There is nothing intrinsically wrong with profitability, of course. It contributes to both business health and to a broader economy. However, as a general condition in our construct of the temple of capitalism, business culture still looks to profitability as the high priest. As such, that metric wields considerable power in decision-making.

But of course, in a world underpinned by shareholders, it is not just profitability that drives behaviours. If it did, the problem would be simpler to address. There is *competitive* profitability – the edge that draws the greatest investments towards the organizations that can convert such investments into the greatest, most consistent returns. After all, given a choice of three companies in the pharmaceutical industry, why would the consistently greater-performing business (defined by profits and dividends) not attract the most capital?

Our alternative view – that fulfilling a societal need in a responsible manner pre-empts, as a logical outcome, profits for its shareholders – is not new in modern business philosophies. It is also theoretically sound. There are practical examples of its efficacy in our global economy, and many examples of the damage that businesses might incur if profitability is placed before these fundamental principles of business. Yet Friedman's doctrine remains strongly within our leadership cultures, if not as distilled as it was back in the last century, at least still deeply embedded in the tertiary institutions that shape our economic leaders. The doctrine is deeply interwoven into the laws and practices of businesses that have merely evolved from the early days of the industrial revolution, and not transformed. Our business organizations often work within a re-conditioned engine that has compounded old, and perhaps redundant, wisdom with newer insights. Business and economic leaders are products of a system that has many outdated parts as well as newer and more contemporary parts. The older aspects function as inhibitors to positive change. It will take mindful dismantling and reconstitution of business leadership models to replace unhelpfully dated paradigms with more useful new ones.

But the system within which our contemporary business wisdom works is not necessarily an automated one that we are doomed to rotate through. The business ecosystem is a very human construct. The four pillars of markets, finance, resources and labour are owned by individuals and collections of individuals. People, whether in the midst of or at the very end of a customer chain, dominate the markets. The providers of capital are, ultimately, individuals and collections of individuals who seek to gain value from finances risked, directly or indirectly, in the business. Resources are apportioned to people, groups of people or organizations comprising people. The decisions made about such apportionments are made by people, and decision-makers may have been elected to those offices by other people. Our labour structures, even with the long-foretold horizon of artificial intelligence or machine learning well upon us, are still for the majority human, and – at least for the next few decades – those structures will be shaped and dictated by humans.

In addition to these elements of the business ecosystem, there are strands of connectivity that permeate value chains. These are business-to-business relationships, which run like a root system from the end product or service, down through its key components and the sub-components that make up the key components, and on downward through the chain to the raw materials or services that begin the value chain. Business standards run like links of DNA through these strands of connectivity, often initiated from the end product or service, defining and shaping the do's and don'ts that are normative in that value chain. In addition to product or service quality, there are ethical business norms, such as the abolishment of child labour in the supply chain or the removal of harmful chemicals, which are made applicable through mindful decisions and ongoing governance. Business-to-business relationships are the infectious conduits of evolving standards and expectations. The infections can be slow because they are hampered by negotiated contracts between individual businesses that take time to re-shape around new norms. They can also be fast, particularly as new norms are validated formally, such as through security exchanges and trading hubs, or legislated for or even strenuously requested by customers. Whether fast or slow, they can represent an inexorably powerful set of currents within the business ecosystem because of the vastness and value of the business-to-business connectivity that exists, increasingly densely, around the world.

Business leadership is only a slave to its older paradigms for as long as it chooses to remain so. Fierce resistance to change may occur in pockets, but it is by no means universal. On the contrary, there is largely apathetic and passive inertia. We require an energized pivot to a leadership style that is more attuned to human expectations within the business ecosystem. We await a predominant business leadership style that responds to the expectations with agility and is both insightful and foresighted enough to anticipate evolving expectations. We have already begun to exercise this pivot on issues such as gender diversity and equity, on bullying and harassment, on employee health and well-being, and others. Our challenge is to upscale these pivots to a broader range of societal factors.

This style of leadership requires a helicopter view of the business ecosystem. It requires more than just an ability to survey the broad and complex landscape from a sufficiently high vantage point; it predicates a keen insight into the risks and priorities that can be seen, glimpsed or inferred from that height. Such a style of leadership is no doubt still functionally underpinned by the requisite mechanical skills of running a business. But it is also substantially enhanced by more multi-faceted wisdom about a rapidly changing, interconnecting and aware world. This new wisdom and leadership insight are not just inevitable in time if the risks in the business ecosystem are to be meaningfully managed but increasingly necessary for the strategic insights that underpin business success in a competitive environment. The businesses that can adapt fast enough are more likely to survive than the ones that cannot. The ones that anticipate well enough are more likely to thrive and prosper.

Of course, this anticipation and this adaptation will not happen by accident. Nor, for businesses that seek to lead in their fields, can it happen at a slow evolutionary pace, because both the changes and the connectivity in the business ecosystem have the distinct hallmarks of rapid acceleration. It will need mindful change that is both purposeful and urgent. In turn, this will require leaders who believe in that change and are able to effect it in a viral, rather than a department-by-department, fashion.

The breed of leaders that can do this has unprecedented value. It is a breed of leadership that has the ability to read and deal with external complexity and continually shifting stakeholder expectations, not simply in a public relations sense but with their ability to imagine, forge and implement a business strategy that capitalizes on such insights. This breed of leaders is increasingly sought after and valued today. It is likely to be the leadership model of the future.

The older leadership beliefs that result in a separation of values and culture between what happens in a company and what happens in the surrounding business ecosystem can only survive when there is limited connectivity across the ecosystem. That time is nearly past. The outdated mantra that *what happens in the company stays in the company* is less and less likely to hold in a global condition within which connection and connectivity are the operative rules of business life. Leadership that seeds and encourages authentic connectivity to, and empathy with, the business ecosystem will have the ability to transform cultures away from the older patterns and into the emerging needs of contemporary businesses. Leaders who can, within their own leadership and managerial ranks, create cultural transformations that resonate with the business ecosystem will be valued higher and higher. Those that precipitate not just a new form of internal awareness and judgement within the organization but energize a genuine pivot into a stakeholder-centric world are more likely to shepherd true integration of businesses in the business ecosystem.

3

A Call for Change

It is relatively easy to hold onto a belief that real change needs a shock to precipitate it. Because of the unsettling nature of change, we are prone to hope for, and believe in, the fiction that the status quo has a longer shelf life than it actually does. As a result, we shirk proactive change. We wait for the pressure to change. There is a good reason that the pressure for such a change is highly likely to occur and with it energize an increase in momentum the further it goes. The world we are in today, interconnected as it is, faces societal pressures that are different in type and scale from the pressures faced ever before. While in the past, thermonuclear conflict and world wars appropriately dominated our attention, today they are being joined by other existentialist threats. Shifting geopolitics has precipitated, and has in turn been precipitated by, a rise in both terrorism and discernible shifts to the right in Western political persuasions. Global populations are climbing, with follow-on demographic shifts that, like the tide, are both predictable and seemingly unavoidable. Threats to human health loom as our physical ecosystem strains at the seams and releases disease and infection. Meanwhile medical advances occur at unprecedented rates, extending lifespans and changing our individual and collective perspectives of the future.

Economic power bases have decentralized, moving away from the Western hemispheres and into Asia. Globalization and nationalization lock horns again, forcing hybrids of economy to emerge that we have never seen before. Climate variables are different now than they have been for centuries, with resulting local and regional weather patterns showing increasing signs of volatility, greater extremes and lower predictability – heralding challenges for food production patterns, resource availability, existing infrastructure and logistics. In short, the world today is more fraught with angst than in the past – at a geographical scale not seen before, if we subtract armed global conflicts such as the two world wars of the twentieth century.

To separate this trend from the business world is both naïve and unhelpful and potentially damaging to our world. If we assume that these issues fall within the purview of the government alone, we ignore a clear and unavoidable fact. The publicly and privately funded economy – the one populated by corporations, small- and medium-sized businesses and traders of all types – collectively taps into the world of supply and demand to create our economy. Any of the threats mentioned above has the ability to constrain or damage business sustainability, either directly or indirectly.

A useful snapshot for business leaders to hold in their minds is the composition of the global economy. Global gross domestic product is largely derived from three areas of activity: agriculture, products and services. The contribution to GDP from products has traditionally been around a half of the contribution from services, and agriculture occupies a relatively modest – but mission-critical – space in our global economy (Figure 3.1).

The apathy towards societal well-being that runs through much of modern business organizations is sometimes articulated in *it's not our job* terms. *It is not our job to look after society's issues; that is what governments are for.* Indeed, the role of the government in putting in place the priorities and policies that facilitate this action is undisputed. However, the abdication of action by business organizations to governments implies that there is a zero-sum game at work. It implies that the footprints created through the process of bringing products and services to society can be managed through the efforts of the government alone. The phrase *that is why people pay taxes* is often used to buttress this point of view. However, this line of thinking would, if it ran free, allow us to surmise that the sum of all societal burdens created by the delivery of products and services to society could be mopped up by taxes.

There are four constraints associated with this train of thought. Firstly, it separates the roles of business and government into two camps. Business is free (within the confines of the law) to create and ignore societal burdens that will, in turn, be borne by the government (or society, if the government does not have the means). Secondly, it does not account for how this might work; for example, if societal burdens are increased,

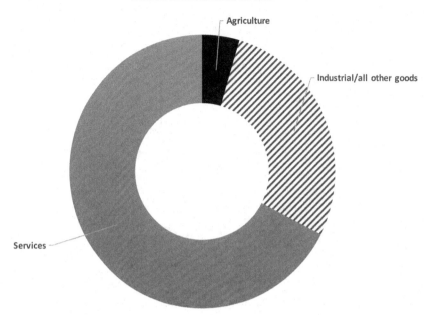

FIGURE 3.1
Global contributors to GDP.

should taxes also increase? If so, how should it be split between individuals and corporations? And where does that line of evolution end? Thirdly, the reality of our global economic construct is such that on average (in OECD countries, at least, for which the data is dependable), taxes amount to around a third of the gross domestic product (Figure 3.2), and we have shown for over a century that this has never been enough to mop up the collateral damage of economic growth. And fourthly, tax regimes are individually sovereign constructs, with the result that the focuses and effectiveness of tax regimes vary widely from country to country. In turn, this makes it highly unlikely that abdicating responsibility to the government will have any dependably positive global outcome. Instead, we can expect substantial variations from country to country. Therefore, the underlying argument separating business and society, one that has been a staple of business organizational dialogue for many decades, is not a sustainable one. While it draws on some classical logic, it is not a helpful stance to adopt if one intends to genuinely consider the role of business in a societal ecosystem that manages to hold some kind of equilibrium. It

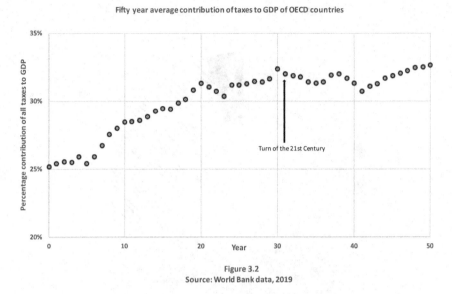

Figure 3.2
Source: World Bank data, 2019

FIGURE 3.2
History of tax contribution to GDP in OECD countries.

merely results in more public taxes being required to address the footprints left by businesses. The alternative is, clearly, smaller business footprints.

Governments that resist this realization, striving to allow businesses to flourish in the magical free market of unfettered growth while propping them up with taxes and subsidies, cannot do so forever. For a very few countries with significant socialist policies, taxes are almost 50 per cent of the GDP. For many poorer countries, the percentage is much less than the average, to a low of well under 20 per cent. Over the last fifty years, taxes as a fraction of GDP have grown in the OECD countries from an average of around a quarter to about a third. This possibly reflects an evolving public view of the role of the government around aspects of basic human amenity, which might slowly increase funding for those aspects. However, part of this growth can be attributed to an increasing defence budget in many of the OECD countries. Since the middle of the twentieth century and through the period of the Cold War late in that century, funding for defence activities has increased dramatically and represents some of the observed fifty-year growth in taxes relative to GDP. Defence and nationalist leanings aside, the world is not inclined to continually raise public taxes to cover social and environmental inequities propagated in the business world.

A common public misconception is that corporate taxes and royalties form the lion's share of funding for governmental efforts. This may be truer in less developed economies where personal tax revenues are low, but it is nevertheless generally misleading no matter where in the world is examined. The median range of corporate income taxes relative to total tax revenues has remained reasonably consistent for more than two decades at between 7 and 12 per cent in the OECD countries. In the debate of who pays taxes to reduce the footprints of our businesses, there is a great deal more headroom in corporate taxes than there is in public taxes. And no business leader wants to be part of a collective drive in that direction; it is bound to slowly remove autonomy, increase forced accountability and almost certainly increase business costs. Raising prices of goods and services to pass these on to the public is also not a sustainable solution because an increasingly-educated public is unlikely to absorb that in perpetuity.

A sizeable proportion of the flows of money in a global economy, which incur taxes at various points in the flow path and at various rates depending on a country's taxation policies, can be traced back to economic activities precipitated by or actioned in the private sector. Put differently, if the private sector did not exist in its current form, the tax processes applied today could not fund the public activities that currently occur. As it stands, within the OECD, the combination of personal taxes, social security contributions and taxes on goods and services forms the vast majority (around 80 per cent) of total tax revenues. Public consumerism is a significant part of the engine of most of the tax systems.

This point is often used by business leaders to show that the private sector, by virtue of fuelling and meeting public consumerism, is already adding significant value to the world; it is, indeed, serving humanity. If one squints hard enough, a case for 'good citizenship' can be made merely on the basis of adding value to society by producing enough (or more) to meet society's needs. In this oversimplified paradigm, a business organization's job is done as long as it produces its goods or services, apart perhaps from some optional philanthropic activities. However, the deep and endemic connectivity between how the business world functions and how society functions makes it difficult to hold that separatist argument, except at a very philosophical, transparently self-interested and simplified level.

To divorce, or even moderately separate, the business organizations' sector from societal issues is an artificial separation. Collectively, the sector economy has both a large causative footprint and a large impact to navigate. Much of the momentum in footprint or impact is created or exacerbated by decisions made in this sector. From a helicopter view it is neither immune to nor exonerated from where societal conditions migrate as a result of our communal evolution.

These facts do not go unnoticed by society at large. Leadership of the private sector economy is more and more likely to be called to account for its significant part in societal well-being. The illusion of the separation from a broader society that many external stakeholders perceive the business world has deliberately designed is, as time goes on, more likely to be diluted. As this happens, the deep interconnectivity in the business ecosystem will more readily be acknowledged and focused upon by a much broader cross-section of stakeholders. They come from the worlds of consumers, trade, finance, investment, resource management and employment and others. As that happens, pressure on business leadership from these multiple pillars, and others, is likely to mount. An aloof business leadership style that distances itself from the clear enmeshing of business with society is less and less likely to ring true. There will be greater calls for business involvement in, and even accountability for, societal concerns.

This trend has already begun. Two decades into the new millennium, it is discernible, if not yet mainstream. Once this momentum takes hold, there is no reason for it to stop. There is no readily apparent ceiling at which it should plateau until the fate of business organizations and the fate of society are linked in a much more co-dependent manner.

The source of pressure does not just stop there. The business world, by its own proclamations and by the countless examples of outcomes reaching back well over a century, holds sizeable intellectual power in solving social problems. Meeting societal needs, a cornerstone of business purpose, has been repeatedly put into practice by the private sector. Vast fortunes have been made in this way. The business world has done this through thought leadership and innovation. It has applied try-and-fail and try-and-succeed grit, inherited knowledge and organizational memory. It has done these many hundreds of thousands of times, beginning before the industrial revolution. The business sector has not held a monopoly on this, as the public sector has also often been the source of solutions to society's problems. Yet business clearly holds the numbers if this was a competition between the two sectors. If business abdicates from being a genuinely engaged part of solutions, society at large might feel compelled to express its growing outrage. There would be pressure to get involved. In the latter part of the second decade of the twenty-first century there has been mounting evidence of this building pressure. While there is no consensus on whether, or if, there is a tipping point for this pressure, there is no denying its existence and trending growth. It is a warning rumble.

The magnitude of the pressure is - even today - evident and large, and increasing. The Global Risks Report, an annually updated assessment by the World Economic Forum, has been in circulation since 1995. This report, the contents of which can be contextualized to an individual country level or de-aggregated to regional levels, attempts to capture these risks. Like all such endeavours, a great deal of scientific and non-scientific thought and effort goes into capturing the issues that might impact society at scale. And like all such works, individual perceptions and predispositions may affect how much stock is placed in it. However, there is a great diversity of thoughts and opinions – of both people and organizations – that are regularly synthesized thoughtfully to provide an overview of the risks to our global economy. Its key aspects have not varied substantially for many years; the simplified picture at the turn of the third decade of the twenty-first century, in January 2020, is shown in Figure 3.3.

In addition to the rankings – which are segmented by how likely the risk is and how consequential it is to the world – it is worth noting the interdependencies. Water and climate have interdependencies, as do migration and agriculture. All four segments are connected in several

High impact, low likelihood:
- Weapons of mass destruction
- Infectious diseases
- Food crises
- Financial failure
- Information infrastructure breakdown
- Financial failure

High impact, high likelihood:
- Climate change
- Extreme weather
- Biodiversity loss
- Water crises
- Natural disasters
- Cyber attacks

Low impact, low likelihood:
- Unemployment
- Critical infrastructure failure
- Adverse technological advances
- Terrorist attacks
- State collapse

Low impact, high likelihood:
- Data fraud or theft
- Asset bubbles
- Involuntary migration
- Social instability
- National governance failure

FIGURE 3.3
Top global risks in each category (from Global Risks Report, 2020).

dimensions. These connections between the various risks highlight a very important layer within the business ecosystem: the issue of co-dependent risks, sub-risks and domino effects that result from one risk being triggered at a given threshold. The complexity of the connections between the risks is important. This is not just because it hints at the world economy's exposure to forces that might conspire to collapse it like a house of cards. More usefully, it helps provide high-level insights into how a company's place in the business ecosystem exposes it to some of these risks. It shows how its position in the business ecosystem potentially inoculates it from other risks. Additionally, it hints at how co-existing and compounding risks might affect its overall stability.

What is not included in this Global Risks Report map is how the different stakeholders that are important to a business' prosperity are potentially affected by these same risks. This is a critical issue for leadership to examine, in order to understand how the risks might play out within the business's own ecosystem and therefore where efforts might be prioritized, socialized or co-ordinated. In addition to providing a view of global risk, it permits a useful view of how society's concerns might interface with the business's own footprint.

In the past, with fewer existential threats crowding society's horizon, society's approach to the business's place in societal welfare was predictable. It adopted at face value a *do-no-harm* approach. Where this was impractical, as was the case in many settings, the approach was modified to a *you-can-do-manageable-harm-but-no-more* setting. 'Manageable harm' was, in most cases, defined by the law.

This approach acknowledged that a certain amount of responsibility was necessary. It was clearly unacceptable to profit while ruining the world, for example, or cheating customers, or engaging in labour practices that infringed on the fundamental rights of human beings. Business ethics, and the policy and regulatory directions that followed, revolved around not being destructive to society. They defined a set of negative actions to avoid. They did not actively engage with the notion of helping solve a growing number of society's greater problems. There was no broad compunction to engage in positive actions, other than discretionary philanthropic efforts.

As society came to terms with the speed and size of the business economy, it recognized that there were more responsibilities that required attention. The number of responsibilities was elastic, stretching on seemingly indefinitely. In some cases, this occurred simply because some impacts of businesses went unrecognized for a while. There was a legitimate process of discovery, characterized by the repeated identification of impacts after they had occurred. The learning process was mainly evident in the government and the civil society, rather than within the businesses themselves. Policies, laws and regulations began to evolve. This set up an initial divide between businesses and regulators. It set the scene for many decades of cat-and-mouse interactions between businesses and regulators. To no small degree it contributed to a culture in which businesses tried to get away with what they could. This 'real world' game, as it is frequently referred to, is depicted as a 'fair' battle of wits, in which society is the gradual loser. It is an embedded part of the majority of business cultures around us. Business universally considers increasing regulations as an insidious tide constraining competitive sharpness, and society is at a loss as to what else to do but strengthen regulations.

In other cases, the discovery or responsibility occurred because the expectations of society migrated from where they used to be to new levels. This migration is a normal pattern of social evolution. It is in human nature to seek improvements in the decisions of our past. A constant recalibration of what is acceptable is a predictable aspect of our species. These characteristics, sometimes referred with some irritation as 'policy creep' or 'regulatory creep' by some in business organizations, are seen to be like moving the goalposts. Yet they are a perfectly natural feature of societal development and should be expected. Failing to foreshadow a tendency for this to happen is a failure of leadership to recognize a basic societal behavioural trait. It is a staple of the societal ecosystem in which business organizations operate.

Some of these expectations have, over time, been ensconced in law and regulation. Others accrue in the waiting line of society's expectations and in the administrative queues, advocacy lounges and counter-advocacy parlours of political decision-making. The file of growing expectations is perennial. We would be naïve to expect society to function any differently.

This rolling process is also part of our societal ecosystem. There is leisurely, incremental clarification of existing and new expectations of business. This is followed by some step change in governance control, typically expressed in policies or regulations. Regulations are tightened and penalties are raised if there are too many actors in the business ecosystem who do not comply. This machine has been, for over a century, characteristic of how society has expressed its expectations of the business world.

There have been few – but not zero –cataclysmic events of global note to precipitate such processes. However, there have been many locally and regionally impactful disasters that have triggered consideration of laws and regulations. These have sometimes been enacted at the local level and sometimes broadly embraced in multiple jurisdictions. Where the disasters have been recognized as events-in-waiting in other parts of the world, similar policies and regulations have been implemented. Often these local and regional disasters have actually occurred elsewhere, scaffolding the impetus for introducing policies or regulations in several jurisdictions.

Generally, though, there has never before been the growing and sustained sense of societal urgency that is now being felt. This point of inflexion in society's relationship with the business world is an important cue to note and act upon. This point of inflexion is perceived by global communities as a shift in the pace and intensity of dissatisfaction with the historical status quo. The shift has happened within a short time span, perhaps in the last 10 years of the preceding 150. The convergence of attitudinal shifts is unprecedented, and it is seen in the socio-political changes that have occurred in the twenty-first century. And, as the next sections of this book highlight, the human faces of the various stakeholders have changed. These are important tides and undercurrents for business leaders to be aware of.

Without a searching, critical evaluation of the external world, a business can very easily fall into a lethargic and dangerously naïve mode of inadequate preparedness and dismissive leadership. It is tempting to ignore the signs as being peripheral to business and perhaps even a fad. There is comfort in rationalizing the signs as slow; more like a tide than a tsunami. At the current and historical rates of observed agitation, particularly relative to the average CEO's tenure in an organization, it is tempting to de-prioritize. It seems prudent to wait and watch, a bit longer, perhaps.

However, in doing so there is insufficient attention given to the rapidly interconnecting world. This connectivity could quite easily accelerate collective tensions and concerns. But could this phenomenon genuinely crystallize as a company threat?

It is a fair question; are customers and investors really likely to walk away from key products or services, or would they put up with unsavoury business behaviours in the face of societal angst? Perhaps, as some business leaders hope, it is easy and cost-effective to move into public relations mode. After all, it has worked well in the past, where social media were less prevalent and the key channels of communication could be dominated more easily. The inertia against change is mired in these considerations.

For enlightened business leaders, it will seem more authentic and genuinely strategic to pivot business organizations towards this new paradigm. But it *is* a new paradigm, and many business leaders – even with thirty, forty or fifty years of experience behind them – have not necessarily been schooled in terms of this emerging world. They have not practised in earnest within this new, deeply interconnected and increasingly dynamic paradigm. Indeed, they may even be too comfortable in their long-learned ways to generate the appropriate energy and urgency to catalyse change, for it requires change, individually and collectively within an organization, to refocus. The term 'transformation', used to refresh, renew and even re-purpose business organizations, applies here. Change is also required in the co-ordination between organizations, to create collective momentum and avoid wallowing in small, regressive waves of micro-change that accumulate to progressively shackle businesses. Bad actors ruin it for the good ones, and so peer pressure gains greater relevance. The change is less tactical and more strategic; it is less programmatic and more cultural. And this change may need a different mindset and style of leadership.

Before looking at the mindset of leaders, it is of value to look for insights among business's stakeholders. They collectively form the societal ecosystem that exists adjacent to business organizations. Without synergistic connections between business organizations and these stakeholders, the sustained prosperity of businesses falls into doubt. The next chapters make some observations of key stakeholder groups: investors, customers, employees and the communities to which they all belong.

4

Investors

For all its imperfections and its unfortunate side effects, capitalism has fuelled societal progress in a great many ways – health, education, communication and quality of life are just a few. Capitalism sustains itself partly because it leverages finance to fuel the investment in progress. The motivation to leverage finance lies in the creation of wealth – a motivation that is owned by the investment community. Whether it is you or I, as individuals, or investment brokers who aggregate the wishes of millions of investors, the motivation is broadly the same.

The amount of capital available to leverage is not infinite. While there is around $5 trillion in circulating currency in the global economy, the actual amount of capital that is employed around the world is much higher. This employed money is called broad money. Some two decades into the twenty-first century, it stands somewhere in the vicinity of $100 trillion or higher, and it is continually growing. It sits in assets and equities, in bank accounts on digital ledgers, and is represented in currencies both physical and digital and in other repositories in the financial system. This finance is available to be utilized via lending and recovery ebbs and flows. The vast majority of capital employed around the world is investment-based, meaning that when it is employed, a return or profit on its use is sought.

The spectrum of investors ranges from individual investors with personal savings through to institutional investors who access aggregated components of the world finance market and put this capital to some use. The capitalist system abhors 'lazy money', because it is a mark of inefficiency. As a result, the amount of energy that is at play at any given moment within the financial markets to leverage money is enormous.

The term 'access to capital' is, for a business, the ease with which this vast bank of monetary resources can be tapped into, to further the aspirations of that business. This ease is determined by the investment community. The holy grail of investment is to achieve the greatest returns with the lowest risks. If a business requires capital to fulfil a powerful market need, and the risks associated with bringing a product or service to market is low, it represents an intrinsically attractive proposition. In such situations, access to capital might be high and the business may be spoilt for choice in how it gains the finance required to further its agenda.

Without good access to capital, the direction and scale of what a business can achieve is curtailed to what its own resources can be employed to do. In a global economy, characterized by the constant invention and re-invention of products and services to satisfy constantly changing consumer demands at an ever- larger scale driven by more emerging economies bringing more customers to the market, access to capital is particularly critical to businesses at the bigger end of town.

As the global population treks towards eight billion, there are five age-based tranches of investors that dominate the age demographics of our society. These tranches are more evident in the wealthier economies, which unsurprisingly contribute the larger share of the funds into the global economy. The tranches are also visible in emerging economies, although typically in the younger demographics, and not necessarily with the same hallmarks of behaviour that are noted in the wealthier economies.

These tranches are important to our global economy because they allow us to track the generational shifts of wealth, and how that investment power has been, and might be, used. It is worth noting broadly definitive characteristics of these tranches, as they provide valuable insights into where investment preferences may shift over time. They provide useful perspectives on why investment behaviours of the past were what they were. They provide reasons for the shifts that have been observed. And, most importantly, they tell us that investment behaviours change, and that we must be prepared for change.

These characteristics are, of course, generalist and, like all generalizations, are subject to a great many evidences to the contrary. However, they illustrate trends and tides in the business ecosystem that, despite all the smaller counter-flow eddies and currents that may exist, still represent the dominant macro scene.

Let us begin with the oldest investor cohort. Reaching the end of their natural lifespans, the Silent Generation investors were born between 1925 and 1945. The youngest of this generation are between the ages of seventy-five to eighty-five as the world passes through the third decade of the twenty-first century. This generation, born into the depression years between two tumultuous world wars, is called the Silent Generation because in the households of that era, children were meant to be seen and not heard. The few of the Silent Generation left in the workplace today are typically senior advisers, partners in law firms, bankers, directors and the like. Their accumulation of wealth occurred in the 1970s through the 1990s, typically through steady, industrious application of their skills and knowledge in their chosen careers.

The Silent Generation's investment choices were largely steady. Once invested in a vehicle, funds tended to stay invested in that vehicle. The Silent Generation grew up in an era where loyalty was highly prized, and the careers of this generation are often marked by long tenures at single businesses. Loyalty was often rewarded by promotions and positions of leadership. In corollary, the Silent Generation's investment characteristic is often to stay the course in traditional industries. Application, rather than purpose, was celebrated in the business cultures of those times, and the investment choices of the Silent Generation often followed businesses that, whether they were good or dubious for society, exuded brands of hard work and diligence in delivering their products or services to the public. Adversity held little fear for the Silent Generation, who would see downward swings in the fortune of their investment choices as a natural part of business life. Their pride in loyalty, buttressed by this resilience for adversity, saw the Silent Generation play out an investment role of dogged, sometimes even stubborn, stability in the financial markets even during times of economic turbulence, such as those that accompanied the Korean and Vietnam Wars.

The next oldest and most substantial investor group on the planet comprise Baby Boomers. They were born between 1946 and 1964, and many enter retirement in the first three decades of this century. They are the post–World War 2 children, born during a time when the wealthier nations of the Western economy were recovering from the trauma of global instability and great economic uncertainty. One outcome of this post-war era was population growth. There was also industrial growth, as the countries most able to step forward began the process of rebuilding infrastructure, economies and livelihoods. Technological advancements flourished during the post-war peacetime, stimulated by a renewed populist vigour for quality of life. International trade resumed and grew, finding its way into more effective supply-and-demand relationships, trade agreements, accords and other connectivities that paved the way for regional, inter-regional and eventually global economies.

During the time of the Baby Boomers, there was a far greater sense of lifestyle optimism, particularly in Western economies. This was accompanied by a perceptible shift in consumerism. These together fed the business world with opportunity, which was duly capitalized upon. The generation of Baby Boomers, who account for around twenty per cent of the population in Western economies, currently holds a disproportionately high percentage of these economies' wealth. During the time of unprecedented business growth and pension plans for young employees between the 1950s and the 1980s, a strong foundation was set among Baby Boomers for a reasonable retirement.

Baby Boomers were schooled in a work-hard-for-success ethic and conditioned in an age of business growth that placed, at its central focus, the need to meet rapidly growing demands. Their investment lenses have similar characteristics. Baby Boomers, now entering their twilight years, are not renowned for bringing to the investment scene a deep desire for creating a better world. Theirs is the generation that accumulated property wealth, a trait celebrated in the massively popular board game of their times, Monopoly. They are more focused on returns on investment, with at best a secondary regard for whether or not there is a societal downside to said investments. Baby Boomers often attract bad publicity for their sometimes-unkindly-attributed rape-and-pillage attitude to economic growth, but conversely, history is often an unflinching mirror. Today, as a society, we bemoan the irreversible decisions made by captains of industry and leaders of government in the second half of the last century.

The leadership culture of Baby Boomers was characterized by a thirst for business growth and the gaining of economic power. It was coupled with both a low curiosity towards, and a high tolerance for, collateral societal damage. The leadership culture flowed from predominantly male business leaders through their predominantly male workforces naturally. It forged a generation that, within the investment community, is well known for its no-nonsense attitude to the utilization of capital.

In the investment arena, Baby Boomers are overwhelmingly male. Because the wealth flows in this time came from Western industry, the term 'pale, male and stale' is often used in slightly denigrating terms to characterize this tranche. However, the colloquialism is not without its insights. In contrast to some of the other tranches, there is a strong investor flavour representative of values that might be described as conservative. There is a strong and deep appetite for the utilization of capital in tried-and-true, safe investments with the highest return feasible. Thus, for example, it is unsurprising to see a higher proportion of Baby Boomer funds utilized in fossil fuels, manufacturing and other familiar business activities that were successful in the latter part of the twentieth century and continue to display a considerable footprint in today's economy. The case for change in investments does not naturally rest with Baby Boomers.

As Baby Boomers enter the end of their lifespans there are some notable adjustments in the investment fraternity. Firstly, women tend to outlive men by between five and ten years. Given the societal trend of a probable three-to-seven-year age gap between the typically older men and younger women in Baby Boomer marriages, there is a gender shift of Baby-Boomer wealth continuously occurring, from expiring men to surviving female spouses and partners. This shift is slightly more pronounced in light of the societal acceptability of divorce and remarriage that emerged in the 1970s, and the continuation and even enhancement of the age differences between older men and younger female partners. There are more shifts of wealth from older Baby Boomer men towards slightly to significantly younger Baby Boomer women.

The shift of this relatively large volume of wealth between genders is notable, as there are – again in very generalist terms – gender-based differences in world views that play out in the investment world. There is more on this later.

The next tranche of investors is Generation X. These are people born between 1965 and 1980. The time span is interestingly short, because Generation X people were born in a time of change and grew up at a time when global purpose was, to an extent, somewhat unclear. There were no more defining events such as world wars. The only existentialist threat worth mentioning was nuclear conflict. The world was yet to hit a period of technological or economic momentum that could genuinely be characterized as global. Eastern and Western economies were still significantly different in both scale and reach. The world existed in two distinct groups – haves and have-nots – and these could be almost precisely defined by geography. In many ways, Generation X's formative experiences were un-anchored to momentous global shifts. Yet Generation X children benefitted enormously from their Baby Boomer parents. In Western society, where the Baby Boomer benefits flowed primarily, Generation X children are among the most highly educated tranche of investors in the market. This occurred because Baby Boomer parents translated their work-hard-for-success ethic into a parallel educational universe. There were no global scale conflicts, for the first time in over half a century, to interrupt this translation.

Born under the shadows of their era-defining Baby Boomer parents, Generation X children are characterized by a greater humility and a more self-deprecating existence. They are also, boosted by an unprecedented investment in education and learning, a generation of entrepreneurs. Generation X in the workforce has paved the way to technological breakthroughs that have defined, and continue to redefine, the way we live. It was during the time of Generation X in the workforce that the ethics of business underwent a renaissance. A quiet revolution occurred with young Generation X people, pushing back against the norms of Baby Boomer business rules. The operative word here is quiet, because there was less rowdy conflict and more insistent coercion at play. Generation X in the workforce is expressed tellingly in society by the grunge rock bands of the 1990s whose anthems spoke to a passive-aggressive apathy and angst-ridden low self-esteem. Generation X was the underground resistance that painstakingly teased out an emerging humanity in the business world.

Most interestingly, Generation X has been the quiet conduit between Baby Boomers and Millennials, fitting in our society as an axis for shift, a flexible interface between the vastly different world views of Baby Boomers and Millennials. There are not as many Generation Xers in our society, in this digital revolutionary era, as there are Baby Boomers. They were the product of a transient time, which was a shorter span in our societal evolution than others in these investment tranches.

Generation Xers in the third decade of the twenty-first century are hitting their straps in the business world. They are the CEOs and the executives, the emerging board members. There are far more Generation X women in the business world, including in senior ranks, than there were Baby Boomer women. Generation X sits today as the face of wisdom that the world looks to as the many existential crises are faced. They are the pivotal generation occupying many of the seats of leadership globally. Their decisions in the next two decades will shape, in unprecedented ways, the echoes with which the next generations live. Historians wait with bated breath, because Generation Xers did not occupy formative places in history at a scale similar to their parents.

Generation X is the first tranche of global wealth that has significant diversity to it. There are more women with financial resources in Generation X than before. The difference, viewed on a macro scale in both Western and Eastern hemispheres, has been a step change rather than a stealthy incremental creep. The cultural diversity of investment resource in the world market that Generation X brings is unprecedented. Generation X in leadership roles coincides with the start of the Asian Century, with a shift in global economic powers. Three out of the four most populated countries in the world are in Asia – China, India and Indonesia – and together they command, by headcount, forty per cent of the potential human resources and market at play on the planet. Generation X occupies a large proportion of the leadership chamber that will navigate the business world and the governments of this planet through this phase. With the diversification of global wealth that Generation X represents, it is hard to imagine a world in which there are no tidal shifts in capital markets associated with investment preferences. Change is due, but the extent and direction remains unclear.

As one would expect given their shorter tenure in the workforce so far, Generation X's contribution to investment wealth is currently less than that of the Baby Boomers, but the balance sits on the cusp of change. Generation X is poised to inherit two vast drivers of global wealth – the succession of wealth passed down from Baby Boomers and the pivot of new economies that open the world up in ways previously unseen. As Generation X powers into its pre-retirement decades and beyond, faced with the prospect of a longer lifespan, the corresponding need to fund it, and imbued with the long-evidenced subversive culture of being an agent for change, it is positioned to trigger shifts in finance and investment that are, as yet, unknown. Whether it leans towards the historically conservative patterns of Baby Boomers or swings in quietly revolutionary directions is yet to be seen, but first indicators are beginning to show.

Following Generation X, the much-discussed Millennials entered the world stage. Originally labelled Generation Y, the more frequently used term 'Millennials' points to their school-leaving age at and after the turn of the twenty-first century. They are born between 1981 and 1996.

Millennials were born and raised in times of unprecedented global peace underscored by unsettling escalations in terrorism and so-called 'invisible wars'. The economic safety that comes with the absence of war has been a constant feature in the background of this generation, as has the psychological burden of unseen fears. Yet despite this fear factor, their foreground has been, on digital platforms at least and in the growing multiculturalism that pervades everyday choices and experiences, more inclusive rather than less. Millennials have watched their parents, the Generation Xers, shift their world views. In the Western hemisphere, Millennials have been indoctrinated into adulthood alongside their parents' inexorable shift from the left to the right of politics. Despite the ongoing piecemeal triumphs of exclusion over inclusion in world politics, they have retained a strongly independent perspective, courtesy of unlimited information access. In the Eastern hemisphere, despite the cautiousness of their elders who carry the memories of centuries of colonization and subsequent relegation to a lower rung on the economic ladder, Millennials have shown reverse characteristics. They have launched gleefully into bi- and multi-cultural hybrids of existence, against which the tides of Western exclusion are likely to have very little impact.

Crucially, Millennials have grown up with staggering advances in communication technology that have served to connect the globe at rates and scales never seen before. While Western geopolitics flirt with exclusion, Millennials have, virtually since birth, seen diversity and similarity in equal, homogeneous waves. The small walls that Generation X strives to build along geopolitical borders are unlikely to withstand these Millennial waves; social and economic co-mingling is inevitable because Millennials of all nations have been, at the very least, immersed in digital co-mingling all their lives.

The expansive learning curve of Millennials has been exponential in nature, and it has far outstripped their parents' ability to keep up with the information and misinformation that traffics the superhighways in the internet of things. Thus Millennials are labelled as a know-it-all generation by their parents and grandparents, whereas the reality is that the generation is more of an 'access-it-all' generation. Perspective is offered, and it can be baffling to see it all. The vast array of information on tap offers very little instruction in how to sift through it to make decisions. The Millennial generation of investors is, in all likelihood, knowledgeable but baffled.

They inherit, together with a mesmerizingly technological world, a society of compounded liabilities. They inherit the spectre of climate change. Millennials will read, in Wikipedia, of creatures that they will never see in real life. Their access to the follies of the past will be unprecedented.

The oldest Millennials are entering managerial and senior management roles in the third decade of the twenty-first century, while the youngest of this tranche are entering the workforce. This tranche of the workforce, and of the investment community in general, is the most diverse yet seen. The male-to-female ratio in this tranche is much closer to an equilibrium, and the widespread historical differences in male and female earning potential within like-for-like employment sectors are being dissipated. The cultural diversity in this tranche is even more pronounced, as the so-called Century of Asia produces Eastern business power brokers, leaders and senior managers at a much faster rate than their Western counterparts. Millennials are part of a global spread of education and opportunity. Unlike the Silent Generation, Baby Boomers and Generation X, whose characteristics could largely be annotated to Western monocultures and behaviours, Millennials bring with them a heady mix of culturally diverse characteristics. Their investment patterns are new and emerging, and as a result there is little in the way of analysis and post-rationalization with which to arm forward projections. Correspondingly, it is more complex to rationalize investment behaviours in this tranche.

What is clear is that Millennials have lower access to land and property than ever before, that there are significant barriers to entering housing markets, and that the competition for jobs and economic success is increasing among Millennial peers. These barriers, and many others like them, create a need for solutions. The Millennials, society's emerging leaders and leaders of the future, have a strong reason to become adept problem-solvers; they are inheriting a planet full of problems, courtesy of their forebears. Their mindful investment choices, when they are in a position to make them, are unlikely to support a status quo of economic marginalization and a widening of existing gaps. Thus, while there are no clear solutions for Millennial investors, their choices are likely to bring winds of change.

The next tranche of investors of the future is the Generation Z, born after 1997, the oldest of which will be completing the first phase of their working lives by 2030 and the youngest of which will still be at school at that time. Their investment behaviours are entirely unknown, apart from within the musings of futurists. It is readily surmised that the pivotal investment decisions of Generation X and Millennials, and how investment power is used to influence the deployment of capital in businesses, will inform Generation Z's future and their consecutive investment behaviours. Beyond that, it is pure conjecture, as opposed to educated conjecture.

It is important to remember that these demarcations in our society, by era, are an artifice created to view each tranche through a sociological lens. The literature in this area is deep and wide, and broadly empirical, even theoretical. The conclusions drawn are unlikely to be fully right, or fully wrong, but they support a rational view of differences in investment behaviours. There is, of course a significant risk that the view is two-dimensional and misses critical aspects that would otherwise bring it to life in a bankable way. However, a two-dimensional view is better than no view at all.

These individual investors, aggregated into the tranches defined above, are further aggregated into a wide array of investment vehicles that are steered and ridden by institutional investors. While institutional investors do not, in any sense of the word or by any stretch of imagination, control financial markets, they do – by the weight of aggregation – have some influence over policy perspectives and how these are played out. The largest institutional investors each have $3 trillion to $6 trillion of assets under management; in other words some four to eight per cent of the wealth in the world is harnessed in some way by the largest of these organizations. Their insights, their words and their actions have some currency in the business world.

At the vanguard of financial markets, institutional investors create signals that, over a period of time, knit together to form cohesive messages. These messages, measured by their consistency and varying degrees of insistency, are useful for current and future business leaders to register. Like all messages of undercurrent, they can be readily countered by much more visible cues, but if looked at carefully, they provide vital clues as to how access to capital will be tempered in the years and decades to come, if the concerns of today persist into tomorrow.

Most CEOs and boards of publicly listed companies will have had some interaction with institutional investors. Most will agree that these interactions are at their deepest when wrestling with how the finances are depicted to investors, how the balance sheet is structured and displayed, how these reflect in share prices, and how and when boards distribute dividends. These are, after all, the decades-old traditional investigation grounds of most investors. It is where investor knowledge is the greatest. Most will also agree that towards the end of the second decade of the twenty-first century, there was a noticeable upturn in the number and nature of queries levelled at CEOs and boards in respect of non-financial risks. Some will report that investor briefings often begin with these non-financial risks, this probing of the stability of the business within the business ecosystem that predicates financial health. Most, if not all, will probably report that each year these questions get stronger and deeper and are visibly backed by a greater knowledge and understanding of the uncertainties that lurk in the shadowy depths of non-financial risk. Unlike financial risks, non-financial risks do not lend themselves to being bracketed comfortably by financial calculators. Financial ratios do not provide dependable diagnostics of non-financial risks. Non-financial risks lie in front of a business, and often many years in front. Like icebergs were to the Titanic, some non-financial risks can only be avoided if seen from far enough away and if the process of steering begins at a point far enough away. Like icebergs, non-financial risks may carry more weightiness below the surface of vision than they carry above. The rapidly evolving consideration of long-term risks by institutional investors underscores a more measured approach to strategy than in the past. It represents a longer-term view of business viability and sustainability than annual cyclic financial considerations.

Institutional investors, particularly the larger ones, create stability on the basis of long-term outlooks and long-term investments. Once this stability is created, shorter-term plays can be considered with more confidence. The balance of long-term to short-term thinking can be inferred by considering the layered stability created by long-term outlooks and the potential instability invited by short-term outlooks. Investments with long-term outlooks must far outweigh investments with short-term outlooks to create overall stability in a mixed investment portfolio.

Investors probe a step further. They seek an improved understanding of the long-term risks, many of which are non-financial in nature. This understanding is used to make measured decisions about risk-taking in portfolios. After all, risk is an acceptable variable and the concept of zero risk is nonsensical. The issues revolve around whether and how a risk is manageable; and in order to ask and answer that question openly, the risk must first be well understood. The narrative pivots around whether risks are truly understood by business leaders. It probes the commitment of committed business leadership to managing those risks. What will be done to manage them, and is the business leadership confident about their successful management? What does success look like, for the business leaders? Does it correspond to the investor view of success? It is, in essence, seeking openness and commitment around the murky space of non-financial risks, rather than claims of cut-and-dried solutions that institutional investors are well aware do not exist for many of these risks.

The increasingly insistent questions from institutional investors are voiced not because investors know of a particular risk but because they are aware of what they do not know. These 'known unknowns' may cause them concern, suspicion, discomfort or worry. The issues that worry institutional investors are often broadcast, and the tone of the broadcast is a useful indicator of the depth of worry. Issues that cause discomfort, suspicion or concern may be raised at investor briefings, proxy meetings or at the annual general meetings. They may be raised through specific queries to the Chairperson or CEO of the organization or through selected officers of an organization. Overall, issues that bother investors are not generally kept secret. There is little excuse in the boards and executive leadership cohorts for not knowing what concerns them.

Added to this are the aspects of risk that are unknown. These 'unknown unknowns' are the surprise factors that stalk the investment world and occasionally cause economic meltdowns. In a risk culture that is coy about the known unknowns, what chance is there that vigilance is high for the lurking unknown unknowns? This is the undercurrent of worry that flows through the institutional investment community as it interfaces with the business world.

The decades-old dance of investors and boards or executive teams around financial issues has been a coy one. Investors know that it is in the best interests of the business, and its shareholders, to value the organization as optimistically as possible. Indeed, if boards did anything else they could be accused of not keeping their shareholders' interests front-and-centre. The coyness often revolves around, for example, accounting treatments of debts, equity and assets. There are many legal ways of treating these, subject to the accounting rules of the profession and the laws of the country, and each one may be nuanced to highlight a particular facet and downplay another. As a result, debates about these issues tend to stabilize at an I-know-what-you're-trying-to-show-and-I'm-not-buying-it professional truce. Both sides are flirting around how a financial issue is reported and reflected, the permutations for doing so are quite finite, and in most cases a competent investor can re-cast the accounting figures in tune with the lens that she or he wants to adopt, in order to make a differently informed decision about risk.

This forgiving structure is much less available for non-financial risks. For one thing, there is a staggering range of social and physical aspects that have the potential to play out as a risk to the business. Issues like climate change, customer preference volatility or demographic market shifts are, firstly, markedly different from each other and, secondly, have very few accounting rules with which to corral our understanding. For another, these risks have tentacles that may reach deep into the external world, beyond the boundaries of the business's walls and desks and ledgers. Capturing them and transparently dealing with them is not trivial. Worse, hiding them (or the true nature of their danger) while they fester and poise to damage a business is not hard to do within the current rules of governance in any jurisdiction. It is a recognized part of the game, between businesses and institutional investors, to downplay non-financial risks in order to buoy investor confidence, as this has both a direct and an indirect positive impact on the value of shares. But the nature, complexity and potential consequences of larger non-financial risks are beginning to weigh heavily on investors, not necessarily because they pose risks to society but because, as a result, they pose potentially significant financial risks. As a result, there is a growing alertness around these issues and a desire to consider them more carefully where necessary in the investment world.

The first attempts by the investment community to recognize and garner some commitment to managing these risks were known as the Principles of Responsible Investment, coined in 2006.

These principles were simple. They committed signatories (whether investors or asset owners) to examine a range of environmental, social and other governance factors relating to investments, and to encourage reporting of what they found. A trail of commitments to promoting the initiative, and to continuous improvements, followed.

Encouraged by the United Nations, which recognized the global footprint of the businesses that leveraged investment capital, they attracted signatories for a number of reasons. Some presumably wanted to do the 'right thing', while others might have felt they could benefit from the positive brand image. The initiative, while important, was notable for one thing. Over a period of 14 years, its signatories grew from a handful to over three thousand. By any comparison, this is an impressive, sustained sign-on rate. By the end of the second decade of the twenty-first century, the assets under management of the signatories had reached around US$100 trillion, within the ballpark of the volume of broad money on the planet (Figures 4.1 and 4.2).

Whether the sign-on momentum had a correspondingly positive effect on governance is more debatable. Signing on for a commitment is, in all probability, indicative of the acknowledgement of the validity of such a commitment. However, it is not, and has never been, proof of commitment – in all of society's rich history of signed commitments. Proof of commitment, it has long been established, lies in the actions that occur after the affirmation of commitment. Those actions may even bear no resemblance to the signed commitment. However, it still remains that the rate of sign-on is an important signal across the investment community. It reflects an in-principle agreement that the validity of the commitment exists, or that non-commitment carries a negative connotation. The signal is strong that the issue is not without merit, but it is of course inconclusive as to whether the issue warrants strong action, until such action occurs.

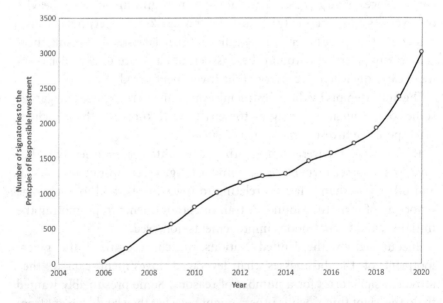

FIGURE 4.1

Investor trends: Growth in investor signatories to the Principles of Responsible Investment.

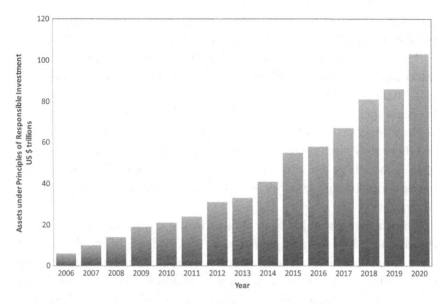

FIGURE 4.2
Global finance and its growing links to responsible investment.

The Principles of Responsible Investment have, consequently, been criticized for being somewhat of a branding ambit. Detractors point to relatively few practical means of holding signatories accountable to the Principles. Nevertheless, it has united a great proportion of the investment community behind a broader non-financial flag.

The debate has moved further since this turn-of-the-century initiative. Within the investment community, a new cohort of leaders is applying a much broader lens to investing, and the access to capital paradigm, than ever before. This lens is less Baby Boomer and more Generation X in its focus. A broader focus on business ethics has entered the conversation; not just around bribery, safety, human rights or other such considerations but also around workplace diversity and inclusivity, talent retention (taking into account the intergenerationally changing values of employees) and remuneration structures that encourage the hallmarks of good governance, among others.

A specific focus has been applied, since the mid-2010s, on climate change. This has increasingly triangulated on a structured approach to assessing and disclosing the risks to a business, directly or indirectly, from climate change. Some institutional investors have been walking the talk, progressively changing out their investments away from fossil fuels.

This pre-emptive action stems from a belief in the limited scope of such fuels in the face of public and intergovernmental concerns. Investors, with their keen sense of risk, are unlikely to wait for a flurry of regulatory interventions to disembowel the fossil fuel market before they move out of it. That would, in investment terms, be far too little far too late. Nor are investors inclined to dump investments overly rapidly, particularly ones as globally pervasive as fossil fuels; this would precipitate a collapse whose reverberations might reach any number of commodities on the market. And so there is a slow and deliberate extraction from risk, which should not be confused with lethargy but rather associated with a controlled exit strategy.

A broad focus has also been applied to the significant array of other environmental, social and governance risks. Because of the diversity of these, it remains both challenging and potentially impractical to increase the specificity of how they are assessed and addressed. Here, institutional investors appear to progressively invite businesses to explain how they view these risks, how they assess them, how they influence or control them, and how they are feeling about their residual exposure. The ambit is more about opening up useful and transparent discourses rather than demanding proof of safety. In this way the institutional investment community is opening up progressive, shared-consideration pathways to engage. However, as all boards and executives are well aware, the end result of poor risk management, whether discovered through convivial discourse or through invasive investigative means, is a shrinking of their available universe of capital access and, in some circumstances, a reduction of company value.

Retail investors are often individuals or families who invest in shares in the stock market. They were typically viewed as a disaggregated group, following stocks for which they develop an affinity. These investors often have hard-earned savings, generally at much lower amounts than the far bigger aggregated firms. They make individual, rather than collective, decisions upon where to invest. In this group of investors, dividends and growth in share value is often of substantial importance. They make their voices heard at annual general meetings, as distinct from the investor briefings and the proxy meetings that are held with institutional investors. As such, their individual voices often fade into the background, lost among a widely diverse set of views. In the past it has been rare to find retail investors developing cohesive, collective views on issues that affect their investments.

Towards the end of the second decade of the twenty-first century, a shift occurred. There has been a noticeable cohesion among retail investors in their collective views on societal impacts. This cohesion has translated to dissent and demand, in a movement termed 'investor activism'. It has developed its own focal areas of voiced concern, depending on the industry their investments lie in.

Two factors that have contributed to a narrowing of focus are social media and the increasingly strategic actions of non-governmental organizations. The former has led to the much wider sharing of information (and misinformation) previously only accessible through a small range of channels. The latter has used a greater connectivity to provide a marshalling point for retail investors who have specific concerns. Thus the banking industry has been increasingly beset by concerns over ethical customer dealings and risk-taking in the public debt markets (particularly around housing, which was a key instigator of the Global Financial Crisis late in the first decade of the century, and continues to attract watchful concern). The natural gas industry has been plagued by concerns over hydraulic fracturing ('fracking') and environmental risks, particularly around methane emissions and water resources in semi-arid regions of the world. The mining and extractive industries have been pressured by retail investors on a number of issues, including child labour, human rights and safety of their waste facilities – the latter following a spate of failures of dams that resulted in the loss of lives and significant environmental damage. Many industries are being questioned with increasing concern on the issue of climate change on two fronts: what is being done to limit the ongoing damage to earth's biosphere and what is being done to prepare for the potential effects of climate change on the industry's costs and operations.

An overarching concern, spanning all of the above and more, is the remuneration of chief executives and directors. In the face of rising dissatisfaction with the leadership of business organizations, particularly publicly listed companies, this issue continues to elevate in the minds and voices of shareholders. There is an increasing focus on the business leadership need to manage the many non-financial externalities related to business operations, and the internal governance relating to these non-financial issues.

These agitations have been around for many decades, and have been notable for their almost consistent attraction of just one or two per cent of investor voting at annual general meetings when put to open challenge. Yet as society moves deeper into this century, it is apparent that these previously paltry figures have begun to creep upwards, into double figures and further up the scale of influence.

To dismiss this trend as an odd deviation from a more comfortable norm is, in all likelihood, naïve and denialist. There are clear indications over many years that investor attitudes to the companies that they choose to support are moving on two fronts. Firstly, they are moving from a position of lesser knowledge to a position of greater knowledge. Secondly, they are also moving from a passive stance to a more assertive one, on a wide range of concerns that affect society. Together, both constitute a groundswell of change.

The pathway for businesses at their interface of the investment community is reasonably clear. It is to understand the current, evolving and potential future concerns of investors as best as its leadership can, to proactively manage those risks as diligently as practical and to engage in transparent discussions with investors to remove as many of the uncertainties that haunt them as possible. While this pathway is clear, it requires a specific cultural business leadership strength to do this with authenticity – a strength that is explored further in this book.

5

Customers

Despite a rapidly digitizing economy, the vast majority of end customers continue to be people. People have values, diversified in much the same normal distribution as the rest of society, give or take customer demographical segment similarities. They have fears and aspirations, just like everyone else in society. They are a defining part of society and a focal part of the business ecosystem. In businesses, customers often get aggregated and disaggregated into numbers with characteristics in order for market insights to be gleaned, or for market segments to be better defined or targeted. The repeated consolidation of customers into numbers – more observable in manufacturing and retail than in the service industry – can be an insidious cultural de-sensitizer that results in customers losing an element of human relevance within businesses.

It is commonplace, particularly in retail and manufacturing businesses, for executives to look blankly or in mild sympathy at employees who refer to the woes of individual customers. It is a reflection of the naivety attributed to such infinitesimal disaggregation. Over several decades of tertiary education evolution and business practice, customers' places in society have been greyed out and replaced with statistical markers of behaviours and attributes. There is a usefulness to this, of course, because it helps form informative macro views. Parts of the narrative in this book, for example, look to trends and broad characteristics among stakeholders using similar aggregations. But a daily-practised 'us and them' view of customers held by businesses, coupled with a subtle replacement of human traits with numerical and behavioural traits, cannot but help build a culture that identifies customers less and less as individual humans. There is deep value in these analytical processes of course, if they are held in equal co-existence with a view of customers as people of society. But business cultural issues around customers begin when the analytical view displaces the human view.

In the customer world, as distinct from the investor world, the terms 'risk' and 'non-financial risk' hold no meaning and no currency. This is because those terms speak of a consequence to a business and its investors, which in turn has very little relevance to a customer. Customers use the term 'business ethics' or simply 'ethics' to capture a very broad range of behaviours of a business. Many aspects of this broad range are correlated to the aspects that were discussed in the 'Investors' chapter. They are essentially the same but considered through very different lenses. In this section, both retail customers (sometimes called consumers) and business customers are discussed.

Whereas institutional investors are inclined to consider a broad range of risks, or issues, that might constitute a threat to the long-term prosperity of a business, retail customers are more inclined to consider a more personal set of values-based aspects, or ethics, that they hold important. The strength of importance may vary from customer to customer. One customer may consider an issue as being of extreme and immediate concern, another customer may consider the same issue as being of moderate and non-urgent interest, and yet another customer may not even be aware of the issue.

It would be presumptuous to begin with a notion that ethical standards are irrelevant to purchasing considerations. It is a long-established market behaviour that if there is no difference between product A and product B in terms of price, value and fit for purpose, then knowledge of the ethical standing of product A has a material influence on most retail customers who have a care. In everyday terms, "I would rather buy from the good guys than the bad guys."

This influence is not, however, necessarily definitive. Customers who are aware of the ethical standing but who choose product B (lower ethics) over product A (higher ethics) are often conditioned by brand loyalty. Brand loyalty is generally cemented over time, through repeated experiences that compound each other and form a less-shakeable convergence of values. Thus, a customer who is loyal to the brand that delivers product B through repeated lived experiences but who is then faced with a single point of irrefutable evidence in the ethical superiority of product A may not find his or her loyalty to product B's brand sufficiently shaken to change. Brand loyalty banks a benefit-of-doubt asset.

For some customers, there is no material influence. Some customers are genuinely ambivalent to the ethical standing of product A. In any normally distributed population and at any point in its evolution on any given issue, there is an expected contingent that is neutral to, or even resisting of, shifting societal views on that issue.

While there have been numerous studies into purchasing decisions and ethical sourcing, the data is noisy. A great many studies have combined Baby Boomer, Generation X and Millennial buyers, resulting in compound data that may not readily be projected to envision a future state. The control markets tested have been highly variable, making it difficult to compare studies with one another in the depth that has been needed to probe the issue. A pragmatic view is that, firstly, there is a social justice to ethical sourcing and delivery of products and services. Secondly, this social justice has some value, but it does not, in contemporary markets, necessarily overshadow value/price and fit-for-purpose/expected experience, particularly in low-engagement products and services. Thirdly, it does not necessarily support a higher price, and so it is logical to infer that there is a competitive impediment to incurring a higher cost of production in order to achieve an ethical status.

Notwithstanding such immense diversity, the contemporary umbrella notion prevails that retail customers prefer to buy products and services from companies that show higher ethical standards. A business organization that ensures its products and services are delivered to an ethical standard that is required or appreciated by a customer creates, as a result, some customer value. It is also true that there are other factors that influence whether that preference translates to the purchase of a product or service from an 'ethical' company over a purchase from a 'less ethical' company, cost – or value – and fit for purpose, for example. Customer experience is important in many products and most services – the way a customer feels about the journey taken with the product or service.

What is true, over time, is that customers have become increasingly sophisticated about what they want. They have moved from a utility-based expectation (I expect the goods or services to work) to experience-based expectations (the journey and destination are both intricately connected). Customers have evolved towards wanting more (Figure 5.1).

The customer attraction and retention levers are complex and vastly different across the staggering range of products and services that society partakes of. Cost and utility are often first-order considerations. They

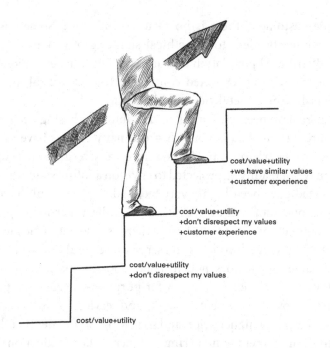

cost/value+utility
+we have similar values
+customer experience

cost/value+utility
+don't disrespect my values
+customer experience

cost/value+utility
+don't disrespect my values

cost/value+utility

THE EVOLUTION OF CUSTOMER EXPECTATIONS

FIGURE 5.1
The evolution of customer expectations.

relate to a primary need. There is still a strong undercurrent of secondary needs, linked to a customer's very wide array of values. Some customers may pay a premium for meeting their array of values; many others will not. And so, while there is undoubtedly a customer value proposition in being 'ethical', it appears overshadowed by the pragmatic thresholds of cost and utility when a single purchasing proposition is considered. But a broader view presents a strategically different picture.

There are two aspects to the value of business ethics that are shaping consumerism which are difficult to ignore. Firstly, the face of consumers is changing. Values are shifting, from Baby Boomer–based ideologies to Millennial and Generation Z ideologies. Knowledge is increasing and with it awareness of the realities of bringing products and services to markets. Dovetailed to this knowledge is a greater desire for fairness as the younger generations of consumers inherit a world burdened by past excesses and a smaller share of a smaller future unless some paradigms are shifted. As a result, the emerging openness of consumers to a 'better way' of providing products and services is higher than it has ever been. With this openness comes a greater willingness to support such efforts, a proclivity towards loyalty. There are multiple soft edges of competitive advantage that are emerging, at scale, from large tranches of our close-to-eight-billion consumers on the planet. Billions of customers may not yet pay more for ethical business practices (and may never get there), but there is no denying the increasingly valued currency of business ethics. Its trend is clear.

Secondly, to underpin the long-term longevity of products or services, the battle for competitive advantages is fierce. In an already-highly-connected and rapidly-ever-increasingly connected global economy, the ability to mirror a competitor's cost and utility thresholds is becoming easier by the year. Technology replication and blockchain models allow 'fast follower' strategies to take market share from pioneering companies more readily than ever before. Technical competitive advantages (reflected in cost and utility) have fleeting lives. Capital that is invested into creating technical competitive advantages requires some years before it is recovered through sales and profits. This recovery is threatened by the ability of the digital global economy to replicate technical competitive advantages. A competitor business with similar cost and utility profiles can place at risk the recovery of capital for the original business by rapidly eating market share. In an ethics-agnostic world, competitive advantages can be progressively shaved until the competitive edge in cost and utility becomes vanishingly thin. However, in a world where ethics are valued and create brand loyalty, competitive edges can be strengthened by adopting, practising and proving ethical business practices.

There are, of course, niche markets where the cost and utility priorities may be inverted towards an 'ethical buying' behaviour. Since the late twentieth century when the movement started in earnest, there have been numerous attempts at cracking an 'ethical market'. The perception that ethically sourced products improve perceived value and underwrite a higher price has been explored, and the results – while not entirely negative – have not been compelling enough for a market revolution to have occurred outside of niches. But the past is not necessarily a good indication of future trajectories.

Strategic business leadership prepares for a range of feasible futures. It does not expect a continuation of the present or the past, other than to acknowledge that it is just one possible (and even potentially unlikely) future. Future readiness thinking would navigate a business organization to a position where it is able to fulfil ethical priorities of the future, and simultaneously profit from that readiness.

For example, a traditional energy business might run a fleet of coal-fired power stations. However, seeing the increasing concern about emissions and climate change, it begins to prepare itself for a future where renewable energy and hydrogen fuels might be more palatable to its customers. It might do this by slowly building a fleet of renewable energy generators and hydrogen fuel production, in a lower-risk exposure manner without straining its balance sheet or capital outflows. It begins to shift its weight gradually, from a high-emission fleet to a lower-emission fleet. The shift may take a decade or two, but with every passing year it gains a stronger foothold on the business expectations of the future. At the point at which the energy output of renewable energy generation assets and hydrogen fuel products are more economically valued than the energy output of coal-fired generation, the business is poised to make the transition. Because of the decades of shifting weight it has undertaken, it has positioned itself well to profit from the transition. It may even, as it established a greater and greater weight shift, begin to call upon policy, regulatory and customer incentives to choose renewable energy over coal, thus potentially influencing to some extent the market movement that it wishes to capitalize on.

This futurist readiness – the reading of emerging customer preferences and acting upon them – is the core, and the embodiment, of strategic positioning. It requires an ability to compose a future view based on facts, trajectories and insights. It requires the flexibility to position for it without destabilizing the current business. This in turn allows the business to act, and to capitalize on customer value propositions, at the right time and over an appropriate period.

There is an even higher order of strategic leadership than anticipating and intersecting future customer needs. This greater discipline is in influencing and even creating customer trends that can and will surpass existing projections. The confidence that this will do so comes from a purpose that is both – to use the language of ethics – 'right and good'. It represents both where customers would aspire to be and the provision of value. This discipline is steeped in structuring customer evolutions rather than merely responding to them. Few business leaders in the past have led in this fashion, trading customer service leadership paradigms for a broader view of purpose. There is a significantly more powerful leadership displayed in developing customer propositions that don't simply react to demand but shape demand to meet a greater purpose while serving the customer's needs of today. In a world of increasing complexity, concern and stakeholder interfaces, this will hold greater value for the future.

It requires a business leader to believe that tomorrow may be different to, and *better than*, today if a different tangent is applied, to encourage a different trajectory to the one that troubles us. The improved-future vision must be founded in an improved humanity or it has no broad currency with which to pursue its agenda. If the improved-future resonates with society, a seed is sown. As every marketing executive will point out, society includes a small number of customers, and a much larger number of potential customers. Business leaders who consistently lead businesses to better societal outcomes that benefit current and future customers are able to create a powerful branding foundation. It is one of vision, a greater good, and, if pursued with dedication and consistency of values, it develops trust. This is the sort of trust that cements brand loyalty. It is the sort of force that converts potential customers into actual customers.

Such a leader can cause some short-term consternation, because some of the leadership messages may be counterintuitive to the status-quo health of the business. For example, business leaders in the food industry who take strong and visionary stances for healthier dietary habits may seem to be undermining their own existing products. Pharmaceutical leaders who advocate for preventative lifestyle changes that obviate the need for some of their products may receive concerned calls from investors and executives alike. But these are not impromptu calls for change, made on a whim. If they were, then shareholders would rightly ask if they have the right person for the leadership job. They are urgings based on a change for the better, underwritten by a strategy to steer the business towards the new horizon, and the first-mover or fast-follower advantages that come with the formulation and execution of a successful strategy.

The broadest possible strategy would meet reasonable long-term business and shareholder prosperity goals and safeguard current ones, while simultaneously helping ease larger societal burdens and concerns in the customer value proposition.

Retail customers are a visible and potent segment of the customer world. Yet they are often the final destination of a much longer aggregation journey through, particularly, a product supply chain. Within this chain may exist a large number of interim buyer-and-seller transactions. The number of these transactions may, in aggregate, exceed the number of individual transactions between the product retailers and end customers. Within this supply chain, those that sit within the highest links (closest to end customers) are imbued with significant power and influence. These are, for example, manufacturers of vehicles, machinery and electronics, supermarkets and clothing manufacturers, among others. These actors are able to leverage their role as key customers in the supply chain in feeding through the business ecosystem the ethics and standards that help deliver a broader social justice at a global scale.

Concerns in the supply chain can be complex because the great diversity of product components, particularly in the rapidly growing technology arenas. Because of the complexity of many supply chains that trail through multiple continents, they can take significant time and effort to untangle, let alone address, the issues that may reside within. Every country has different laws relating to many of the standard supply chain issues – land rights, human rights, child labour, environmental protection, remuneration standards and others. Regulations and their enforcement may vary. Companies have to tread carefully in countries that are not their own. A company that is judgemental about local laws, regulations and their enforcement in other nations has the potential to draw the ire of those nations' regulatory groups. This creates diplomatic issues that, businesses argue, they are in no place to trigger. Yet, consumer pressure is building to spark just this kind of diligence.

For many years through the latter third of the twentieth century and continuing well into the current century, there was significant resistance from the business sector to the prospect of addressing supply chain issues. The key reason for resistance was supply chain complexity and traditional contractual modes of doing business. Since the end of the first decade of the twenty-first century, the discomfort expressed by retail customers of well-known brands regarding labour practices in supply chains has visibly increased. Retail customers rationalize that their favourite brands, many of which are large, profitable and successful enterprises, should not be profiting at the expense of less-fortunate people. Child labour, which has been publicly and sensationally uncovered in some of the most visible brands on the planet intermittently since the 1980s, became a renewed flashpoint for twenty-first-century protest.

The protests were no less inflamed in the twenty-first century than they were in the twentieth century, but their visibility was greatly enhanced by social media and digital communications. While some product boycotting has been observed in some markets, it did not cause genuine market turbulence. However, in the boardrooms of businesses, it raised alarms. There was a new tone to the argument; being blissfully ignorant of ethical issues in supply chains was no longer a valid defence in the eyes of consumers. How far might this customer dissent continue? There was curiosity about what could be done. New supply chain and business-to-business economic interfaces such as blockchain technology presented options that had not existed before. Some countries began legislating for, at the very least, a sense of transparency through the supply chain. A threshold was tipped in the second decade of the twenty-first century, and for the first time in the history of industry, there was a collective impetus behind cleaning up supply chains. It had surpassed the piecemeal efforts of prior decades.

Emerging laws and requirements of listed companies in some countries did not advocate for the outright removal of unethical labour practices from supply chains. Instead, they began by requiring transparency about where and what those risks were. They required statements from boards of directors about what was being done about those risks. This approach is not dissimilar to approaches taken towards gender diversity in multiple jurisdictions around the world beginning in the last decades of the twentieth century. The concept of transparency is considered a soft-start strategy for issues of governance. It is easier and more productive to manage and make decisions about what can be seen clearly.

Using gender diversity as a corollary, it is readily foreseeable that progression from soft starts to publicly available targets and, eventually, investor curiosity in how businesses are meeting such obligations might occur through the first half of the twenty-first century. It can also reasonably be expected that such expectations will mirror themselves in multiple jurisdictions as the issue becomes more and more of a mainstream concern. After all, we are in a global economy.

For businesses lower in the supply chain, customer expectations around these issues are only likely to escalate as a direct consequence of elevating effort higher in the supply chain. As these expectations rise, businesses that meet them will access mainstream commerce more readily. Businesses that fall short are likely to find their universe of potential buyers on one side of the fence curtailed, reducing their own commercial flexibility. They may still operate viably on the other side of the fence, supplying to businesses that do not adopt similar supply chain standards. This alternative market may persist for a very long time; perhaps forever. However, the shift to mainstreaming supply chain labour ethics is likely to take hold and branch out inexorably within the brand-led markets. It is more likely than not that the legitimized supply chain market will eventually be much larger than the non-legitimate supply chain market. This is more and more likely as major brands consolidate their positions in a global consumer market and their reputations with customers represents a larger dimension of their net worth.

6

Employees

Employees are people who are drawn from society to coalesce their efforts in a business organization in order to help fulfil its purpose. This alignment of effort is facilitated by business leaders. The organization aims to achieve its purpose through the culture, structures, policies, rules and work practices it uses. Employees are sorted into work streams, hierarchies of management, departments and other architectures that lend themselves, in some co-ordinated fashion, to fulfilling the business purpose. It is easy, as a business leader, to become mesmerized by the complexity of internal structures and processes to the extent that the employees' place in an external environment fades into the background.

Yet the reality we know is that for employees, life occurs outside the work structure. Their friends, families and the communities in which they live form their vivid foreground. Employment, and the employer, represents an exchangeable environment. If not quite a background, employment is a vehicle through which their foreground life is enabled. The trajectory of employee behaviours in the last century is illustrative of the path to this point. From the loyalty of the Silent Generation to the nimble and flexible Millennials, industry has witnessed an arc towards increasing empowerment and choice. We know today that without engagement with the business purpose of the employer, employment becomes little more than a means to an end.

Despite their grouping and stratifying within an organization, all employees have this in common; they have a place in society. They work in the business organization for a percentage of the week. They work within the remit of an employer culture. They laugh, cry, love, argue and otherwise experience life in society. They live through the same economic fluctuations that everyone else does – the same storms, the same housing bubbles and bursts, the same influenza outbreaks and all of the other eddies of life. They may experience them differently, but they are in some way touched by the same things that everyone else is touched by.

They occupy a space in society and the business ecosystem, and it has a specific duality – a side that is business-facing and a side that is society-facing. Perhaps every working day, they immerse themselves in one side of a socio-economic frame and then for the rest of the day, in another side of the same socio-economic frame.

They may, in addition to being employees, also be investors – perhaps with shareholdings in the business organizations in which they work. They may also be customers. They may have these pluralities, but their duality as employees and members of society is consistent and pervasive.

The commercial contract that connects employees to their employers is transactional. Businesses rely on employees to align with the organizational purpose and values while undertaking the tasks for which they are paid, and the return is specified in the commercial contract. The choices, in such a contract, are to align or leave. No business wants to accumulate employees who refuse to align with its purpose and values; this is a basic recipe for a failed business.

The tens, hundreds, thousands or hundreds of thousands of employees in any organization operate within a culture. Every organization has a different culture because it is an organic thing, built of many nuanced inputs. Culture turns the employee–employer relationships into something much more than the sum of the employee–employer contracts that are in place.

A great deal of business time and effort is spent on fashioning the 'best' organizational culture possible, for many very good reasons. Much of this book focuses on leadership that forges a societally relevant business culture, that is, a bringing together of the business world and broader society in a more profound way than has occurred in the past. This culture can coexist with other types of cultures – for example, cultures of high performance, cultures of inclusivity, cultures of shareholder value and virtually any other desirable business culture.

Many business cultures are founded on issues that are only of peripheral resonance with employees – for example, being the leading business in the industry or delivering value to shareholders – and then heavily buttressed by remuneration practices and non-financial rewards that work together to form a workable alliance. Some of these alliances may appear to work if specific, often self-fulfilling, key performance indicators are focused upon. For example, consider a culture built around the notion of being the leading business in the industry. The performance metrics relevant to that notion are based on share of market. Remuneration structures may lean heavily towards measures of market dominance. A management approach that contains these alignments would be expected to deliver its agenda. Within the organization, the leadership behaviours and employee norms that are encouraged would be those that contribute to and support this culture.

This approach works in businesses around the world, connecting a central cause to a desired effect. Two decades before the turn of the twenty-first century, businesses moved into a more human sphere of employee culture. Initially, a prevalent common denominator was that employee culture was forged around the internal workings of the organization. Businesses became better at building into cultures the aspects that employees find important from their employee-facing perspective. For example, issues such as diversity (gender, race, religion/belief system, sexual orientation and others) have become a fertile part of employee engagement strategies. It is not unusual to hear cultures being labelled 'inclusive' because of the embracing of such elements of diversity.

Increasingly, work–life balance has become important to business culture. This has contributed positively to more flexible working conditions, allowing employees to better forge for themselves a more tailored centre of gravity between work and home. The list is long – career development, crèches, parental leave and so on. All of these serve to diffuse the interface that once very clearly and strongly delineated work from the rest of our lives. They seek to make the interface more fluid, and to make the values compatible across that interface.

The payoff for a business organization is clear. These cultural measures seek to make the business environment more conducive to productivity and loyalty. The measures pursue respect, fairness and equity. There is a code of ethics that serves to delineate the no-go areas. There are incremental attempts to break down the sometimes-artificial separations and rigidity that existed, and still continue to exist in most businesses, between employees and their place of work. It seeks to impart a better sense of belonging, and a less transactional relationship between the business organization and its employees. Without these core elements of connectivity and integration, employee engagement is elusive.

This evolving view of employee engagement is at the very earliest phase of its development. It is a mere few decades old. It has, appropriately, focused initially on inequities of the past – gender biases, unsafe working conditions, corruption and others. As the discipline evolved, it sought to create a community within organizations; a sense of belonging and purpose. These are all relatively recent renaissance measures.

In this evolution of business humanities, the world is yet to explore in earnest the interface between an employee's work life and employee's place in society. It is still to triangulate this with a more deliberate synthesis of a business's place in society. The inherent value to building deeply resonant business cultures and fostering a much broader employee engagement across this interface is transformational.

Look at the employees across a business organization. The expectation would be that the vast majority would prefer a world with less poverty than a world with more poverty, or even constantly sustaining levels of poverty. Some may very well be ambivalent, but this might be a small minority. It would be expected too that the further away the employees are from the realm of poverty, the more it would be seen as a noble, rather than an essential, proposition. But noble aspirations come with a sense of purpose and pride, even if their direct relevance or practicality is unclear.

There would be a wellspring of purpose and pride in a business that leans into such an effort. Similarly, the vast majority would probably prefer a world in which the effects of climate change are eased rather than worsened. For many, this might be a concept less removed than poverty, because the effects of climate change are broadly non-discriminatory and we would all experience some of it. It may be more homogeneously engaging to a group of employees than poverty because of its broader applicability closer to home.

Later in this book, the significant issues that concern society, and how businesses can be a more committed part of the solutions, will be explored. For now, note that there is a significant amount of latent business cultural cohesion, and a large amount of untapped employee engagement energy, that lies in a leadership perspective that begins with employees as humans in a society.

To acknowledge employees as humans in society is to acknowledge that they care about a broad range of societal issues, and this is helpful in a leadership context. In the first two decades of the twenty-first century, significant steps – both informal and formal – have been taken in leadership cultures to explore the human challenges faced by employees both within the workplace and in balancing work and life. These steps have, largely, spread radially from a workplace epicentre (a workplace hygiene focus), and out into, firstly, family households (a personal work–life balance focus) (Figure 6.1). The nature of the spread hints at a universal leadership cautiousness in extending beyond what it knows and understands. This is a reasonable and respectful propagation of interest. If this spread were to be extrapolated, it would continue into communities and into society at large. Such a propagation would be reasonable to foreshadow, and would perhaps even be appreciated or invited by employees and their communities.

This radial extension of investment in employees' interests has a potentially powerful societal effect. Firstly, it forms a very strong link

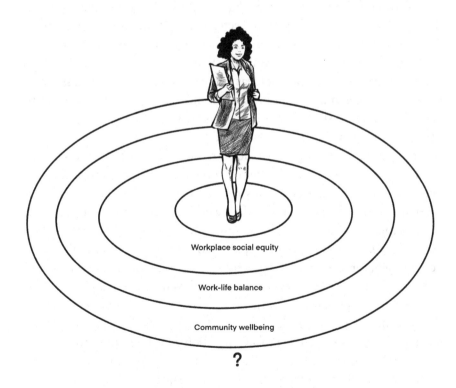

THE EVOLUTION OF EMPLOYEE EXPECTATIONS

FIGURE 6.1
The evolution of employee expectations.

between business and society because each employee is only a short- to medium-term constant in a business organization. Depending on employee turnover percentages, the association between an employee and the business organization may be of the order of several years. This timeframe is around the lower end of strategic timeframes for a business organization. Therefore, the advocacy outreach of employees – both when they are employees and when they cease to be employees - has the ability to play out as an enduring extension of the business presence.

Secondly, businesses employ a considerably large segment of the workforce, particularly in the more developed economies of the OECD. Large businesses have many employees, but there are relatively few of such businesses. Small businesses have fewer employees, but there are a relatively large number of those entities. In aggregate, the business sector's outreach into society, through its employees alone, is enormous.

Thirdly, employees move from organization to organization, between the public sector and the private sector, and within each sector. Cross-pollination is a constant force that accompanies employee mobility. Because of the inherent cultural thirst for innovation in the business sector, the cross-fertilization of ideas and values within the business sector is prolific. People move from business to business. They typically retain and leverage the best ideas and initiatives they have at their disposal and place on a memory shelf the less useful ideas and initiatives. If the business that they move to is receptive to the better ideas and initiatives that these employees bring, an advancement of ideas and initiatives is seen in this new organization. This effect has been noted in, particularly, issues of diversity in the workplace and work–life balance. These societally relevant improvements to business culture move and adapt rapidly, carried often by employees who move from employer to employer in a natural career-development process. While the sharing of ideas at conferences and seminars has genuine impact, it is the movement of people between employers that propagates, with both conviction and momentum, the changes that shape businesses for the better. And as the workforce shifts from a Baby Boomer–led one to a Generation X–led one and through to a Millennial-led one, there is a more frequent change of employer evident, hinting at an ever-increasing velocity of propagation of ideas across the business ecosystem.

The powerful societal effect alluded to in the paragraph is enhanced by business leadership. If leadership is disinterested in the ideas that cross-pollination brings, then there is little impact. But if the leadership of business A has a similar level of interest in those ideas as business B, then employee cross-pollination becomes a potent force.

As the examples used above illustrate, in the concepts of diversity and work–life balance, the effect of cross-pollination across companies has been rapid. Broadly similar paradigms have taken effect across businesses and across sectors. While we may readily attribute the rapid uptake to strong leadership in these areas, this is only the case at the start of change. As change across the business ecosystem progresses, it needs leaders to do less leading and more enabling. They need to harness and direct latent energy. Their jobs are made easier because of employee cross-pollination. It is much less a competitive effect between organizations as it is a collaborative, dispersed, groundswell effect.

This energy for societal change, both drawn from and discharged through employees, is readily available to business leadership. Once the intellectual property is present in the business ecosystem, the question is less about how to lead it and more about how to harness and direct it in ways that propagate business greatness.

The potential for businesses to change society for the better is plentiful and available, through employees. Businesses are prominent in society, and the business's employees wield a substantial footprint in that same society. There is deep business employee connectivity into the social fabric, and a strong circulatory effect through the business ecosystem. All of these factors point to a very large force for business change. It is reasonable to ponder why this force has not, to date, been felt substantively in society. There are a number of reasons for this.

Firstly, leadership styles have, in the majority of cases in the business world over many decades, been observably egocentric. Command-and-control and heroship models have dominated the business world, excruciatingly obviously in the Baby Boomer working era and commonly visible during the existing, in-flux, Generation X era. In turn, this has meant that leadership styles have for many generations exhibited a do-what-I-say dynamic.

Words like inclusivity are relatively new across the board. It was not until the second decade of the twenty-first century that the previous, fringe exhortations to inclusive styles became more commonplace. They are not yet the norm. This command-and-control mode is – despite very creditable advances in normalizing more rounded styles of leadership – still prevalent in business leadership styles. And it does not, generally, lend itself to a more human development–oriented model of thought and action – one that shifts focus to societal good.

Secondly, investors and society in general have visibly rewarded heroic leadership outcomes. We have taken the good mantra of acknowledging good work and celebrating success and exalted it to dizzying heights for business leaders. The heroship models of leadership were inherited from both Western and Eastern histories and, following several significant wars in the twentieth century during which those models achieved results in dire circumstances, established themselves firmly in the fast-developing business culture. The heroship models lent themselves to increased remuneration and increased incentivization. After all, if one leader saves the day, it makes absolute sense to remunerate that leader very well. The compounding remuneration cycles of seventy years or more of business in society is visible today in the sometimes disproportionate remuneration of the most senior executives to the average employee. The pyramid so created has only served to embellish the egocentric platforms of some leadership styles. The self-fulfilling prophecy of handsomely rewarding hero leaders as a normative market behaviour has encouraged more hero-leader cultures to prosper. This dizzyingly-high leadership-to-employee pyramid of remuneration sits uncomfortably against a paradigm of societal togetherness. The word 'we' in business leadership has too often suffered a literal translation of 'you, led by me'. The contemporary use of inclusive terms can be neutralized by our inherited business architecture. To overcome this, business leaders would need to re-engage in common-ground issues and remove the shackles of a heroship history.

Thirdly, without a coalition of caring that is created between leadership and employees, a model for change relies almost entirely on the will of leadership to make that change. If a business leader and employees are not genuinely engaged on the same issues, it is left to leadership to either create that engagement (*come, care with me*) or create a facsimile of it (*let us care about a parallel, or derivative, issue*) in order to be somewhat effective.

Employee engagement surveys are often narrow representations of actual and potential engagement because they focus on a culture that is largely made up of internal factors. There is a high proportion of neutrality – an almost clinical detachment – that is evident in organizations with a functioning culture. The neutrality occurs partly because employees are able to, and are perhaps conditioned to, separate work from society. Employee engagement surveys focus on that sphere of work that has been separated from society, except perhaps for some philanthropic activities. Yet most of the things in life that employees are passionate about exist in the same society that they go home to.

This is seen most readily in exit interview conversations, where voluntarily outgoing former employees will admit to entering a period (often for years) of seeing work as their enabler to enjoy the things in the broader sphere of society. The transaction is clear and consistent. Disengaged employees 'tolerate' their work because it offers them the means to, quite independently and in an almost different universe of existence, engage in other societal activities that provide them with pleasure. For over a century, business organizations have remained distant from this universe, choosing only to invest in the near interface.

In maintaining this separation between the world in which they live and the world in which they work, employees are able to exist in businesses that promote little positive societal change (or even cause negative societal change) but still covet positive societal aspects and engage in positive societal change outside of work. Employees can slide deeper into this separation paradigm without even mindfully registering it.

This broad ability to slide into this separation is inversely correlated to the degree to which some core values are held firmly, visibly and authentically by an organization. The less the organization holds core societal values firmly, visibly and authentically, the easier it is for an employee to slide into separation. The more important such values are to an employee, the easier the slide.

Yet, as business organizations surge into the second quarter of the twenty-first century, employees still perceive the role of business in the following duality. Many employees expect businesses to *not* damage our world, ethically, environmentally or socially. But they also believe that businesses do *not* have a mandated role in improving our world, other than as a philanthropic activity. The dissonance is interesting; there is vested interest in our society, but it is focused on not damaging society, as opposed to improving it. This role separation is an inherited mantra reaching back over one hundred years. Business does not have to improve society, unless it wants to via a philanthropic leaning. It is a discretionary effort. It is generations of classical economic theory, as articulated by Friedman, handed down from business leader to employee.

There is considerable ability within the ranks of the majority of employees to sit with this for quite a while, even if, at some level, this irks many employees. This discomfort comes from a coalescing of customer and employee values in society – that businesses have an obligation and the means to be more productive in supporting and advancing human values.

It is useful to consider what this means for the holy grail of engaging leadership that most business leaders are taught to achieve. A great business leader is prized for their ability to engage many employees in a vision. The vision that is chosen is often deeply self-serving at its very heart. It presents business purpose in narrow terms, following the classical notion that scope constraint builds focus.

And so for many decades, employees were able to bring their 'work selves' to work and to keep their 'community selves' for the weekends at home. This has been an ongoing characteristic of labour markets for well over a century. The separation of work life from the rest of our lives has been a learned attribute, established in the very early days of the industrial revolution and moulded more distinctly into our social fabric in the mid-twentieth century. This separation is an odd artifice and one that serves a potentially outdated leadership paradigm. It is, when viewed objectively and without the benefit of history's cementing of one perspective, a large and missing element of visionary leadership in our business organizations today. Why not engage, as a business leader, with the things that matter to our employees' lives? Why not engage employees in a vision that is not just shareholder-focused, but humanity-focused? Is there not a deep cultural value, and the roots of a common and aspirational purpose, to such envisioning? These points will be raised and explored from a leadership perspective in later chapters of this book.

7

Community

Within the very wide landscape of community – and we can use the term 'society' to indicate the extreme broadness of it – are some factions of engagement that have already been dealt with in the previous pages. There are employees ranging in number from one to several hundred thousand per organization. There are customers ranging from several hundred to hundreds of millions per organization. There may also be some highly engaged communities. For example, an organization building infrastructure or buying land to build a factory or dealing with a water pollution issue may have direct contact with a subset of directly impacted communities. Against the backdrop of a world population approaching eight billion, a single large business may perceive community, something like that shown in Figure 7.1.

Business leaders very commonly hold this view. Business organizations have pockets of directly connected community, together with focal segments of customers and employees. Beyond that, there is relative disconnection. Smaller businesses would see smaller segments of customers, employees and, sometimes, directly impacted community. Beyond that would be a similar sea of disconnected community.

The engagement nexus with community, taken from this perspective, is low for a single business. But if we aggregate businesses, small and large, around the world and re-examine the connectivity nexus, it looks something more like that shown in Figure 7.2.

The picture is much more connected. It is a better representation of what happens in the world, how relationships evolve and how trust is formed or lost. This aggregate connectivity, between the business sector and communities, is what operates every day. There is only a minuscule segment of the population that is not directly impacted by the business

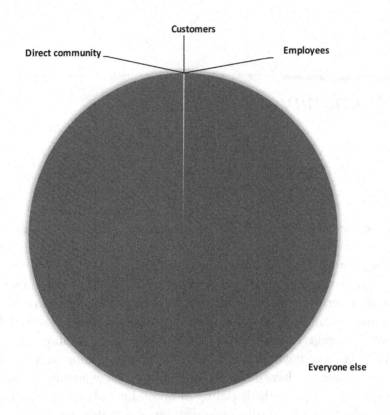

FIGURE 7.1
The assumption of low societal relevance: how one organisation sees its stakeholders.

world. The impacts are largely felt through the lenses of employment and consumerism; we are all, in one way or another, either a buyer from or an employee of the business world.

In this world view, the actions of one or more businesses affect the aggregate relationship between the business world and the community. Negative action and negative impacts, in particular, send a potent ripple across the societal ecosystem. The loss of trust imparted by one business upon the community has the potential to infect other businesses. It does not take much for this infection to take hold broadly. Over the course of more than a hundred years, the community's resilience to the mistakes that business may make has lowered. Now, an ethical blunder by one bank places all banks in a shadow of mistrust. An environmental disaster at one mine sends ripples of concern across all of the mining industry. Yet the reverse does not occur. A humanitarian push by a pharmaceutical

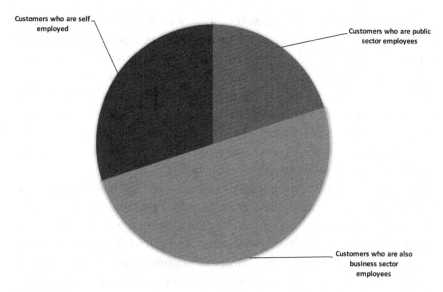

Customers who are self-employed

Customers who are public sector employees

Customers who are also business sector employees

FIGURE 7.2
The reality of high societal relevance: everybody is connected to organizations.

company to treat endemic diabetes in a poor country does not bolster the reputation of other pharmaceutical companies.

All across the world, the institution of business finds itself in an awkward place within the broader community. We, the community, are ready to vilify whole sectors based on the strength of the evidence of one bad actor but reluctant to grant broader acknowledgement when champions of that sector take social leadership. This one-way characterization speaks of a cultural reluctance to embrace business as a trusted part of society. Business organizations, as a species in the ecosystem, are close to being considered a necessary evil in society. The collective leadership of the business world is not proud of that position, and if it were, society would express bemusement at the degree of denial that prevails. But, like seasoned performers, business leadership knows that the show must go on. And so we smile through the mistakes, forgive ourselves the faux-pas and keep influencing, behind the scenes, the reviews of our performance. And with every season of the show, our audience in the community grows increasingly cynical.

We know that this erosion of trust is growing. Yet, oddly, there is no obvious epidemic of business failures that would account for such a determined downward slide in trust levels. We are not faced with an avalanche of cataclysmic mistakes. It is an everyday behaviour that contributes consistently to this erosion. Nor is every business organization ruthlessly gouging its customers, employees and community for its own selfish reasons. Those within the business world know that they are not an axis of evil in the midst of society, plotting the demise of the community at large. In fact, the business world is aware that it wants to do better, to rebuild trust. Most within society know this too, or we would be paralyzingly awash with corporate conspiracy theories. Yet the balance, indisputably, is an ongoing recession of trust.

If there is no malevolent intent (or indeed, quite the opposite) and the business world continues to lose trust, then only one reason remains. The business world must be inept at building trust. There must be missing skill sets and behaviours, a missing leadership strength in the business world, for collective societal views of business organizations to progressively become less trusting and more cynical. We cannot continue to blame the bad press and the poor reviews. The next section of this book addresses this failing of business leadership and considers how successful cultural paradigms can be created and nurtured to reverse this slide of trust.

Much like the objects in the side mirrors of our vehicle that appear larger than real life, the adjacency of businesses to the broader community highlights the flaws of business organizations. Ignoring them does not make them go away. Denying them through well-conceived press releases and divinely orchestrated social media campaigns does not make them go away. The digital age, and the internet of things, ensures that business organizations are highly visible, even if they are not particularly transparent.

This has not always been the case, and classical business leadership styles have not had to deal with the intense proximity to communities that our digital world creates. The business world was once seen as a minor sliver in the everyday lives of people. Despite the growth of consumerism and rampant advertising that exploded in the middle of the twentieth century, the initial presence of businesses in everyday lives was still relatively modest. The exception might have been smaller communities dominated by one or two businesses upon which people relied for their livelihoods.

Through the period that we know as post-industrialism, the perceived presence of businesses grew from the fringes into the mainstream. The digital era then supercharged public awareness. The presence of businesses in our daily lives was uncloaked, not just because of our access to the internet of all things but also because of the boom in advertising that was enabled for these businesses. As social media took off, so too did the era of personalized advertising. In this era, a mere passing interest in a product or service that we might exhibit via a lazy keystroke or two is reinforced by customized advertising feeds into our social media and other digital platforms. The new world order is that of highly visible business organizations with convex-mirror images that reflect, amplify and propagate their presence, flaws and all.

Now, even if we had never heard of a business organization before today, this avalanche of business organizations' push into our lives can take us from no awareness to passively curious to highly aware in a matter of minutes or days, depending on our degree of engagement with the digital world. Our awareness of businesses, and their footprint in our society, is being increased at unprecedented rates. A teenager today, for example, is substantially more cognizant of the presence of a teeming sea of businesses than a teenager was twenty years ago. Brands, products and their competitive advantages are thrown at existing consumers and budding consumers through interlinked digital platforms and devices twenty-four hours a day. We are not averse to interacting with several of these platforms and devices on a daily basis. Through two factors – digital connectivity and businesses competing for our attention – we have become highly aware of the business world. Our awareness now soars at an unprecedented level. That level will only rise. And a deficit of trust in the community around business organizations is a challenging place from which to navigate the next chapter of business organizational evolution.

8

Government

Government, whether elected or imposed, often shapes the environment in which businesses operate. When elected, governments are, in theory at least, the voice of society. While the lofty ideals of societal representation may not always be delivered upon by government, there is nonetheless significant connectivity between public concern and government attention, particularly in an elected democracy. Similar connectivity can also exist in benevolent dictatorships if the business is operating in such jurisdictions. And while the same cannot be said for countries with weak systems of government and despotic leadership, the world as a whole is becoming more, not less, governed.

Of all institutions on the planet, an elected government is best placed to hear and respond to societal concerns. While this may not always happen to an electorate's satisfaction, the ability of government to shape the business-operating environment in response to societal requirements is considerable. This ability positions this stakeholder group as one of the most pivotal enablers available to business leaders.

Today, in reality, business and government wrestle with each other on a broad array of issues. Taxes and royalties form a large percentage of direct interface concerns. They often set the stage for a culture of careful manoeuvring. If politics in government is cagey, politics between government and business can be even more so. Compounding this, business has for many decades been instrumental in financing and otherwise supporting political campaigns – an action which has given the business world considerable influence in policy settings. As a result, business and government working together attract a particularly heightened sense of suspicion and mistrust from society. This in turn creates a range of impediments to businesses working collaboratively with the elected government.

Business and government are uneasy allies in the business ecosystem. Yet their co-dependence is intense. Business needs government, and government needs business. Government regulates business, and business health is a key determinant for a government's economic success. The current state – and the foreseeable futures – of government and business are tightly intertwined.

Government is highly visible to society in a much more specific way than businesses are. Government is generally newsworthy every day, whereas businesses are broadly omnipresent. There is much to gossip about when it comes to government and politics and very little to gossip about when it comes to the business world unless you are a very active part of the business world. The number of political vehicles (government and opposition) is much smaller than the number of businesses in the environment, making it much easier to afford political parties a sense of personality and to differentiate between them even when their policies are comparable. Neither governments in power nor parties in opposition are inclined to be discreet. As a result, they are relatively loud in traditional and social media – either because they are making a statement or because millions of people are talking about their statements.

Society therefore sees governments in positions of leadership, advocacy and authority through a steady torrent of the same actors making statements on a wide range of issues. Contrast this with business organizations which, despite having a considerable footprint in our world, are a relatively silent fraternity. It is not unreasonable, therefore, for communities and society to form the view that governments are the most significant sector in how societal issues are considered or addressed, even if their key practical role is as an enabler and facilitator, rather than an economic force for change. As we shall probe in the next chapters, business leadership can choose to be more societally prominent or to stay out of the limelight and remain powerful, shadowy voyeurs.

9

Global Trends

Good leaders keep their eyes on the bigger picture. Sometimes this higher perspective is of direct relevance to leadership visions and strategies. Other times the higher perspective serves to set and maintain an appropriate context for leadership efforts. For business leaders, the forces that influence and shape society cannot be ignored. They provide depth of insight and wisdom to the value that a leader's business can bring to society. In accessing these higher viewpoints, a leader's ability to navigate a business towards strategic competitive advantage is greatly enhanced.

This skill is, of course, highly valued in the narrower realms of business-to-business and business-to-customer strategies. It is equally useful in navigating businesses towards becoming a force for good in society. In this section, some global perspectives are highlighted for two reasons. The first is that they set global contexts for where people – whether as individuals living in society or as business leaders creating lasting impacts on society – might in the future find themselves. The second is that the process of connecting perspectives to form a whole that is greater than the sum of the parts is a skill that works equally well in regional, country, state or even local economies. This skill delivers ground-breaking strategies, because it brings broader, deeper and connected insights to the role of leading organizations through future societal trajectories.

The term 'megatrend' became increasingly popular with businesses towards the end of the twentieth century. It allowed the strategists to move past considering the waves of trends that were prolific in the global economy and look instead to the deeper tidal forces behind them. In doing so, longer-term views, forecasts and strategies could be formulated. This was particularly important because the world began yet another cycle of rapid change, accelerating in the time of the Millennials and through the time of the Generation Z youth. Looking to trends that have deep and prevailing rationales allows strategists to anchor the 'why' of their strategies to societal changes. Because the 'why' is captured, the analysis of megatrends increased strategists' potency.

There are many megatrends at play across our natural and geopolitical landscape. The true value for business strategists lies in identifying those few that are relevant in the sphere of business operations, both for today and for tomorrow. For the purposes of this book, whose intent it is to encourage business leadership behaviours that will improve the future of humanity and underpin transformative long-term business success, just five are highlighted. These are not the only five of importance, and they may not, in time, even prove to be the most important. However, considering these five illustrates some significant forces that might compel business organizations to differently view their relationship with the world.

The first megatrend is that of humanity itself – its population and its age demographics. Irrespective of humanity's progression through its variously labelled phases – the Silent Generation, the Baby Boomers, Generation X, Millennials and Generation Z – humanity's hierarchy of needs has not changed. It remains one of the many species that survive and thrive on this planet and it shares with those species many similar needs, albeit with specific human nuances. Air, water, food and shelter remain high on the list of physical priorities. Humans are very social animals, bringing with this state of being a number of pervasive psychological needs that are the same irrespective of race or religion. As age demographics change, the emphases that are placed on the basic needs of society flex too. As populations invariably increase, the magnitude of these needs, tempered by the emphases of age demographics, also changes.

The population of our planet currently changes at a rate of just over 1.2 billion people every 15 years or so. Because numbers trip off the tongue deceptively easily, a historical perspective is useful to reflect upon here. Around the start of the industrial revolution, and before global geopolitics precipitated two world wars, global population was only 1.5 billion. Over the next 15-year period, the world will add to its population around eighty per cent of what it took millennia to accrue.

It does not do this uniformly across the globe. There are significant differences in rates of growth from country to country. However, some distinct patterns exist. These patterns are almost certain to occur, notwithstanding any cataclysmic events, whether natural or human-induced, that might change the general global stasis. The magnitude of population changes can be estimated, at ninety-five per cent probabilities, to within a few tens of millions of the actual number we would expect to see. The spread of our global population of around 7.5 billion people at the turn of the third decade this century is as shown in Figure 9.1, considering the six major regions of Asia, Africa, Europe, Latin America, North America and Oceania.

Of these regions, the population in Europe is the only one that is close to remaining constant. All other regions show appreciable growth rates. Of the estimated one billion extra people that will populate Earth by 2030, ninety-seven per cent will come from the emerging economies of Asia, Africa and Latin America. Out of these three economies the greater majority (ninety of the ninety-seven per cent) will come from Asia and Africa, in similar quanta to each other.

What this means for the business world is clear: moving into the future, its new end customers are largely born in Asia and Africa. In a two-decade timeframe, there are no signals of significantly diminishing growth in Asia

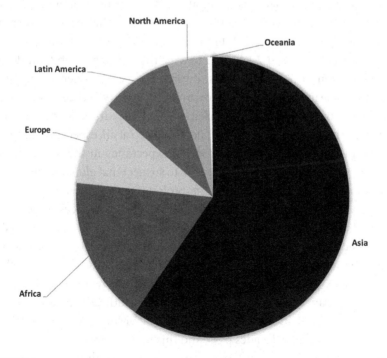

FIGURE 9.1
The world's population by geography.

or Africa, just like there are none for either of the Americas or Oceania. It's simply that these two large Eastern and Southern continents, together accounting for over seventy-five per cent of the global population in 2020, will – for the foreseeable future – continue to accrue a greater and greater share of this population. By 2030, this share will be nudging seventy-eight per cent.

The relative magnitudes of population in Asia and Africa herald some important supply-and-demand cues for basic human necessities such as food and water. Over a 15-year period, Asia's densification increases by around ten per cent. Africa's, by comparison, increases by a staggering forty-two per cent. The ramp-up in pressure to procure some of the basic necessities of life on Earth will be fourfold more apparent in Africa than it will be in Asia. The parts of the world's products-and-services economy that exist within the supply chains of food and water, as well as other primary requirements of civilization such as sanitation, health and education, are poised to witness unprecedented opportunities for upscaled delivery in these regions, and particularly in Africa.

Changing age demographics will affect the shifting economic potential in these different regions. The 15-year period that the planet is currently experiencing, in which 1.2 billion people are added to the planet, is underpinned by around 2.1 billion new births but only 0.9 billion deaths. The population of the world shifts towards an average older demographic because people live longer. Since the turn of the twenty-first century, average global life expectancies have increased by over five years, to around seventy-five years. The increase has not been notably steep at all, especially compared to the rapid global advances made in life expectancy in the second half of the twentieth century. There is no reason to suspect that global increases will cease to occur. The combination of life-prolonging medical interventions in many developed economies, together with the improved access to basic and intermediate medical facilities in emerging economies, has contributed to a solid bedrock of life expectancy increase. It will continue to contribute greatly, because there are still a great many regions of the world where average life expectancies can be increased. The inter-regional averages still show a wide range, varying at the last World Health Organization review in 2016 between 61 in Africa and 78 in Europe. More countries break the 75-year age average as decades pass, and this will continue.

At the other end of the life spectrum, infant mortality rates still show large variations between countries. In countries with the highest infant mortality rate within Africa (where the mortality is counted if it occurs within the first five years of a child surviving birth), the likelihood of infant death is ten times that of a child in Western Europe. High infant mortality rates are correlated with high birth rates; humankind's drive to promulgate family and species survival is played out via increased procreation to offset increased infant mortality.

Within the age demographics, there are three key brackets to consider in business economic rationalizations: pre-working age, working age and post-working age. The first and third brackets characterize largely unproductive markets. These are the dependant segments of society. The middle bracket is the productive segment. It is the part that fuels economic engines through a combination of work and consumption. The consumerism in this bracket is often for multiple persons, not just the person and a partner, but perhaps for children and parents as well. The middle bracket subsidizes life within the brackets on either side.

In the decade leading up to 2030, Asia and Latin America hold the highest percentage of the middle bracket. Around sixty-seven per cent, or two thirds, of their respective populations are in this group. United Nations predictions suggest that this period represents a levelling off, or a slight tailing off, of the peak percentage of the productive population. North America, Europe and Oceania all show a rapid decline, progressing downwards through the century from the low-sixties percentile range. In these regions, an ageing population will be subsidized by a shrinking productive population. It is a trend that will require adjustments to fiscal policy to manage. Only Africa, climbing steeply from a high-fifties percentile range, shows strong future growth in the productive tranche of its population.

Many countries in the world, including the substantially populated China and India, are expected to slow down their birth rates leading up to 2030 compared to birth rates experienced immediately after the turn of the century. This foreshadows a steepening decline over time in the Asian region of the currently high percentage of the population that is classified as productive.

As these trends play out over a 50-year window, the population aspects and the age demographics underpin why many economists refer to the current period as the Asian Century. A region's productive-consumer population, together with its access to resources and markets, is an excellent prime indicator of inherent economic strength. Add to this Asia's current sixty per cent share of the global population, which is likely to remain at a still-dominant fifty-seven per cent by 2030 as African populations grow aggressively, and it is clear that the impact of Asia on global markets is going to be significant for a long while yet.

Many of Asia's subcultures promote a firmer economic household-level co-dependency between all three age-demographic brackets than is typically seen in other parts of the world. Extended-family economic dynamics are prevalent. The contrast is greatest with nuclear-family dominated economies in North America and Europe, where vertically and horizontally extended families are less the norm than in Asia. These co-dependencies bring with them different household productivity and consumer behaviours than the predominantly Western-flavoured economic behaviour of the last century. Sharing, or more accurately, distribution – of jobs, incomes, consumables – is a more prevalent feature of Asian economic cultures than it has been of Western economic cultures. This interconnectivity creates a potentially greater degree of resilience at the grass-roots level of an economy than the world has been familiar with. Consequently, the so-called Asian Century, with its two previously unseen hallmarks of relative global size and inherent grass-roots resilience, has a potentially substantial and long-term effect on the global economy, potentially to a greater degree than was witnessed courtesy of the Western hemisphere's economy in the twentieth century. Consumer trends are aggregated differently because of these dynamics. There is an inherently greater ability for consumer preferences to shift, like larger schools of fish in a current, compared to Western economies of the past.

Meanwhile, Africa's demographic shifts herald a growing strength. It is the only region to increase its share of the productive-consumer population in the decade leading up to 2030. This foreshadows an emerging 'sweet spot' that is available to the African economy and to global markets if this productive-consumer population is enabled in two ways. The translation of this latent human capital into productive market value, via the improvement of its labour market value (typically through education, training and access to business), is one. The other is an increase in the per-person and per-household income (which occurs as a by-product of the first, if accomplished at scale), creating a demand hub for products and services at parity prices. This represents a significant shift in African economies, which have traditionally attracted cheaper and lower-quality goods in the world market, largely because of affordability constraints.

The third bracket of the global population, the increasingly dependent cohort of older people who have completed their years of peak productivity, is increasing across all parts of the world. The increases are at their most marked in Europe and North America, where the older contingent of the population is projected to reach between twenty-five and thirty per cent. This precludes any dramatic improvements in late-age health management, such as a rapid reduction in age-onset diabetes or a cure for cancer, which would elevate these percentages further.

By comparison to Europe and North America, Asia's contingent of the older bracket moves from about twelve per cent in 2020 to around seventeen per cent in 2030. By raw numbers, rate of increase of the third-bracket ratio in Asia is the fastest in the world, although its percentages are less than its Western counterparts. Still, by 2030, over seventy per cent of the older contingent on the planet will be in Asia, foreshadowing a very large market for aged health, community care and other industries.

In contrast, Africa's population, still surging through its high regeneration phase, will hold fewer than eight per cent of the world's elders. It stands out as the epicentre of youthful demographics well into the middle of this century.

For businesses, particularly the larger and more established global entities, the pivot needed from a Western-hemisphere focus to a more distributed landscape is especially large. Older paradigms of leveraging high-resource availability, low-cost and low-demand geographies to service low-resource-high-demand geographies will be challenged. The consumer world is beginning to shift in an irreversible tide, while business models that still resonate with older colonial models continue to persist. The required pivot is roughly in the same timescale as large multinational business organizations used to evaluate returns on capital investments. It is a deeply strategic timeframe. It is both unavoidable and occurs at a truly global scale. It requires a recalibration of how leaders have conceived of connecting resources to markets in the past and a re-invention of business wisdom to prepare for a very different world. For example, there will be a more complex array of factors to consider when extracting minerals from emerging economies. During the twentieth century, business models thrived on a variety of resource rent models. Agreements were made with governments to remove minerals from, for example, Africa, constitute them into value-added products in Europe or Asia and export them to dominant markets in North America or Europe.

As demands for some commodities in Asia and Africa begin to catch up with, and eventually outstrip, European and North American demands, the more circuitous business chains of the last century might truncate to more direct conversions of resources to commodities. A greater flavour of Asian resources servicing Asian markets, or African resources servicing African markets, could emerge. Traditional business models that were previously underpinned by the so-called First World and Third World relationships are likely to become increasingly blurred and eventually unworkable. In the past, the problems of the so-called Third World could be all-but-divorced from business economic considerations. These Third World stakeholders held little market power with which to bargain on the world economic stage. In the future, this is likely to shift. Regions that hold both resources and customers, such as Asia, South America and Africa, are likely to grow, at astonishing rates, the capacity to convert local resources to locally consumed goods. Any other outcome seems unlikely, irrespective of whether the journey starts from a point of low capacity or not. The broad rationale for this change is there. So is the scale of economic value for embarking on this change. So, too, is the availability of human capital to fuel this change.

Add to this the ever-growing economic relationships between these regions of population growth. It is possibly at its most visible in the decade-long process of conjoining of Asian and African governmental interests. The intuitive probability of this Asia–Africa axis pivot becomes near-certain. Irrespective of the political lenses that might be chosen to view these trends, there is an unprecedented economic impact that is making its way into our future. The way multinational companies, in particular, need to think of the way mid- to far-term futures will change; and it is changing.

As this pivot occurs, the traditional regional stakeholder groups will change. No longer will the bulk of organizational thinking be Anglo-centric. We will not almost exclusively be solving for problems that affect the Western world. Already, in the start of the twenty-first century, focuses are shifting to the Asian continents at scale, providing solutions for Asian societies that once barely made boardroom strategies. Already, Africa is attracting growing attention, and in a decade or two will command more boardroom strategy time. The roles of business organizations relative to these problems, today and in the future, are changing, but so are the locations of these problems. Business leadership involvement in solving macro-scale global problems will broaden its theatre beyond the traditional stage. It is along this very different axis that many of the future challenges and opportunities – and perhaps even mandates – of the business world will emerge.

For the leaders of today and tomorrow, there is no shortage of learning grounds about, for example, economic globalization and operating in an Asian economy. Since the late twentieth century, tertiary educational institutions have focused commendably on economic and cultural leadership learnings to help facilitate some of this pivot in business thinking. Interestingly, the growth in this educational focus has, by and large, been much more visible in Western institutions of higher learning. Yet, with these global population and corresponding economic changes in train, it is by no means assured that the past – a dominant Western business economy led by Western business leaders serving global markets – is a reasonable predictor of the future. Indeed, any expectation that this trend would continue is dangerously wedded to past business perspectives that 'Older Anglo-Saxon Men Know Best'.

As the world moves into the third decade of the twenty-first century, around $30 trillion of its capital markets are represented by 350 of the world's largest public listed companies. By region, this cohort's command of the $30 trillion is distributed as follows, from the smallest entity at a $10 billion market value to the biggest at just under $1 trillion market value (Figure 9.2).

Around seventy-five per cent of this segment of the capital markets has been represented for decades by North American and European public companies. Not unexpectedly, business leadership has reflected these markets. Over time, the 'stacking' of business leadership strata has evolved towards an observably homogeneous mix. Gender homogeneity is evident, as a result of the male dominance witnessed through the Silent Generation, the Baby Boomers and Generation Z. Cultural homogeneity exists among these 350 companies, with a predominance of Anglo-Saxon leadership. These companies, many of which face into emerging economies, have a potentially narrowed diversity of perspective at leadership levels. Relatively few companies release public information on leadership diversity, and the ones that do are probably in the more progressive echelon of organizations. There are three statistics that represent a dated paradigm of leadership which is distinctly at odds with existing and future global demographic shifts.

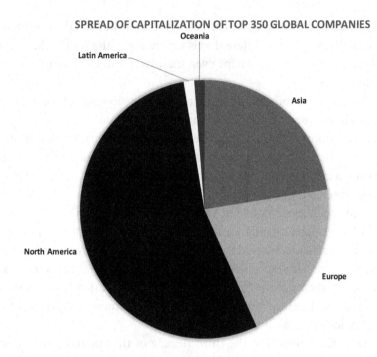

FIGURE 9.2
The capitalization of Top 350 companies by geography.

Drawn from Fortune 500 company data at the end of the second decade this century, men in senior leadership positions in public companies (CEO to two levels down) sat at around eighty per cent, with women represented at the ratio of one female to every four males. Cultural diversity in this same leadership segment averaged around seventy-three per cent Caucasian, twenty-one per cent Asian and the remainder split between other cultural identities. Leadership and experience continued to correlate strongly, although there were some visible trade-offs between experience and energy, resulting in an increasing number of CEOs appointed in their fifties.

These statistics highlight a glaring issue for businesses looking into the future. The leadership mix, at least viewed from gender, cultural and age perspectives, is strongly reminiscent of the last one hundred years of business management. There are credible, but nevertheless marginal, shifts achieved in the last two decades in the areas of gender and cultural diversity. However, business leadership still displays a gap risk – one between its collective market and investor perspectives and those of a fifty per cent female, majority multicultural and increasingly youthful demographic of market and investment needs. Many conservative views revolve around the observation that leadership representation need not physically reflect stakeholder demographics in order to make wise decisions. The counter-argument to this is that deeper and more profound business insights can be drawn from perspectives that resonate strongly within those demographics. It is not a question of democratic apportionment of stakeholder characteristics into the leadership cohort of businesses but more of an authentic accessing of broader perspectives. This counter-argument is still based in meritocracy, but one that places as strong an emphasis on understanding stakeholder perspectives as it does in deploying classical business skills. This issue will arise throughout this book; it speaks to leadership that is more attuned to stakeholder nuances and therefore more conversant with the business risks and opportunities that these signpost.

While the population demographics are compelling, they must be overlaid with other megatrends that affect how such populations actually behave in the decades to come. The conjoining of these major inexorable shifts and how business organizations respond in the ecosystem are crucial.

Humankind's affinity for community and development has been taking consistent directions in urbanization for over a century. Since the late nineteenth century, beginning in Western economies, populations have migrated from rural settings to urban settings, densified within existing urban frameworks or densified and transformed rural settings into urban landscapes. As 2020 approached, the percentage of the world's population classified as living in urban settings was around fifty-four per cent. By 2030, this is expected to be nearly sixty per cent.

The future urbanization effect is attributed by region as shown in Figure 9.3.

Over a 15-year period to 2030, over a billion more people are assimilated into existing, expanding or new urban landscapes. Some ninety-five per cent of this urbanization occurs in Asia and Africa, and this is expected to continue as these continents' urbanization ratios normalize to within global levels. While there is certainly physical migration of people from rural to urban landscapes, the main driver of increasing urbanisation is the originally larger urban populations exhibiting average or above-average regional birth rates.

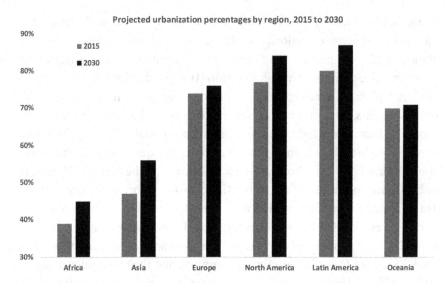

FIGURE 9.3
Where urban growth is projected, 2015 to 2030.

In contrast, rural populations are expected to peak at around 3.4 billion between 2020 and 2030, and are expected to slowly reduce to 3.1 billion by 2050 as the remnants of rural-to-urban drift continue.

Urbanization contributes to the economy-of-scale of public utility distributions. Infrastructure, fresh water, energy, public sanitation, education and health, among many others, benefit in lowered cost-per-capita terms (for equivalent quality of service) in urban areas. Efficiencies can be realized more easily via streamlined delivery, notwithstanding inefficient consumer use habits that may prevail over these.

Urbanization, especially at rapid rates, has the potential to stress existing public utility services. Demands can exceed supply, creating cost pressures. These stresses lead to physical demarcations in these services, organized along the lines of those who can afford to pay for continuity of quality of supply, and those who cannot. The urban landscape becomes increasingly divided by sharp socio-economic gradients, contributing to social tensions. Slums are formed and significant urban divisions occur.

The growth in urbanization is accompanied by a number of trends. An increasingly larger proportion of the world's population will live in bigger cities. As the earth's population passed the 7.5 billion mark, the number of people projected to live in cities with over a million but less than five million inhabitants will increase by twenty-eight per cent within a decade. The number of people projected to live in cities with over ten million people will increase by over forty per cent, again within ten years. This will see a much greater densification of markets – for food, housing, infrastructure, education, medical facilities and so on. Economies of scale will continue to reshape the way the world delivers consumer goods and services to our populations.

Cities which have for many years dominated global landscapes because of their sheer population will continue to be significant in the global economy. But the urban centres of humanity will take on some distinctive new patterns. By 2030, the ten largest cities in the world by population will include six from Asia, two from Central and South America, and two from Africa – each housing between twenty and forty million people. At the turn of the third decade of the twenty-first century, there were 33 cities with over ten million people; by the turn of the fourth decade, this will have grown to 43, with only one of those emerging 10 being located in the Western hemisphere. Building, energy, transport and communication sectors of the economy will be more and more subject to scale effects. There will be both economies of scale that will place competitive downward pressure on unit costs to serve customers and extremes of demand and supply that will incur pressures on the continuity of service. As more and more cities grow into larger, denser communities, there will be greater interconnectivity between supply chains and industries, shifting the way business is done further and further away from centralized models and more towards dispersed but massively interconnected models. Business disruption that uses the power of population proximity, de-regulated markets and rapidly increasing digital technological connectivity will begin to reshape the way business models work, heralding even greater interrelationships within the business-to-business environment and the business-to-customer environment. Within the business ecosystem, interdependencies between the various entities between, for example, source materials and consumers will increase. So too will the transparency that accompanies interdependencies, gradually building pressure to break down the organizational separations from society and the opacity about how business is done that have remained a feature of the business world for generations.

As urbanization continues and populations densify, the risk exposure to natural disasters of populations grows. The likelihood of some risks (for example, extremes of rainfall, flooding, heat waves, hurricanes and cyclones) may increase as the effects of climate change are felt. Populations exposed to these risks will increase, driving up the consequences of such natural disasters. The number of people potentially affected will climb, not just because of average global population increases but because of urbanization and rapid scale-ups in population densification. As this happens, the global sensitivity to natural disasters will increase and, correspondingly, the outrage factors that might be associated with such disasters.

A number of factors shape how businesses might fit into this ecosystem. In the first instance, a business's ability to service its customers will rely to an extent on the proximity of delivery mechanisms to these customers. This proximity will facilitate how it delivers products and services to more densely located customers and how it markets and advertises its products and services. The presence of businesses in population centres will grow as a result, making their presence an increasingly visible part of a societal construct.

Secondly, as population centres increase in number and density, businesses in these cities will become more firmly enmeshed in societal issues. Power, water, natural resources and infrastructure will become increasingly shared between businesses and communities alike. Either the constraints that affect one will affect the other or, if businesses are afforded greater access to such necessities than communities are, there will be greater tension between the two. In either event, there will be a greater propensity to co-create individual and collective futures, infusing the relationship with an increasing sense of shared responsibility.

Thirdly, the co-mingling of business entities' corporate presences in the urban landscape, their customers, investors and communities will facilitate a greater homogenization of values. This will be in direct contrast to the late twentieth century, where a corporation in Japan, for example, could interact with a significant market in New York but share little else in common. Its employees might have been in Tokyo and Kobe, its investors in Tokyo, London and New York, and the majority of its customers in a small number of population hubs in Europe and the United States. The late twentieth century saw a greater dispersion of stakeholders with very different world views of societal constraints and challenges. In the twenty-first century, as urbanization surges forward, employees, customers and investors in a business might well be neighbours. Their connectivity is set to increase and expand as more flexible working conditions grow in scope through the workforce, allowing people to larger percentages of their working time outside of the perimeter of traditional workplaces. Societal aspects affecting one stakeholder group might be increasingly similar to societal aspects affecting one or more of the other groups. The ability to communicate individually and disperse collective commentaries on societal experiences will far exceed the social media boom of the early twenty-first century. There will be a widespread breakdown of the societal and work–life separation barriers that currently create separate enclaves of communication between investors, connectivity between employees and collaboration within communities.

Fourthly, the search for talent in businesses will increasingly focus on urban settings in which this co-mingling has been occurring for some time, in which the attractiveness of an employer – particularly among bigger businesses – becomes increasingly correlated with what value the business entity brings to society. Financial rewards and lifestyle-related benefits will still continue to be a key attraction, but the offset value of non-financial aspects in attracting talent will grow in stature. In a business world that currently is, and will only continue to be, competitive in its search for highly engaged, values-aligned human capital, this aspect will gain prominence with businesses that want to be able to attract some of the best leaders.

Fifth, a by-product of greater urbanization, coupled with the steady global improvement in the percentage of people living in poverty that the world has engineered for several decades, is that a much higher component of populations will be middle class. While at the high end of the spectrum, it is predicted that the rich will get much richer, at the low end of the spectrum – those in poverty – will reduce further, growing the middle class across the world. This middle class will congregate in urban settings, with surges in numbers expected in the expanding economies of Asia, South America and Africa. A greater degree of education, awareness and middle-class activism accompanies this trend. Thus, the proximity of populations to business, the sharing of resources and the co-mingling of stakeholders will be subject to an underlying growth in awareness and a resultant amplification of critical thinking – within the broader business ecosystem – of the role that business plays in society. As this happens, businesses will find it less feasible to distance themselves from the factors that affect societal well-being.

Sixth, the increase in urbanization improves the scope for local business disruptors to flourish. For the larger multinational businesses, this points to an underlying business risk, representing an erosion of the hold on markets that was previously uncontested, or only weakly contested. For potential local disruptors, an increasingly attractive proposition is presented: a directly accessible market of scale that can be offered differentiated service by leveraging local challenges and aspirations. A population in an urban location with challenging access to fresh water, for example, may find a greater affinity with a local manufacturing or retail business that innovates to use less water or make more water widely available. Larger, multinational businesses will face, and need to respond to, competitive local businesses that benefit from the availability of increasing local scale markets and from their inherent ownership of local considerations.

Seventh, as populations congregate and greater order is sought in the melting pots of the world's civilizations, the historical trend towards increasing regulation will intensify. Expectations of order will propagate policies that move us towards a greater level of orderliness in the face of inherently more chaotic urban settings. These policies will need to be supported by laws and regulations that prevent the breakdown of orderliness; that represent what is good for the majority, and that dissuade the promulgation of societally harmful actions and behaviours. The bane of business operations, the scope creep of regulation, is unlikely to dissipate with increasing urbanization. It will only increase.

These seven factors in urbanization herald increasing visibility and accountability within the business world, for which leaders of the future will need to be better armed than the leaders of the past.

Juxtaposed with these two megatrends that capture people and their congregation on the planet are two others that affect the broad societal stratosphere of the people on this planet.

As the number of people increases at previously unheard-of rates, and a much larger middle class establishes itself in rapidly increasingly urban settings across the planet, the needs of this population must be met in order for society to progress rather than regress. This means, of course, not that consumer demands must be pandered to but that supply and demand must reach a comfortable and sustainable equilibrium. In order for this to happen, there must be a significant change in our global economy.

At the turn of the twentieth century, well more than a hundred years ago, there were two notable characteristics to the earth's resource utility. The first was that our cache of non-renewable resources – the land and the minerals, and all materials that have a fixed and finite quantity within our reach – was being used up at a slow rate commensurate with a much smaller population. The ability to consume these non-renewable resources was modest, meaning that while there might have been a foreseeable date at which these resources would be depleted, that day was very far into the future. In much the same way that today we acknowledge the sun as a slowly cooling ball of fire that will one day no longer sustain life on Earth, but with a timeline that is too long to address meaningfully with any sense of urgency, our population's relationship with finite resources was similarly unconcerned. Of course, the timelines for the two comparisons are vastly different, one being several hundreds of thousands of years before we ought to worry and the other being only a thousand or so years before concern would have set in. However, in human terms, there is little difference between thinking 30 generations out and 3,000 generations out, both are too long to contemplate without becoming enmeshed in surreal imaginings. Not only was humanity's dent in non-renewable resources unconcerning; it was not calculated because it had not yet emerged as a serious consideration.

The second was even less of an issue. Our biocapacity, counted as fruits and vegetables, meat, fish, wood, cotton for clothing, and carbon dioxide absorption, were being used at a lower rate than they were being replenished. It is important to note that this biocapacity indicator is, like gross domestic product, an environmental economics artifice. It is useful to compare and communicate concepts, but it is a highly simplified measure. However, what is important to understand is that, at that point in history, we could have used these resources forever, without deficit.

These two characteristics have changed. Firstly, the stockpile of non-renewable resources that are within our reach is some cause for concern. At the rate of population growth Earth continues to experience, these resources no longer seem nearly as long-lived as they might have one hundred years ago. Offsetting this is the advancement in synthetic technologies that three consecutive generations have seen, shifting some of our reliance on non-renewable natural resources to manufactured synthetics. So, as a society, we are aware of the finiteness of non-renewable resources. Our population expansion, and its ability to rapidly whittle away any comfort we have in the longevity of such resources, is somewhat ameliorated by our propensity for the invention of alternatives to reduce our impact on the earth's finite non-renewable resources, but we nevertheless edge towards greater resource scarcity.

Secondly, in 1970 the world's population, and its use of the earth's biocapacity, exceeded for the first time the planet's rate of renewal. For centuries before this, the growing human domination of the planet, together with other environmental factors, had combined to push some biological species to extinction, so this was not an entirely new phenomenon. However, in 1970 the human species moved up a gear. It became, annually, a net taker of the planet's biocapacity.

Since 1970, this phenomenon, termed 'ecological overshoot', has meant that the growing population's activities have extracted more of these resources than Earth can replenish and deposited more waste than Earth can absorb in an aggregate annual timeframe. By the turn of the twenty-first century, human activities used up nearly thirty per cent more than Earth could recover from, in the same annual aggregate timeframe (Figure 9.4 shows this as the number of days per year that are left over after this biocapacity budget is exceeded). By the end of the second decade of the twenty-first century, its usage had increased to over fifty per cent more than Earth could recover from, again in that same (nominally annual) timeframe.

The four factors that give rise to ecological overshoot are (i) population increase compounded by (ii) consumption rates and (iii) the efficiency of

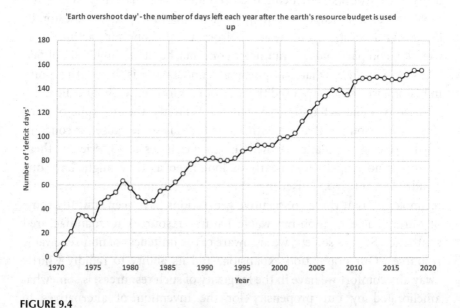

FIGURE 9.4
'Earth overshoot day': a depiction of the number of days per year our planet lives on resources borrowed from the future.

production of what is consumed, balanced out by, or in a state of imbalance relative to, (iv) nature's own production rates. Exacerbating this, consistent overshoot creates an impairment in nature's own production rates. The result of these factors and the exacerbation mechanism sees the global ecosystem experiencing, theoretically, a 'holding the dam' type stasis followed by rapid decline. The period of stasis leads our populations to experience a sense of false security, while in the meantime our ecosystem loses resilience while maintaining a façade of equilibrium.

While there are many aspects to ecological overshoot, including the health of oceans, overfishing, desertification and others, the most prominent (and inextricably linked) issue of our time is climate change. First raised as an issue with almost science-fiction overtones in the 1970s, it attracted considerable scepticism for its doom-and-gloom projections despite its scientifically defended calculations of the physics of our planet. Scepticism gave way to a viewpoint known as the precautionary principle. This is where an issue of potential concern that is otherwise unconfirmed is given a respectfully comprehensive investigation on the off-chance that it does, indeed, turn out to be disastrous. As a result of these investigations, a sense of niggling worry elevated across the world in the last two decades of the twentieth century, but it was not until the period 2005–2015 that there was a global public surge in both awareness and concern. There were a number of reasons for this tipping point, and some are illustrative of the rapid shift in societal engagement. The growing body of independent and interdependent corroborating science pointed more and more firmly to a global phenomenon of worrying proportions and consequences. The growth in awareness, moving the issue away from the tables of scientists and intergovernmental panels and into a broader societal spotlight, coincided with the explosion of social networks, the use of the internet and the emergence of trends in the frequency and intensity (both increasing) of severe weather events in many parts of the world.

During this time, some global businesses adopted a precautionary principle, but it was largely founded without a sense of real urgency. The lack of urgency was in keeping with climate change projections, which were beset by three issues. These were (i) a continuing debate on the validity of various average global temperature projections, (ii) significant differences in the extrapolated holistic impacts of such projections (including ice shelf breakdown, global ocean currents and macro-scale weather patterns) and (iii) differences of opinion regarding the severity of derivative local weather conditions from the macro-scale patterns. Added to a residual core of climate change cynicism that permeated through the investment and shareholder communities, governments and business leadership alike, these factors conspired to elicit both cautiousness in responsiveness and piecemeal actions.

The business world was notable for some of the widest range of responses possible. A large part of climate-change aggravating activities, which were linked to energy and transport, sat prominently in the sphere of the vast majority of business operations. However, for every strategic shift in the way energy and transport were considered in climate change terms by a few businesses, there were often equal and opposite shifts by many other businesses. In many parts of the world, fossil fuels represented one of the cheapest sources of energy and transport outcomes available. Examples of forward-thinking divestment of fossil fuel interests, notably in thermal coal used for power stations, were neutralized by buyers of these same interests, leading to a number of zero-sum transactions within the business ecosystem that collectively made little real impact. Indeed, collectively, business organizations actually increased their distribution and consumption of fossil fuels. Within the business ecosystem, some of the risks of climate change were not so much dealt with as passed on from one entity to another.

Added to this zero-sum game were cynically opportunistic actions, practised by large tranches of the business community and aimed equally at generating public relations value as they were meaningful climate change risk mitigations. Where business cases existed for some climate change mitigation actions (for example, energy efficiency initiatives that both reduced costs and shrunk greenhouse gas emissions), these were taken. These were largely decided against commercial hurdle rates of return for such initiatives, meaning that a large proportion of these would have made sense even without the threat of climate change. However, internal business narratives as well as those narratives transmitted out into the world of customers and other stakeholders celebrated the climate change credentials of such action. The term 'greenwashing', coined to capture those actions that were motivated as much, if not more, by the public relations value of the action than the true mitigation impacts achieved or even aspired to became commonplace. Within businesses, the term was reviled and rarely used. It spoke to an underlying lack of authenticity, which is an aspect of leadership that this book will examine in more detail later on.

This period of activity was entrenched in the culture of business leadership and, among its followers, an unfortunate sense of gamesmanship around pivotal societal issues like climate change. It resonates, still, into the third decade of this century, within the cultures of organizations that practised these rituals. Irrespective of whether employees in an organization believed in the gravity of threats such as climate change, it played out as a corporate pantomime that has often left, indelibly, two internal signals in the fabric of internal culture. One, it was important to present a public face of concern irrespective of the true level of personal commitment of leadership to the issue under discussion. Second, it was important to show what was being done by the business, to 'tell our story', in the best possible light. Embellishments, provided they were not provable as untruths, were acceptable. The combination of these two signals reinforced an internal culture that made it permissible to address an issue in an uncommitted or sub-optimal way, provided it could be presented as a creditable effort, or 'messaged' well.

In its developed form, this underlying culture promulgates a wider chasm between what is and what is seen to be. It allowed a culture of inauthenticity to prevail. In its extremes, it passively permits the doing of wrong provided it does not make the public realm of awareness.

After 2015, two significant events occurred. The first was the Conference of Parties, Number 21, in Paris, France, in December of that year on the issue of climate change. It was significant because, at intergovernmental level at least, a tipping point was reached. That point was represented by the Paris Climate Change Agreement, which in turn reflected a collective global commitment to hold the effects of climate change to a threshold that was potentially reversible and probably not cataclysmic. While it was far from binding, the collective will to agree implied that there would be collaborative ostracizing of parties who deviated from the agreement. The impacts of these would vary, but in most cases – particularly for countries with smaller and mid-sized economies – economic and trade agreements could be subsequently affected. Larger economies, such as the United States and China, for example, could potentially thumb their noses at such invectives, because of the market power they wielded. Indeed, less than two years later, the United States announced that it would not honour the agreement.

While the Paris Agreement attracted a certain amount of criticism for not being bold or authoritarian enough, a senior diplomat at the historical signing reflected that parallels could be drawn to Abraham Lincoln's Emancipation Proclamation. Without it, the subsequent outcomes of abolishing slavery and the slow process of achieving equality under law for all people might have been even slower, more painstaking and less effective. In other words, it began a path forward.

Within two years, a second key event occurred. The institutional investment community rallied behind this Agreement from a wholly expected commercial viewpoint. It did so using a pragmatic, if still potentially subjective, rationale. It began to insist on a risk-based evaluation of a business's future prospects (to bring some uniformity to the debate), upon which it would be able to make better-informed investment decisions. This signal, if anything, was even more compelling to businesses that relied heavily on institutional investors' support to maintain their access to capital. Importantly, many publicly listed and large private businesses in the majority of securities exchange jurisdictions, including the United States, Europe, Hong Kong and others, immediately fell under the umbrella raised by the investment community. Not all businesses in the world were necessarily affected at the outset; China, for example, can be relatively buffered from this event, at least while it maintains a degree of separation from Western investment forces in the global capital markets. However, the investment sense of seeking clarity in the long-term prospects of businesses subject to the far-reaching effects of climate change is difficult to argue. It is good business sense.

The nature and scale of climate change – which has the ability to affect the security of food and water, as well as the security of infrastructure that humanity relies on for both its safety and the smooth functioning of its society – has the potential for both far-reaching and intensive stakeholder engagement. There is a clear blueprint for avoiding the worst effects of climate change and the technology either available or on the very cusp of availability with which to achieve this. The blueprint for change comes at a cost, and the faster the rate of change, the higher the annual cost incurred for that change. The affordability of that cost varies between economies; yet it is feasible to absorb in the global economy. The missing factor remains a universal sense of commitment and urgency, particularly among the older generations – the Baby Boomers and the Generation Xers who hold many of the voting rights relating to today's affordability. Businesses which hold many of the innovation and technological enablers to fast-track society into meaningful changes in energy, transport and food production that would lay firm, large-scale and enduring foundations for global change remain on the periphery of action. They, too, at the turn of the 2020s, are still heavily infused with Baby Boomer and Generation X leaders who are waiting for compelling signals for action and perhaps even hoping none is needed. The capacity for business to lead change in how society uses its resources is immense. In addition to risk mitigation at a societal level, there are many strategic opportunities at the vanguard of change that can be tapped into, all with their own risk–reward relationships. There is certainly potential for business to collectively influence government and even intergovernmental collectives to put in place policies that would incentivize businesses to unleash this capacity. However, the historical predilection of business leadership to remain apolitical on many issues of societal importance, retaining a removed-yet-interested position, means that attitudes to, and cultures in, business leadership would need to change before this energy could be proactively tapped into.

The second megatrend that sits outside of the population and congregation dynamics of this planet relates to technology. There are two underlying facts about the growth of technology. One is that the rate of growth and the acceleration of the rate of growth of technology in the current decade are both unprecedented, by many orders of magnitude, than any decade before. The other is that while there is no shortage of projections as to where these technological advances will steer humanity, no one really knows where and how fast technological change will take us.

The pace of technological advancement has been likened to walking up a mountain for many years, and then suddenly strapping on a jetpack. The 'jetpack effect' has arisen because technological advancements are built on the knowledge of the technological generation before, amplified by three key factors which give rise to acceleration. The first is a search for innovation. This search becomes increasingly feverish and widespread as more and more economies compete for its leading edge. In turn, this is fuelled by an increasing population inhabiting more and more emerging economies with innovation capabilities. The pool of innovation widens and deepens at a geometric rate. The second is collaboration. This allows Breakthrough One to be followed by Breakthrough Two. It allows Idea One to be supplemented with Capability Two. It allows the parts of an innovation jigsaw puzzle to be spliced together. In a world of increasing scope and speed of connectivity, the potential for collaboration – whether it is friendly parallel collaboration (we work together) or incidental, sequential, one-upmanship developmental collaboration (you have an idea and I improve on it) – continues to increase. Connectivity enables these collaborative spheres to touch, interact and converge. Thirdly, there is a greater population base than ever before, which is also in the most affluent state it has ever been, that is willing to reward the advances in lifestyle that technology offers. The advances are many. We have prolonged life further and further and, as a species, are not shy to tackle mortality itself. Indeed, we problem solve mortality with gusto, relentlessly pushing our life expectancies towards the one-hundred-year mark, our eyes gleaming at the possibility of reaching one hundred and fifty, at the back of our minds a whispered *why not?* when the concept of immortality wanders fleetingly through our collective consciousness. But we are not interested in prolonging life through an interminably helpless third-trimester stasis; we seek quality of extended life. We seek biological and mental rejuvenation. We seek mastery of the environment around us; and we seek to reach and conquer new environments. We seek both quality and quantity of life wherever we are. And technology, more than any other, offers us glimpsed promises of both. Why would we not reward technology that achieves even a small part of this evolutionary aspiration, while reaping rewards that engineer our lives further and further away from the sicknesses, famines and countless smaller discomforts that have dogged our civilization for the few short millennia during which we, coincidentally, experienced virtually no technological accelerations?

We are cheerfully agnostic about technological advancements. They are all welcome. Certainly, some may have a dark side. But we do not know which technological advancements, when pieced together in the right sequence, crack the code of life. And so, we pursue all forms of technological advancement, considering potential risks but never actually aborting our pursuit of such advancement for fear of these risks. After all, we may find technological antidotes to the risks, too.

These three factors – an insatiable thirst for forward movement, a geometrically growing well of innovative capability and an exponentially growing connectedness – drive us into a massively expansive state of technological advancement. There is a deep resonance to these factors too; the technological advancements feed both innovative capabilities and connectedness, moving us into new realms of humankind's ability with – certainly in relative terms to our parents' technological experiences – mind-boggling speed.

Two tipping points are reached as we move through the first half of the twenty-first century. We turn from computing power to artificial intelligence. And we morph from high-functioning connectedness to hyper-connectivity. Each of these two changes is like breaking the sound barrier, enabling us to fly in a newer, different technological paradigm.

Yet, as we reach these tipping points, the solutions to a great majority of the issues that plague us – from poverty to climate change, from infant mortality to food scarcity – sit within our grasp. We know what needs to be done. We have the technological means to do those things. Yes, there are costs to solving these problems, just as there are costs associated with solving any problem. What we lack, more than anything else, is a collective will to marshal our know-how, our resources and the choices we make in the directions that arrive at solutions. We exist in a global entropy of values, our atoms misaligned, the available energy within us languishing without sufficient purpose to improve the world in which we live.

As we enable the new world of artificial intelligence, we risk taking a leap of faith that we may not be able to afford. We may accrue our debts forward rather than pay our dues forward, hopeful that solutions will present themselves to us in a timely way as we unlock technological wonders. We may hope that artificial intelligence and technological developments will uncover better solutions than today's algorithms deliver. As with most problems, the cost of a later solution is often greater than the cost of an early solution. But our net-present-value thinking has been carefully drummed into our decision-making DNA, compounded by the generational self-interest that places today's voices front-and-centre, and relegates tomorrow's voices to the background. We treasure the value of the dollar spent today, in our current leadership tenure, more than we value the dollar that may need to be spent tomorrow, in our children's leadership tenure. The first is real; the second is somewhat more abstract.

None of these rationales are hidden from society. These are underlying truths which are simply not spoken enough, by enough people – by enough customers, investors, employees, communities and governments. They are not spoken by enough business leaders. The truths that the technologies exist, and the economic means exist, to deliberately reshape the way we choose how society functions. The truths that this reshaping is not trivial, and that it requires effort, but that the effort is well within our capability. The truth is that the missing ingredient – of a greater style of leadership – is all that is needed to progress.

There are three possibilities in how we might interact with these truths. It is possible that we do not see them, clear as they are. Instead, we consider the world as a disposable container and become less caring, as a species, of one another. While it is possible, it is highly unlikely that the same collective intelligence that has moved us through stunning phases of technological development would fail miserably at recognizing our finite world and societal risk.

Perhaps, alternatively, it is possible that while we hold the world and its people dear, we take our eye off the ball and do not act until it is almost too late or just too late; and we descend into a tailspin of regression in our physical and emotional quality of life. It is, indeed, possible that we fail as a species not through stupidity but through a global apathy. Nor would it be a perennial state of apathy, because we have already established that our intelligence is high enough to pull our collective consciousness out of a distracted stupor. The question is, would we do so in time?

And there is a third possibility. It is that somewhere between seven-point-five billion and eight-point-five billion light bulbs go off in our individual, and thus collective, minds. We pivot to become a more enlightened society, using technology and connectivity to increase the lifespan and quality of life. We do this not just for the individual consumer but the world and its people as a whole.

Like Goldilocks, most probably believe that the second – the middle – premise, feels Just Right. Historically, this has been the pattern of our civilization, the way our collective consciousness works. We take time to mobilize. In the past, too, there have been some valid reasons for this. Awareness and education were lower than they are today. There were far fewer communication channels available than there are today. These channels were far less potent in terms of speed and connectivity than they were today. When we think back to sweeping societal changes such as the Civil Rights movement, or to mass mobilizations against disease, humanity experienced a much slower spread of calls to action. Today, we could rightly believe that calls to action, when then spread, would do so at comparatively much faster rates than just fifty, or even twenty, years ago.

But while there were now-overcome mechanical reasons for slower change back then, there is an aspect of humanity that remains firmly ingrained in us. We park ourselves in denial for as long as is possible. We cling to past, easier patterns of thought and action rather than embark on new ones. We resist change and hope that change is not needed. It is an instinct born, not necessarily of optimism that today's paradigm is safe but of an aversion to new and potentially uncomfortable paradigms. Change, for us, is easier to adapt to, like a gentle osmosis of incremental and imperceptible shifts, rather than to boldly and abruptly change, to endure shocks of mindfully-induced alterations to our existence. Change is much easier to be led to kindly, than to lead courageously. Change requires vision and leadership. It requires strategy and the resources to carry out that strategy. It requires a more broadly engaging culture than we have seen before, one that serves multiple greater purposes and one that strives to bring other leaders together in pursuing those purposes.

The rest of this book is about unlocking that courageous leadership. It is about leadership in the highly empowered, and highly empowering, business world that energizes our chosen economic engine. It is not about trading economic prosperity for making the world a better place; it is about building a more holistic prosperity while improving society's lot, today and in the future. It is about business leaders being an authentic and humanly powerful part of society, rather than remain passive and dispassionate watchmen and watchwomen observing from an economic power base. It is about tomorrow's face of business leadership that we, as a society, will truly value.

10

Tomorrow's Global Goals

In 1992, senior representatives from 178 countries – comprising input from the vast majority of nations on the planet – gathered at Rio de Janeiro, Brazil. In this gathering, termed the 'Earth Summit', these countries adopted a comprehensive plan of action to build a global partnership for sustainable development. Its purpose would be to improve human lives and protect the environment. It was known as Agenda 21.

Despite the initial enthusiasm, input from member states waned over time. However, efforts continued to focus the world on key concerns that affected, in some way, all countries, whether directly or indirectly. In September 2000, member states unanimously adopted the Millennium Declaration, the definition of eight Millennium Development Goals (MDGs) that would, together, serve to reduce extreme poverty by 2015.

While credible work was undertaken in respect of the MDGs, they were somewhat less successful than had been hoped. At the time of their development, the pervasive effects of climate change, while suspected by many and indeed proven by scientists, were not widely acknowledged. The MDGs therefore were seen as an extension of philanthropy, with largely rich countries attempting to help out with the woes of poorer nations. There was no rallying cry for the world and no globally relevant set of factors that would cause harm to all countries. The MDGs were an excellent example of corporate philanthropy at work, albeit at a global, governmental scale. This is not to say that valuable work was not done. As with all well-directed philanthropy, good comes out of such efforts. But problems are rarely solved with philanthropic processes; they are merely eased, or their worst outcomes are blunted by the goodwill of others.

Twenty years after Earth Summit, again in Rio de Janeiro, there was greater common ground between countries around the world, with no risk more broadly shared than climate change. The benefit of having shared goals (the MDGs) was well acknowledged, although the modest success in partly achieving them was also well documented. Member states formed and adopted an outcome document, termed the 'Future We Want', which postulated a world that was much less besieged by the problems of the time, and agreed that such a future was feasible in a 15- to 20-year timeframe.

A new set of goals was formed over the next three years, and termed the Sustainable Development Goals (SDGs). The timeline for achieving these goals was set at 2030. The SDGs were launched in late 2015. There are 17 of them, chosen because they are measurably the most concerning issues of our time. They were each responsible for human misery, economic instability and eroding living conditions among billions of people. Achievement of these goals would conceivably improve global economic conditions, living standards and the outlook for the human race at that time. Failure to achieve them, on the other hand, included globally catastrophic consequences for rich and poor countries. With the SDGs, all countries had considerable skin in the game.

For corporate leaders who wished to lean their organizations towards operating modes that contributed to societal benefits at the most relevant end of the spectrum, the SDGs provided a cheat sheet. At 17 goals, it was sufficiently populated with the measurable key problems of our time for any larger business organization to confidently be able to find 3, 4, 5 or 6 highly relevant focuses. Governments could easily find a dozen, or in some cases, all 17. As we move into the third decade of this century – the meaty 10 years of tackling the Sustainable Development Goals – it is relatively easy to find, particularly among the more mature corporate organizations on the planet, specific focuses on a select handful of these goals.

For critics who had, through the process, pointed out that it was better for the world to focus on a few problems and solve them well, rather than consider many problems and solve them partially, it provided both flexibility and focus.

There are many ways for an organization to meaningfully contribute to one or more of the SDGs. Monetary contributions (donations) are one, but while they are easy to dispense, they are not necessarily the most productive or enduring contribution. The leveraging of goods or services that the business is already producing tends to be one of the more powerful, engaged and enduring involvements that organizations can offer. So too is the utilization of staff skills. As business leaders know, we are prepared to pay a premium for employee talent – the problem solvers, the innovators, the engagers, the negotiators, the analysts, the financiers, the strategists, the logisticians and many others. They make the business of delivering products and services effective and efficient, and they have the skills to make the business of implementing the SDGs in selected geographical areas similarly impactful. And overarching these is the power of collaboration. The business-to-business (B2B) and business-to-customer (B2C) agility of corporations and businesses provide an aspect of leverage that few other types of organizations in the world can boast.

The employee engagement value, to organizations, of allowing staff to exercise their skills in areas for societal good are well known and widely practised. There is tremendous opportunity, and benefit, available to organizations in leveraging their people into societally beneficial activities. When aligned with the SDGs, they coincide with a globally relevant agenda.

The SDGs are summarized here, with a brief narrative on issues to consider in relation to footprints of the organization that you lead. Each SDG has a set of key performance indicators, most of which are well-constituted enough to rapidly focus organizational effort towards. Globally, there is no shortage of wider and deeper literature to help leaders hone their ideas and visions.

- *One: End poverty, in all its forms, everywhere*
  If your organization's activities or supply chain have a significant presence in these areas of the world (notably in Asia, Africa and South America), it may have the ability to contribute to this goal. If the organization's goods or services are linked to foundational issues such as education, infrastructure, food production, water security or economic development, there may be impactful opportunities to engage on SDG1 (Figure 10.1).
- *Two: End hunger, achieve food security and improved food nutrition, and promote sustainable agriculture*
  Companies best suited to these are the food producers and supply chain organizations to food producers (including chemicals such as fertilizers, insecticides and pesticides). Organizations with strengths in logistics, market access, finance, primary healthcare and water security can add significant value. Organizations with a significant presence in countries that struggle with food security and nutrition can collaborate with such actors to direct resources and effort towards SDG2 (Figure 10.2).

SDG 1 - No poverty

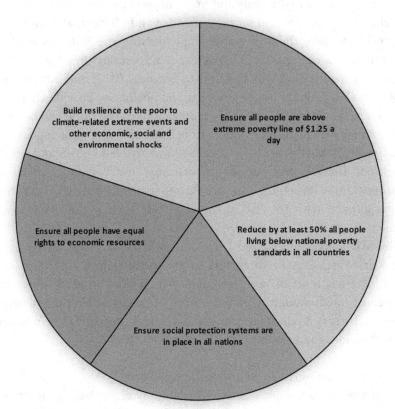

FIGURE 10.1
SDG1: No poverty.

- *Three: Ensure healthy lives and promote wellbeing for all, at all ages*
  This goal has wide-ranging applications in both developing and developed economies, covering issues from infant mortality to alcoholism and drug abuse. It is a broadly applicable focus for most organizations, irrespective of rural or urban settings, or the strength and maturity of a national economy in today's world. Applications can be found readily in countries as diverse as Belgium and Burkina Faso (Figure 10.3).
- *Four: Ensure inclusive and equitable quality education and promote lifelong learning opportunities for all*

SDG 2 - Zero hunger

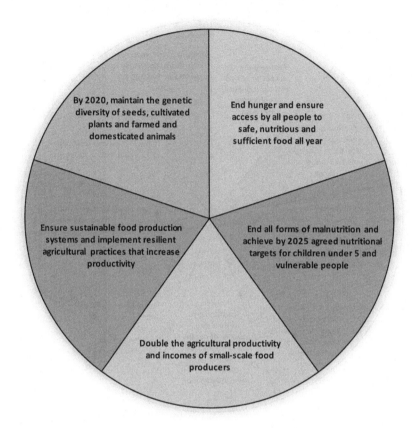

FIGURE 10.2
SDG2: Zero hunger.

SDG4 has a strong focus on education and building capacity, fundamentally through primary and secondary education, but also through vocational training. Pivotally, it recognizes the historical discrepancies between educational opportunities differentially afforded to males and females, and seeks to find equitablity in these. A great many organizations today invest in education, because it is a reasonably easy sector to support and because its impacts are considerable. However, it should be noted that the root cause of many educational deficiencies are related to a broad range of socio-economic conditions, and each locality typically has its own set of drivers that can be addressed. Education, and the causes of poor education,

SDG3 - Healthy lives

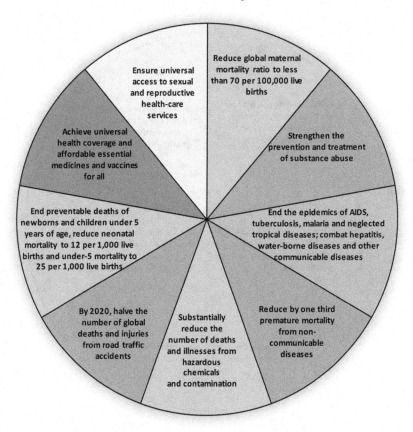

FIGURE 10.3
SDG3: Healthy lives.

typically contains ample opportunities for organizations of all types and scale (Figure 10.4).

- *Five: Achieve gender equality and empower all women and girls*
  SDG5 addresses the historical inequity between women and men, recognizing both the injustice of the imbalance and the folly of under-using half the world's population, including its diverse viewpoints, for the good of humanity. It seeks to eliminate our society's long-standing legacy of cruelties against females, the systemic disadvantages faced by women and girls across the world, and the endemic undervaluation of women in society (Figure 10.5).

SDG4 - Education

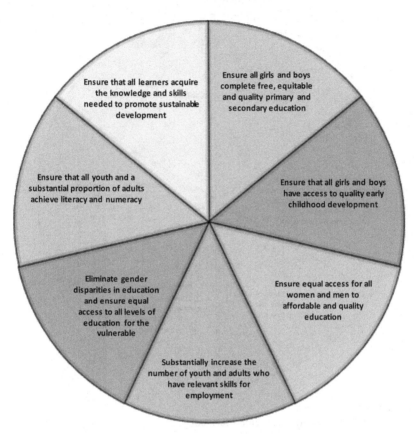

FIGURE 10.4
SDG4: Education.

- *Six: Availability and sustainable management of water and sanitation for all*

  Access to adequate quantity and quality of water, essential to human life, remains a challenge for parts of society. As populations grow and climate change takes effect, the challenge to find and sustain economically viable sources of water expands. So too does the availability of available sanitation, which not only impacts on the quality of life of those affected by inadequate sanitation but also contributes to the potential for harbouring disease, and accelerating its spread, in our society. As global health and the threat of pandemics weighs ever more heavily on the people of the world, the

SDG 5 - Gender equality and female empowerment

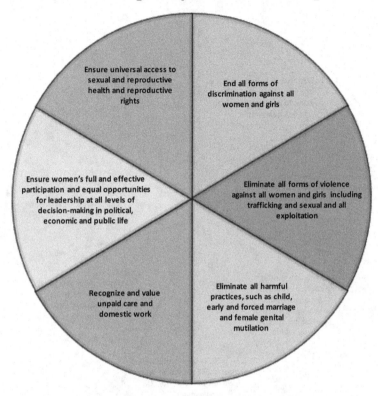

FIGURE 10.5
SDG5: Gender quality and female empowerment.

potential for SDG6 to preserve and improve life on Earth increases each year (Figure 10.6).

- *Seven: Affordable, reliable, sustainable and modern energy for all*
  SDG7 unlocks economic potential, long having the effect of unleashing technology, economic productivity and quality-of-life attributes. The lack of access to affordable and reliable energy has been a barrier to economic development in many countries of the world and has manifested as one of the more visible differentiators between the developed, and developing, parts of the planet. Our insatiable hunger for energy has also propagated the widespread use of fossil fuels and other unsustainable sources, driving our world to the brink of, and

SDG 6 - Water and Sanitation

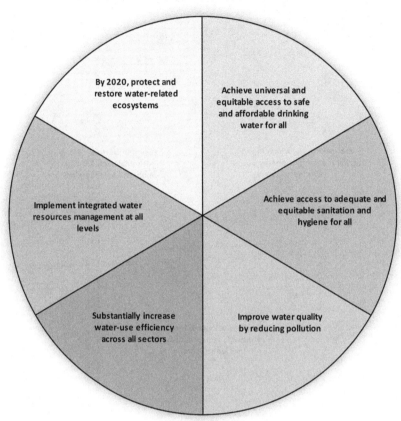

FIGURE 10.6
SDG6: Water and sanitation.

beyond, the tipping point that preserves a healthy planetary ecology. This goal seeks to concurrently address universal energy access and cleaner sources of energy (Figure 10.7).

- *Eight: Sustainable economic growth, employment and decent work* This goal is closely associated with the drive to eradicate poverty but simultaneously recognizes that unlimited global economic growth is unsustainable. It looks to developing nations, notably in Africa, Asia and South America, where population growth is significant and both employment and decent work lag behind developed economies. SDG is a complex and interconnected goal, linking many facets of

SDG 7 - Energy

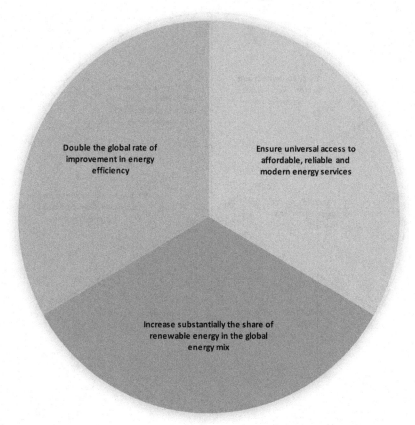

FIGURE 10.7
SDG7: Energy.

sustainable and balanced economic growth with the drivers that contribute to the eradication of poverty across the world (Figure 10.8).

- *Nine: Infrastructure, industrialization and innovation*
  SDG9 looks to some of the cornerstones of economic development
  that support SDG8. It seeks to diversify these across a range of scales,
  recognizing that small- to medium-scale industrialization is more
  easily accessible to developing economies and that innovation at
  these scales provides speed and agility in growth. Infrastructure,
  as an enabler for economic growth, is focused upon in this goal, as
  is the need to balance that growth with a sustainable focus to help

SDG 8 - Economic growth, Employment and Decent work

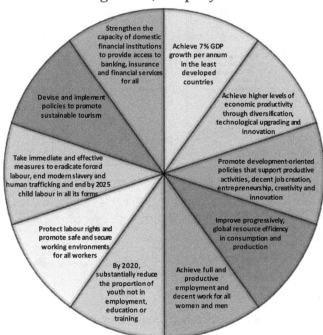

FIGURE 10.8
SDG8: Economic growth, employment and decent work.

preserve and re-establish the ailing health of our global ecosystems and climate stability (Figure 10.9).

- *Ten: Sovereign inequalities*
  This goal seeks to remove many of the common roadblocks to economic development – the inequalities that persist within country borders, and between countries, that impede development. From enabling laws to inclusive financial markets, it seeks to focus on energizing development in the weakest tranches of economies on the planet, lifting the lowest-performing countries out of their inertia. Recognizing too that populations continue to be separated from economic opportunity by distance and borders, SDG10 also seeks to facilitate orderly mobility so that people can physically access country and regional hubs of opportunity (Figure 10.10).

SDG 9 - Infrastructure, Inclusive industrialization and Innovation

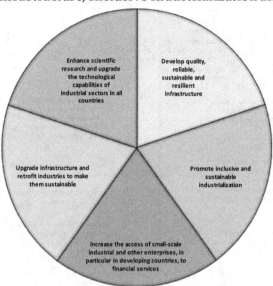

Enhance scientific research and upgrade the technological capabilities of industrial sectors in all countries

Develop quality, reliable, sustainable and resilient infrastructure

Upgrade infrastructure and retrofit industries to make them sustainable

Promote inclusive and sustainable industrialization

Increase the access of small-scale industrial and other enterprises, in particular in developing countries, to financial services

FIGURE 10.9
SDG9: Infrastructure, inclusive industrialization and innovation.

- *Eleven: Inclusive, safe, resilient and sustainable cities and settlements*
  SDG11 focuses on the continuing trend of population drift and consolidation to more, and larger, cities around the world. It seeks to provide housing, transport and associated infrastructure to make human settlements more habitable. Recognizing the pressure that this places on both human health and living amenity, it seeks to find a balance between the increasing global trends towards urbanization and the ability of those urban centres to provide safe and resilient places for human habitation. As the effects of climate change threaten human populations with extreme weather, food supply and infrastructure failures, associated sanitation and disease risks, this goal seeks to make human settlements more robust havens for the world's ever-concentrating population centres (Figure 10.11).
- *Twelve: Sustainable consumption and production*
  SDG12 looks to growing populations and the ever-increasing stresses on the world's resources to provide for the consumption demands

SDG 10 - Reduce inequalities

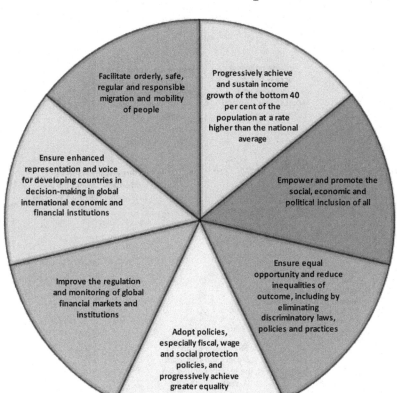

FIGURE 10.10
SDG10: Reduce inequalities.

of these populations. As economic prosperity is pursued, it has a tendency to expand consumption patterns, in turn amplifying production and pushing the planet towards an increasingly unsustainable future. This goal seeks to find a sustainable balance between resources, consumption and production by modulating consumption and waste, fashioning within society a more mindful existence that uses what it needs, reuses what it can and produces just the difference between these two quanta. The concept of ecological overshoot, discussed previously, is an illustrative (if quantitatively inaccurate) model of the conundrum this goal attempts to address (Figure 10.12).

SDG 11 - Safe, Resilient, Sustainable cities

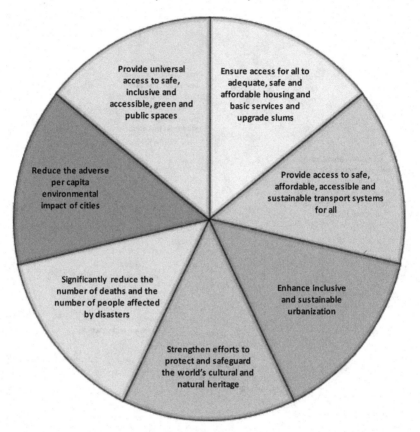

Provide universal access to safe, inclusive and accessible, green and public spaces

Ensure access for all to adequate, safe and affordable housing and basic services and upgrade slums

Reduce the adverse per capita environmental impact of cities

Provide access to safe, affordable, accessible and sustainable transport systems for all

Significantly reduce the number of deaths and the number of people affected by disasters

Enhance inclusive and sustainable urbanization

Strengthen efforts to protect and safeguard the world's cultural and natural heritage

FIGURE 10.11
SDG11: Safe, resilient, sustainable cities.

- *Thirteen: Climate change*
  SDG13 focuses on one of the most significant risks of our time: climate change. The UN's (older) articulation of climate action is superseded by the detail of the Paris Climate Change Agreement 2015, and the subsequent international actions, which contain much greater (and continuously updating) details. Investor requirements on disclosure and action have also superseded SDG13 and provide more granular guidance on what is expected of corporations. So too have regulatory and stock exchange expectations of directors of listed companies (Figure 10.13).

SDG 12 - Sustainable Consumption and Production

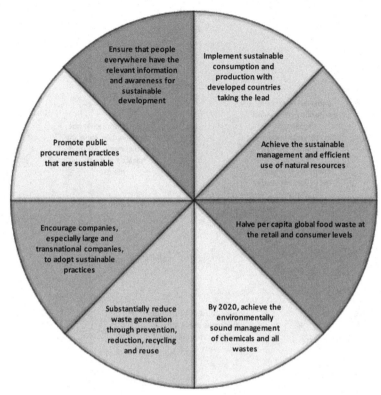

FIGURE 10.12
SDG12: Sustainable consumption and production.

- *Fourteen: Oceans, seas and marine resources*
  In the late 2010s, scientific concerns about the health of the earth's oceans and seas increased as signs of ocean temperature increases, regional overfishing and marine pollution became more visible around the world and at greater scales than before. SDG14 is a multi-faceted approach to managing growing risks to a little-understood but large and critical planetary resource. Its focus is aimed at governmental and intergovernmental initiatives, because of the transboundary nature of marine waterways (Figure 10.14).

SDG 13 - Climate change

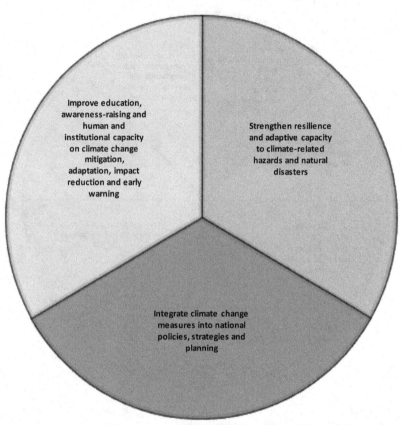

FIGURE 10.13
SDG13: Climate change.

- *Fifteen: Terrestrial ecosystems*
  SDG15 focuses on a long-standing issue, that of the land-based eco-systems that have dwindled as human populations and activities have competed with their scale, health and diversity. Covering a wide range of global factors – land, soil, flora, fauna and biodiversity, the forests that function as the planet's lungs, and the freshwater eco-system that are enmeshed with all of the above – SDG15 has a very wide scope that touches on many organizations' footprints and has direct links to the threat of zoonotic diseases - viruses in terrestrial ecosystems that jump to humans – such as COVID-19 and Ebola. (Figure 10.15).

SDG 14 - Marine Resources

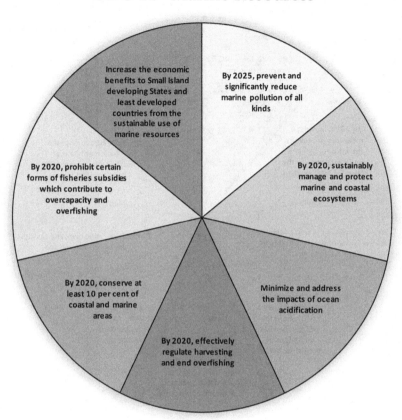

FIGURE 10.14
SDG14: Marine resources.

- *Sixteen: Institutions and justice*
  Many of the preceding SDGs rely on functioning and interconnected institutions that support the foundations upon which our society can address societal risks. SDG16 identifies a cross-section of vital institutional justice matters. It is by no means an exhaustive list, but it aspires to focus on the nine that are considered to be the priorities of our time. Businesses and corporations can help strengthen institutional capacity by engaging proactively and constructively on such matters. While there is a historical reluctance in the private sector to interfere on what is seen as a governmental and intergovernmental role, aspects such as bribery and corruption, illicit flows of

SDG 15 - Terrestrial ecosystems

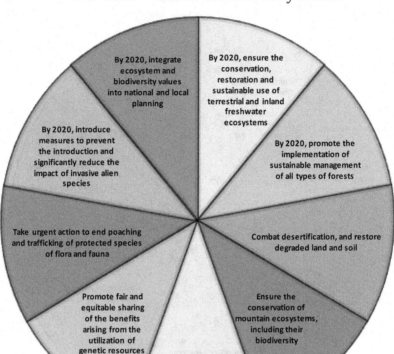

FIGURE 10.15
SDG15: Terrestrial ecosystems.

finance, the funding of arms and the opacity of taxes and royalties have, in the early part of the twenty-first century, seen the private sector being subjected to laws, regulations and trading or economic constraints for their association with such practices (Figure 10.16).

- *Seventeen: Global partnerships for sustainable development*
  SDG17 contains the longest list of initiatives of all the Sustainable Development Goals. It is a clear acknowledgement of an overriding factor facing the meeting of the previous sixteen goals: collaboration. The phrase 'think global, act local' is a fine mantra for individuals and has a foundational place in society. Yet the scale of many of the threats to society in the twenty-first century transcends local

SDG16 - Institutions and Justice

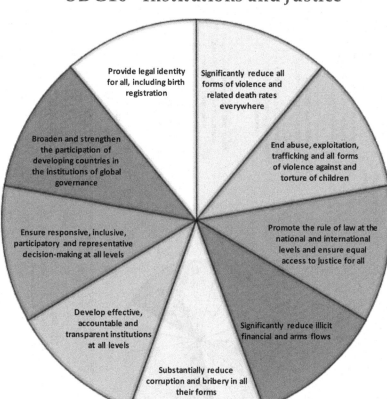

FIGURE 10.16
SDG16: Institutions and justice.

causes and effects. In order to deal with them effectively, co-ordinated responses are required. Aligned philosophies and policies are required, and in many cases contiguous laws are required between countries and regions. SDG17 focuses significantly on economic sustainability, wherein complementary systems of trade, finance, development, capacity building and resource mobilization between countries and regions, to name a few, are essential to establishing a sustainable balance of progress around the world (Figure 10.17).

The United Nations' Sustainable Development Goals are a useful blueprint for organizations of all kinds to get onto the same global page. They are

SDG 17 - Global Partnerships for Sustainable Development

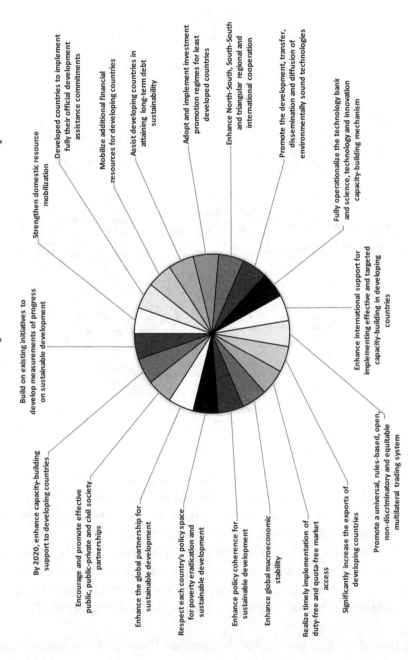

FIGURE 10.17

SDG17: Global partnerships for sustainable development.

wide-ranging enough that any person or organization can find aspects that are substantially relevant to them and narrow enough that they help funnel global efforts into a defined area. This area represents a global 'best assessment' of the most material risks and failures in society at this point in time and helps us place our efforts where the greatest collective good may be harvested.

11

A New Balance

With the bewildering magnitude of the business ecosystem to consider, there is no doubt that it is much easier for a leader in today's and tomorrow's world to focus on a smaller part of it – sticking to our knitting, as it were, keeping it simple, focused and theoretically more achievable. And while many leaders might outwardly show outrage at the prospect of taking such a low road, today's reality is stark. The norm in organizations everywhere today is a tendency to take a lower road than is needed for the welfare of society. This is a difficult view to hear because a great number of leaders try to do the 'right thing'. Many even use that very term, vague as it is, in their speeches and annual reports. But if the results fall well below the exhortations consistently, and regularly fail to meet stakeholder expectations, there are only two real possibilities. One is that the commitment of some leaders today is incomplete and perhaps little more than good public relations. The other is that leaders are still learning how to process and deliver what is being asked. It is probably not, as some business leaders have suggested, that stakeholder expectations are unreasonable!

The reality is probably that there is some of each – some under-commitment and some uncertainty in how to commit – in our collective organizational shortcomings around the world. And until we are able to acknowledge that hard truth, progress will remain elusive.

These challenging views are espoused widely by many stakeholders outside of the corporations to whom they apply. We hear them from customers and investors. We hear them from governments in power, from governments-in-waiting and non-governmental organizations. We hear them from communities, in the everyday household conversations and at the weekend barbecues. And we hear them – perhaps in more subdued forms because of their career-limiting potential to individuals who would utter them too loudly – among the employees of those organizations themselves. Every aspect of society in our business ecosystem admits it, to a greater or lesser degree. It is there in our collective consciousness, and it weighs heavily upon it like a burden of guilt.

Individually though, as leaders, we tend to shrug it off. Our platitudes are many and varied. *It's a trade-off; would you rather have lower profits and dividends, or can you live with a diminished society? It's consumer demand; we are simply responding fairly and appropriately. We are adhering to laws and regulations, and perhaps even going above and beyond; what more do you want? That's what government is for; we each have our roles and responsibilities.* The list is long. Those who have worked in organizations – whether in the private sector or within the governmental sectors – for a decade or two will be able to recall a dozen similar phrases that they have come across or uttered themselves. As organizational leaders, in this sanctum of our own egos, we have spent at least a couple of decades simultaneously recognizing that all is not well (and that we are co-creators of the illness) and living in a state of denial about our power to make a significant difference.

It starts with ownership.

Firstly, how do we avoid ownership? The terms 'it's not my role' and 'it's not my job' have found many different ways to make their way into our corporate lexicons. The defensive entreaty appears continuously in the working environment. It is a mantra that usefully contains roles and responsibilities and, at the very same time, an excuse to abdicate from broader concerns. Organizations are founded on that mantra. You do this, and I do that. If you do yours correctly and I do mine correctly, we reach the desired outcome. It is not my role to do yours; in fact, it would be counterproductive and result in unadulterated chaos if one or both of us started doing what the other was supposed to do.

We have been conditioned in organizational culture, all our lives, to partition another's responsibilities and accountabilities from our own. In the late twentieth century, business schools began to espouse more holistic performance indicators (such as balanced scorecards) and shared performance indicators. When we mindfully deconstruct the older paradigm, with shared key performance indicators or balanced scorecards that strive to bring sharing and integration into an otherwise divide-and-conquer architecture, we are able to overcome narrower forms of leadership. The same power of mindful deconstruction works well enough when we consider business performance concurrently with societal benefit. It can be done, but it requires a deliberate departure from our classical learnings and organizational conditioning. It requires us to apply balanced scorecard thinking and shared performance indicator constructs deliberately to societal outcomes as well as to business performance.

For those leaders who have been practising their craft in line with the older and more rigid boundaries of responsibility and accountability for a decade or two, it requires both awareness of what is amiss and a fundamental shift in thinking. For those leaders who are now entering the leadership arena, it requires the same awareness and resilience against falling into the prevailing groupthinks around them. This latter is an insidious force because organizations have significant powers of indoctrination that often serve to neutralize the value of new and different leadership insights, particularly in middle- to senior-management ranks. For businesses to change rapidly over a short decade, it would require these two cohorts – the classical leaders and the emerging ones – to act in unison.

For those who have been observing the balance shifting over the past two decades, it was evident that change occurred, albeit very slowly. Compared to rapidly evolving risks such as climate change, such change was too slow. However in 2020, the world hit a snag. The SARS-CoV-2 virus brought to the human population a pandemic in the form of COVID-19, an illness that caused the world economy to grind to a disastrous halt. The impact quickly reached scales comparable to previous economic disasters such as the Global Financial Crisis and the Asian Financial Crisis. As this book goes to print, we are at the very start of a new global journey that will change how we view corporate and governmental leadership, and how we view the safety of our global economy, for a very long time. It will test old leadership paradigms and demand new ones. It will cause us to revise economic safety in the same way that the Twin Towers attack on 9-11 caused us to revise national security in scores of countries around the world.

Did we suspect a pandemic was possible, before March 2020? Most certainly. Not only did we think it was possible, but it was considered close to a certainty. It was not a matter of 'if', but 'when'. The planet's burgeoning population, its increasing rates of dense urbanization, a growingly frenetic pace of food production, a rapidly expanding bioengineering industry and the whittling away of the buffer between human civilization and a continually cornered animal world were just some of the factors that made such an event, in hindsight, relatively unsurprising.

If it was such a statistically likely event, why was it such a devastating surprise when it happened?

We simply paid it little attention. The 'we' I refer to includes you, me, individual leaders and collective leadership. Perhaps we crossed our fingers that it would not happen for a very long time, perhaps not even in our lifetimes and that it would be another generation's burden to carry. Perhaps we imagined that there was, accompanying the invisible threat, a co-existing invisible solution that would fortuitously present itself. Perhaps it was easier to focus on the status quo and concentrate on reaping a version of economic success while in that stable stasis than to imagine and prepare for a pandemic that might not happen during our tenure, a net-present-value-driven set of behaviours. Whatever the reasons, there was a failure of individual and collective leadership that allowed us to be taken by surprise. There was a failure of individual and collective leadership that allowed an almost-certain problem to manifest and – worse – grow to world-changing proportions.

It is a shock to humanity that will not pass without some leadership lessons for tomorrow. Within weeks of the COVID-19 disease meeting thresholds for being classified a pandemic, leadership was being tested. There were the tests of crises, to be sure. Leaders everywhere, whether in government or in private industry, whether in education or in health, had to pivot in the face of daily changes to risk profiles. But there was also a common test of humanity. Leaders everywhere had to privilege human welfare at a breadth that had not been called for in many decades before and at a scale that had never before occurred.

This was not just a matter of privileging safety and health, which leaders had become accustomed to doing in the latter half of the twentieth century. It was also around managing family and work in a conjoined context, managing the stress of uncertainty, social isolation, mental health and wage reductions. Leaders had to suddenly juxtapose sharply defined elements of their employees' work–life balance with business decisions, many of them extremely difficult. Leaders had to experience the juxtapositions for themselves. Videoconferences placed us, in a virtual sense, in each other's homes several times a month, several times a week and even several times a day. These are much greater rates than at any time in our history. Connections were forged, in between the embarrassment of the dog tugging at the laptop cable and the toddler demanding immediate attention to her bowel movement, in ways that have only rarely occurred between employer and employee since the industrial revolution. Playing fields between employers and employees were levelled. Our work selves and our home selves blended, and we glimpsed each other's blending. For a rare period of time, employees and employers were all genuinely in a similar boat.

In this world of uncertainty, hierarchies of traditional leadership were loosened. Employees sought empathy. Authentic empathy – as distinct from curated empathy – became a more significant leadership currency. We glimpsed what it might look like if employers cared a little bit more, sympathized a little bit more and laughed a little bit more about the everyday occurrences of their employees' non-work-related lives. Such connective lessons learnt, by employers and employees alike, cannot easily be unlearnt.

This is not to say that there is some magical new leadership approach that the COVID-19 pandemic might gift the world. The year 2020, and its aftermath, will not necessarily present new leadership models. We already have these models at our disposal, albeit with inertia working against them. There is simply a slower rate of uptake in our society of such models than is good for us.

But with the frenetic pace of the global economy paused for a little moment, incumbent leaders and emerging leaders might take stock. Old leadership models might be more readily challenged by a larger cohort of people. Organizational circumstances that we barely considered in the past because they were seen to be dangerously sub-optimal – working exclusively from home, cancelling business travel, changing business deliverables to suit new circumstances – had to be embraced, and while it was far from ideal, perhaps it was not as disastrous as we first thought. COVID-19 forced organizations to question old ideas and challenge old barriers.

Those moments in time often become an axis of change.

We, as a species, are not overly fond of change. It evokes a range of unsettling emotions, one of which is often anxiety. Even small changes can evoke low levels of anxiety. Like chemicals preferring to find their lowest-energy state of existence, we avoid the agitation that accompanies change.

Yet in organizations we practise the art of change daily. Between regulatory changes, constantly evolving workplace norms, striving to achieve gender and other types of diversity and digital revolutions, for example, we live different paces of change every day, in an array of activities. A customer-oriented organization is constantly testing the mood of its clientele, their preferences, their always-accumulating thirst for improvement, and adapting to suit. Indeed, if this change were to cease, so might the organization. For it to be sustainable, an organization must be constantly reinventing itself, sometimes incrementally and sometimes in a pivotal way, but always on the move.

No organization is immune to this. Not even your family business making handmade shoes in a small village in Northern Italy can escape internet-order platforms, or synthetic non-slip additives for soles in the urban environment, or arch-support improvements demanded by an increasingly older customer demographic. But we adapt to change grudgingly, lagging the forces that cause change. Often, we wait until we are forced into change. If we need not change, we would much prefer to embrace a comfortable and predictable status quo.

This underlying orientation in organizations sees us often falling behind the pace of change that is good for us. It is not that we are bound by cluelessness or ineptitude to change and innovate apace with the times. It is much more likely that we simply cannot be bothered until it is thrust upon us. Or until we are lagging so far behind that it is no longer a matter of choice, whether as a result of economic or regulatory forces. And then we may change, but perhaps grindingly, unwillingly and with a low whine of barely overcome inertia.

Leaders who can evoke change are highly prized in our economy. They are valued in all aspects of society. Change agents are so valued, in fact, that it may well be a secondary concern whether the agent evokes a good change or a bad one. The judgement of what change is favourable or unfavourable is, after all, a subjective assessment that depends on your point of view and your predispositions. But change is seen, heard and felt no matter what your point of view is of good or bad. We all know *when* change is happening, especially when it is happening to us. We can objectively identify and agree that we are in the midst of change, or that change has occurred. We may quibble over the magnitude of change – again, this is a matter of an observer's pre-change and post-change perspective – but the change of state is hardly in question.

We often refer to change, and sometimes even verbalize it, in dramatic terms. We may talk about sea changes, or step changes, or transformations. In doing this, we mystify the process of change. We give it some magical properties. Unwittingly, a fiction is created as shown in Figure 11.1.

Almost nothing in nature exhibits this instantaneous view of change, not even the Big Bang that initiated our universe. But we often default to speaking of meaningful change in this way. Perhaps we are even in awe of leaders who possess the uncanny ability to evoke this sudden change in enthalpy, this organizational juju. If you listen to organizational conversations about change, we seek and applaud the alchemy of momentous conversion. We celebrate much less, if at all, mindful evolutionary change. Yet all change follows a process. Organizational change is an engineered evolution. If it is not, then the change you seek is guaranteed to be elusive. Change follows a curve (Figure 11.2), rather than a step. Engineered appropriately, it builds momentum, breaks a threshold, attains its change pace, and then settles, embeds and adjusts to its new state.

As we seek to evolve the organizations that we lead to become more societally relevant and improve the balance sheet that they represent to our communities, it is useful to consider, and differentially approach, three distinct phases of creating change in the organization. Let us call these phases priming change, energizing change and embedding change.

We could identify sub-phases within these, as there are nuances within each phase, but these three are sufficient with which to chart change. The model is commonly used, and most notably in capital

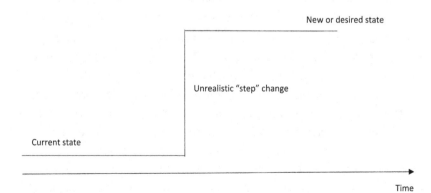

FIGURE 11.1
Change and the unrealistic step-change.

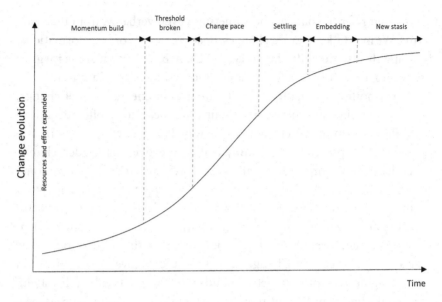

FIGURE 11.2
Change and its realistic phases.

projects – those projects where we spend a lot of money over a long time, such as infrastructure. In those projects, we are moving from one state to another, perhaps from a state of having a poor transport system to a state in which we have high-functioning mass transit system. The beginning and end states are vastly different. Yet, if you have ever idly watched a construction project, two things may strike you. One is that the movement and energy that is expended is obvious to the naked eye. You may even, in your mind, visualize the budget ticking over by the minute. Two is that hour to hour, or even day to day, changes to the naked eye are imperceptible. It looks like a great deal of time, effort and money is being spent, and, unnervingly, not a lot of change is being achieved.

Philosophically, being an agent of cultural change in your organization – one that creates greater and greater societal value in your ecosystem – is not dissimilar to leading the large construction project that, to the casual observer, seems like it is going nowhere. This is a vitally important point for change agents to internalize, because the world is littered with leaders who try to achieve such outcomes, and then give up, or back off the throttle because we are losing faith in our efforts igniting change. We might wait for a 'better time' or for a time when 'competing priorities' dissipate and give change a clear run. We might try to fast-track it, to force change, by jumping prematurely to latter-stages of the S-curve without creating and following a paced strategy of change. Remember, change is not a magical step. It is, particularly in matters of organizational culture an accumulation of well-sequenced incremental movements.

But this is not to say that the pace of sequencing ought to be leisurely. In matters of climate change and pollution, for example, time is of the essence. As the COVID-19 outbreak of 2020 taught us, the impacts of our collective participation in our own economic machine can be thrust upon us suddenly, and with both a force and at a scale that can momentarily exceed our ability to manage those impacts. For a leader, certainly, keeping an eye on the clock is a required discipline. But we do not need everyone to watch the clock or to argue about whether the clock is a minute slow or a minute fast. That energy should, instead, be used to participate in change. We need leaders who will be cognizant of the time we have to effect change and sequence change at an appropriate pace. We need leaders who can set, embark on and stay the course of the right S-curve.

Consider priming change, the first-phase left-hand-side of the S-curve. There is a great deal of effort, much of which is not celebrated in corporate cultures, that sets a scene for meaningful and successful change. The priming phase encompasses many leadership actions that make the difference between useful effort and wasted effort later. In this phase, there is not a great deal of change that occurs, but there is a significant – and crucial – amount of setting up for success.

It is important to remember that this is an embryonic phase of change, and as such the forward momentum that is gained can be both quantitatively modest and fragile. If there is one, overarching goal in priming change, it is to create a groundswell of support and enthusiasm for change. Change itself is not the objective in this phase, even though it would certainly be heartening to have some. When it is time to invoke change, the energy forged by support and enthusiasm can be harnessed to make change happen, but for now the objective is to blend vision, alignment and a growing sense of anticipation for change so that culture is realigned.

As every leader knows, people who want to embrace a path and achieve an outcome make up the most potent force available in an organization. For businesses wishing to simultaneously be good for society, this is not a hard sell to make to employees. The paths that lead to a better future for society contain, in their promise, a desirable outcome for most employees too. After all, who does not want a better future and would be willing to expend effort achieving it? And who would renege against a promise of a better future not just for themselves but for their families, friends and community? The answer, of course, is no one, depending on the answer to four basic questions.

Why is this a better future? What do I have to give up for this better future; what's the trade-off? How much hard work and forbearance is necessary to put myself on this path of a better future? How many others will join me on this path, or will this be a lonely journey?

The better future must make sense. If a leader tried to convince employees that earning larger bonuses led to a better future, it would presumably make sense, with some caveats. If a leader tried to convince employees that less extreme weather events, or less poverty in the country, led to a better future, it would probably make sense, with precious few caveats. In energizing change, the destination must be attractive.

The *why* offers purpose, and without purpose there is no wellspring of energy from which to draw. Recalling, for example, the insights from the first part of this book and drawing from an ocean of other insights that are both currently available and in a continuous phase of updating and evolution, purpose is plentiful. Whether the purpose is existential, for example, when we consider the risks and impacts of climate change, or whether the purpose represents fair humanism, for example, in the case of diversity at work, they are everywhere for us to choose from. Rarely too are they unrelated to each other or independent enough to be considered unrelated. Our society behaves as an intricately interconnected ecosystem whose known interrelationships are too numerous to count and whose yet-unknown interrelationships will take a long journey of evolution and wisdom to catalogue. In the matrix of these interrelationships lay opportunities of purpose that represent countless better todays and tomorrows for this Earth and its inhabitants. They, too, are so numerous to count that there is no reason to claim any particular difficulty in identifying some useful ones that resonate with our organizational purpose and footprint.

While the why is a primary concern to any journey, in the business of contributing meaningfully to society there is little challenge for any leader in articulating it, provided that leader believes in it. The difficulties arise after the why.

The better future must not be less than what has to be given up for it. This is the hard part because the aspects that have to be given up are valued – and their value felt – right now. Conversely, the better future is only valued tomorrow and its value is theoretical. A consistent failing of leaders who try to generate willing and engaged change is that this aspect of change agency is often glossed over when it comes to societal issues. On matters of organizational restructuring, automation, refinancing and so on, leadership skills are much better honed. We have become adept at explaining why 30 per cent of the workforce must be made redundant but have not exercised those skills of rationalization nearly as often when it comes to matters of societal relevance. We rarely address the trade-off with sufficient sophistication, relying on the visioning for tomorrow to sell itself. In engaging change, what must be given up must be less important than what can be gained.

The issue of trade-offs is worth a close look because it has been the greatest handbrake on many worthy societal initiatives in organizations all around the world. In the early days of organizational management, and for well over a century, business bottom lines attracted the intense scrutiny of executives and shareholders. And while this scrutiny was entirely appropriate, as it would be fiscally foolish not to hold a clear view of finances, it led to a type of tunnel vision and myopia that has been passed down from generation to generation of leaders. For a large proportion of the twentieth century, business leaders were viewed as very different species to those interested in societal welfare. One leant to the right, the other to the left. We created political divides between the two on the presumption that one was the natural enemy of the other. Not until the twenty-first century did we investigate, with some enduring curiosity, the notion that the two could, and should, coexist. While this divide existed, gains on one side of it necessitated some kind of loss, or trade-off, on the other side. While this way of operating was firmly believed in, it played out like a self-fulfilling prophecy. Over many generations, we proved to ourselves that if it played out a thousand times, it would play out for the thousand-and-first time, and for all other times after. And so, it is not uncommon at all to hear the phrase *what's the trade-off?* in our boardrooms. We do not query *if* there is a trade-off, starting with the assumption that co-existing purposes are viable, but instead assume there must be one.

As a result, opportunities for societal enhancement were much less picked up by organizational scrutiny than might have been. Multiply, and compound, this trend over several generations of leaders who have tended to pass their thinking onwards and it will not be surprising that the dominant paradigm in the twenty-first century routinely looks for the trade-off that, with different thinking in place, may not even exist. Despite the many positive advances in more holistic management made over many years, more opportunities for business organizations to create value in society have been missed, ignored or squandered than have been capitalized upon because the self-fulfilling trade-off prophecy materialized.

While the trade-off question challenged tactical decision-making around delivering societal good (what must I give up in my business operations to deliver on that societal good?), there is an even more subversive trade-off mindset that permeates corporate decision-making. This mindset may exist in the people whom leaders need to engage in the change. These cohorts of the organization are the mid-level executives, the managers and the supervisors that are best placed to convert theoretical change into practical change. The mindset looks a lot like comfort with the status quo. Or rather, discomfort at moving away from the status quo. It heralds energy and adjustment, both of which require expenditures of will. These cohorts, who together make up the centre of gravity of an organization, are essential to success.

When attempting to lead an organization in a direction that challenges the stereotypes of old-school business, the power of the why may falter at the trade-off hurdle that lies in wait in the midst of the organization. It is why we wait for regulations to materialize and tell us to change. At that point, there is no trade-off, merely a mandatory requirement. But, as we have discovered previously, waiting for laws and regulations to catch up to societal expectations is a laggard's game.

Assume for a moment, without the weight of historical experience weighing down upon us, that we do not have to consider trade-off issues because they may not exist. We have noted previously in this narrative that working in organizations to improve society, concurrently with producing the goods or services that the market requires, does not create any visceral negative human reaction. It is not a difficult sale to make to the average human, all other things being equal. After all, we all want that better world for ourselves, our families, friends and communities. So, what is not balanced, within our organizational setting, that so often raises and propagates this trade-off hurdle?

Organizationally, we are typically victims of our own design. We engage and employ people to work within our organizations who have been part of a larger business ecosystem, in other organizations and in other parts of the world. They come with an array of pre-set views about business and the rest of the world, the average exhibiting yesterday's rather than tomorrow's thinking. We tend to apply our own conscious and unconscious biases to employing people who fit a mould – our mould. Look around your organization. There are also those that have lived within our own organization for many years or decades. This vital part of our own corporate memory and culture may carry outdated views on business and society, anchored in organizational DNA.

We take these pre-existing, primed assets, and we spend the majority of our behaviours and unspoken cues in reinforcing those pre-conditioned corporate reflexes. When faced with a challenge that juxtaposes business function and societal well-being, we may spend an acceptable minimum of effort in changing the narrative in our organizations. We do not dismantle the older narrative because its impact on stability might be akin to an organizational earthquake. While probably prudent – after all, it is wise to steer a ship at a speed that does not actually sink it – it breeds a cautiousness and conservatism that is at odds with the speed of change around us.

Together, these two forces conspire to provide us with a sluggishly incremental momentum forward. Sometimes the balance changes in either direction. Sometimes, perhaps in economically difficult times, or when leadership changes, we may even witness regression. These backwards steps are surprisingly common in organizations of all types. Many longer-term employees who have witnessed economic cycles or leadership changes will comment on the ebb and flow of corporate responsibility, and even social ethics, in those times.

Why, it might be asked, were there not more leaders who changed business paradigms at a faster rate? After all, CEOs move on every four to seven years, and senior executives are not that much slower. Turnover at leadership levels has, for decades, floated around a reasonably healthy cross-pollinating rate. Why is it that, in the cohorts of leaders past and present, business passion for societal welfare is so overwhelmingly bland outside of philanthropic activities (which in themselves capture a tremendous amount of employee engagement, including among leadership)?

This was not an individual human failing among deliberately uncaring leaders, so much as it was a societal construct. Business was business, and discussions of society would, if permitted, take up valuable time in the 9-to-5 world. Not that long ago, such discussions of societal welfare were reserved for the few philanthropic hours of the working year. They were the 'giving back' efforts. Emerging leaders were often given the unspoken message that the business of doing business and the largesse of giving back were two separate things. You were paid for the former, and the latter was a form of recreation. Even during the emerging 'green' era, when the old 1980s phrase 'Greed is Good' was replaced by a somewhat hopefully toned 'Green is Good', this separation was clear. You undertook your organizational operations to stay in business, thrive and reward shareholders or (in the case of government), public stakeholders. And if this effort was successful, it was possible to 'give back' meaningfully. After all, the logic argued, how could you give back what you had not accumulated? One priority preceded the other in the boardroom, and in doing so it gained supremacy in the debate. It the absence of a genuinely co-existing paradigm in which responsible, societally enhancing businesses carried equivalent weight to those generating reasonable value for shareholders and other stakeholders, it would always be difficult to spark passion widely. In fact, those in which such passion was sparked were seen as somewhat renegade. They were in the minority.

As a result the weight of responsibility for creating change would sit not through the leadership of organizations but on the shoulders of those who self-selected to make change or who were deliberately charged with such responsibility. Somewhat appropriately but probably sub-optimally, these people would be given the responsibility to change 'hearts and minds'. This was, and still is, appropriate because they are often senior executives whose leadership attributes included, theoretically, exactly those abilities. It sub-optimality arose because the nature of organizational value was not clearly linked to stakeholder values, which in turn is more pervasively tied to societal welfare. In an environment where societally enhancing values are secondary (as opposed to equivalently co-existent) to the priorities of shareholder value, a self-fulfilling hierarchy emerges. In a climate where the historical time and effort (in the organization's people-hours per year) of society-enhancing activities were vastly outweighed by those activities directed at creating shareholder value, organizational cultures formed around that norm.

This does not imply that there is active opposition to blending business purpose and societal purposes. There is simply habitual passivity that weighs heavily like an anchor on change initiatives. Imagine, for example, a talented and personable Chief People Officer, or a Chief Executive Officer, attempting to co-create shareholder value and societal value via an Initiative X, aimed at improving work–life balance. Other senior executives, for example, the Chief Finance Officer and the Chief Strategy Officer might, as a default, not reject such an initiative aimed at delivering benefit to society. Indeed, active resistance to such noble pursuits would be frowned upon. But support is much more than the absence of resistance. It is more than passive permission. It is the accumulation of peoples' energy behind a purpose. In the absence of this accumulation, you can imagine the tone of decision-making at the executive team. The dynamics might be similar to all projects in which one idea is pitched against another, with funding only available for one – the trade-off. In this case, Initiative X will need to prove its merit in an environment where it begins its battle on the back foot, perhaps even competing for resources against initiatives which are more classically hardwired to shareholder value, such as an advertising campaign or a customer online interface.

What is involved in making the change happen is a matter of practicality. Employees must know that it can be done. They must know that the skills, resources and time can be engaged to achieve change. If not, the ideal languishes as a feel-good prospect. For example, since the first child-labour stories broke in the apparel industry in the late twentieth century, there has been a considerable drive to remove such activities from supply chains of goods. Change has been incremental, sited firmly on the bottom of the S-curve, because leadership has uttered these two statements, or variations of them, in the one breath: *we must eliminate child labour from the supply chain*, and *it is very complicated and difficult to do in many of the supply chain countries*. The first phrase is a fine commitment and highly engaging. The second phrase is a truthful statement. Yet, while it points out (and perhaps even celebrates) the degree of difficulty and the heroic efforts that might be needed, this is typically unhelpful in igniting change. A more useful second phrase, used by companies that have made more recent significant strides, is *we will be using the blockchain economy to progressively help align our supply chains with our commitment*. The fact that it is complicated and difficult to do in many of the supply chain countries is still valid. However, a mere glimmer of a 'how-to' has been offered, and the engagement level for change is different. For employees to apply their own herculean efforts, they must know that the change *can* happen. If one pathway is potentially feasible, the can-do energy created may ignite alternatives.

Finally, crusades can be lonely and tiresome. It is much easier to engage with a vision when you do not, as an employee, feel alone or in a minority. Leaders who want to make fundamental cultural changes rarely hand the task over to their Chief People Officer or their Head of Human Rights to deal with. They take time to create collective pools of support and effort at the start of their S-curve. Task forces within an organization often populated by some organizational leaders, collaboration with other organizations and private/public-sector initiatives are all useful means of forming collective and collaborative energy.

If your objective as a leader is to change the culture of your organization to one that can hold, simultaneously, concepts of shareholder or stakeholder value and societal good in its strategic and operational decision-making, this rinse-and-repeat cycle must be replaced with a more effective one. More than a century of tradition must be broken, rather than timidly bent.

If you are reading this book, you are probably in one of these cohorts but you carry with you a sense that you can be a more holistic leader. You may be increasingly dissatisfied with the societal legacy your current mode of leadership might bring. You want better, from yourself, from your organization, from others like you, and from other organizations like yours. You believe that the concept of good leadership can be better than you have seen it defined. You believe that the untapped vein of betterness lies in greater harmonization of organizational success with societal well-being. Not just finding the compromise of the day, but finding genuine sustainable co-existence and flows of value. Aspects like climate change, pollution, labour rights, resource scarcity and efficiency, community values, supply chain integrity, bribery and corruption, diversity and respect, equality and equity and a list of others remain at sub-optimal or critical levels in society. You believe leaders like yourself can and should help steer those aspects into safer, and more societally just, states of being. You may even be a little bit embarrassed that you feel that way because there is a troubling narrative that suggests such leaders are not the alpha leaders we have long celebrated in organizational cultures. The incumbent narrative may infer that such leaders are something else, perhaps simply unproven, perhaps renegade left-leaning, perhaps even incompetent.

There is no doubt that such a change in leadership views and attitudes, at scale across tens of thousands of the world's largest organizations, would be a game changer for the world. There is no doubt, too, that such a change would only be achieved one leader at a time, with you owning the footprint within which you can make your difference, your leadership leverage and your ability to persuade others to do the same. That is how groundswells gather their expansive potential.

The bad news is this: I do not know of a magic formula to ignite this groundswell. I do not know of 'Seven Secrets to Changing the World through Your Corporate Leadership'. In over three decades of working within large corporations, I have merely observed the hurdles that exist. I have tried different techniques to get over them, some of which worked better than others. Like others pushing at this edge of organizational improvement in our society, I have had mixed successes. I have learnt more from failures than from successes. The best we can do is pass on lessons learnt and wisdom accumulated and hope that they serve as building blocks for your own journey. The rest of this book encourages you to use a self-taught higher perspective of business in society, to understand and be wary of the repetitive corporate patterns that serve us poorly, to look for and use techniques to break them and create new patterns, and to use your own inner compass to forge a better way forward.

So let's look to you first.

Leadership comes in many shapes, sizes and flavours: part character, part discipline, part science, part art, part philosophy, part intelligence, part wisdom. There are willing leaders and reluctant leaders. There are leaders who lead from the front, leaders who marshal collective action from within the pack and leaders ushering from the rear. What we do know is that the *how* of leadership is varied. It is as diverse in nature as anything else we do in our professional careers. It is yours to fashion using your strengths and buttressing your weaknesses. But the *what* of leadership is reasonably clear; it is the invigoration of deliberate, engaged and aligned action by many around a purpose.

We have, in this narrative, loosely formed a purpose around engaging organizations to work in a more integrated manner within the society they serve, to improve society's own well-being. The purpose is reasonably noble and clear, and only awaiting some details on what aspects of society's well-being you and your organization can meaningfully contribute to. But before you address that detail, let us look at your leadership – specifically, in the way you might steer your organization along the pathway that balances success and societal good.

Let us look at some common challenges in achieving this balance because articulating them helps formulate strategies.

Inevitably, defining balance ties us up in knots. What is balance? Who says it is balanced? Everyone will have a view, and the vast majority of views will be different from each other. If there is a correct answer, nobody is owning up to knowing it. Yet, in order to pursue a balance, whatever it is, every organization must form a view of balance that it will honour. That view of balance must, of course, be shared by society. If societal principles define balance, and organizations subscribe to those principles, then irrespective of expected variations in honest interpretation, the laws of averages are likely to get us in the zone of something that looks like and feels like balance.

This view of balance may be set in its purpose, its vision, its code of conduct or any other manifesto that serves to create an overall alignment. Getting to an enduring organizational view that genuinely serves society is no easy task, and we will return to this when we discuss board dynamics and governance. The challenge is not without its global support, because a broad view of balance was formed in 2015 when the United Nations proposed the 17 Sustainable Development Goals to achieve by 2030. They are necessarily macro in scale. You may, or may not, agree with them absolutely. It barely matters. What it does, effectively enough, is catalogue the 17 aspects of society in which improvement would bring about the most profound global changes to human existence. An organization can do much worse than to anchor its own view of balance, which will no doubt be strongly shaped by its own operational footprint in the world. This footprint relates to the goods and services provided by the organization, the supply chain through which they are produced and the organization's proximity – physical or economic – to some of these Sustainable Development Goals.

Of course, all that provides is a blueprint for selecting the subject matter through which balance will be achieved. For example, an organization might determine that its goods and services will be produced with particular regard to climate risk, to water security and to food production. But how much it will lean into these three areas, relative to its resources and its other priorities, is what defines balance.

Historically, organizations have defined balance through the trade-off lens that was mentioned before. How much of the organization's effort would be diverted to these goals? What was too little, what was too much? Given that diversion of effort, what was a credible outcome? Was *that* too little? Should some incremental change be made in the organization's effort to 'keep pace' with peers? Typically, a strategy was evoked through a thought process that resembled an ancient weighing scale of incremental weights and counterweights, with the balance being gauged through a process of finessing effort to maintain credibility with stakeholders. This process allowed ample room for manoeuvring the organization's credibility meter. A couple of years of sub-par performance (usually relative to peers) could be addressed with some gearing-up of resources or effort. Like pace cars in a Grand Prix, strategies were formulated to stay in the game.

A more useful notion of balance is to look at the issues considered – in this example, climate change, water scarcity and food production – and to consider what cumulative effort it would take to arrive at a 5, 10 or 15-year end-state that represents material and meaningful progress. It may be to achieve a 20 per cent reduction in carbon emissions within the supply chain in a 10-year period. It may also be to ensure that the population in area X has physical and economic access to potable water and to achieve a food production annual average in area X that is 30 per cent above self-sufficiency threshold, with the excess accessing markets outside area X. Whatever the paradigm, it is focused not on the organization but rather on the societal issues that the organization has physical and economic proximity to or has otherwise recognizable leverage that it can apply.

While there are many good examples of organizations that have achieved some aspects of this balance, they are often lost in a sea of ordinary examples from which there is little to learn. There are also many good examples that have sometimes, sadly, been offset by other failings in the same organization that, in turn, have tarnished their value. How many times have we heard of a corporation that has contributed to the systemic improvement of water supply in poorer countries, only to discover that it fell prey to a scandal of bribery? Or businesses that innovated to bring renewable energy to emerging economies, only to find that their supply chain was heavily tainted by child labour? Balance then, is unlikely to be achieved by picking one aspect to focus on, much against the old philosophy of picking one thing and doing it well. It implies a rounded view of societal well-being and an awareness that there are many pieces to the jigsaw puzzle. We do not need, nor do we necessarily have, the capacity in one organization to solve the whole puzzle, but neither is it particularly transformative to hold just one piece in such an interlinked puzzle. It is probably more useful to apply our efforts to a connected corner, or a scene, of the puzzle.

12

The Personal Journey

Any leader must have sufficient belief in the worthiness of the endeavour to be able to impassion those that would follow. In this context, you must genuinely believe that a better society is worth directing a great deal of your effort, and that of your organization's, to that end. You must care enough to want to do so. Tempting as it is to gloss over that characteristic, it is nevertheless worth your while pondering it carefully. Faking it until you make it is not a viable option, because of the magnitude of organizational cultural challenges outlined so far.

So if you are trying to change the world through your corporate leadership, it is best to genuinely believe in it. Such big human goals will require the recruitment of others with a latent desire to do the same. In such a setting, inauthenticity is like a handicap for leadership, a handbrake on the wheels of progress and a roadblock to the envisioned destination. If you would lead an organization, or parts of it, to successful outcomes, you will naturally be more powerful as a leader by being invested in those outcomes.

The registries of stock exchanges the world over are filled with leaders who have bowed to investor pressures to make deep cultural changes but who were not internally motivated to make necessary those cultural changes. Consequently, they were unable to achieve the changes to the degree hoped for by investors. In matters of organizational culture, external motivation is a poor substitution for internal passion and drive. A leader who is insufficiently motivated by his or her own passions to make cultural changes but instead reacts to external pressures to embark on those changes should rightly be questioned about his or her care factor regarding those changes. A leader who says, 'We must do this because it is good' is more likely to engage followership than one who signals, 'We must do this because we have been told to'.

This is a pivotal point to make because the most common question I hear from leaders responding to these external pressures is, *we need to respond to these stakeholder concerns, how do we do this well?* If it was a paint-by-numbers process, the many offerings of management consultants everywhere would suit. A useful question, and one which is best asked and answered by yourself, is, *how much do I care about the issue?* There is no wrong answer; you could care very little at the outset, and it does not mean the journey is doomed. But in recognizing that shortfall, at least you form a more accurate view of the challenge.

So let us look at your personal journey first, before addressing the organizational challenges. The latter will be much more difficult if the former has not been taken.

Business challenges have been taken on and solved for well over a century. Textbooks have been written, courses taught, mentors grown and experience amassed throughout that time. On the other hand, very few of society's challenges have had the same wealth of knowledge and experience in solving them. As an organizational leader seeking to combine organizational success with societally beneficial outcomes, you are likely to be travelling a familiar business road and simultaneously navigating a complex and unfamiliar societal landscape that requires innovative – not learned – thinking. You will need to rethink the former to include the latter. Your leadership – if it is to be authentic in managing the fusion – may cycle through the following stages (Figure 12.1).

In the first instance, you imagine. It is humanity's greatest enabling strength, among other living creatures on our world, to imagine what can be. It is a projection of the future. It is a construct that we can develop, inspect, refine and then, when done, accept or reject. We have the ability to both conjure in our minds a future condition and then, even more remarkably, make value judgements on this future condition. How would we make it more desirable? How would it make us feel?

These value judgements that we make can cause us to form an attachment to the imagined future state. We can determine if the imagining is worthy or unworthy to us. If the imagining is worthy to us, we may change our sense of it – from abstract thoughts to an outcome worthy of pursuit. We attach to it a 'why' that makes it worthy, a motivator that makes it worth pursuing for us.

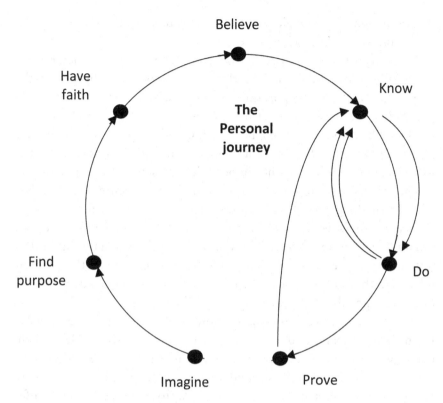

FIGURE 12.1
Knowing you: a personal journey of leadership in change.

At this point, it can become a purpose. The purpose may be essentially for societal good (*all children should receive an education*) or organizationally self-interested (*we need secure access to water to sustain operations*) or a combination of both (*we need to develop a local, talented labour force*), but it must have one important common denominator. It must be important enough for you to care about it. If you do not care much (*we should reduce our energy usage because it will save us some operating costs; besides, everyone else is doing it and we don't want to appear non-progressive*), it will park itself on a to-do list, not transcend into a purpose and be destined for minimum acceptable action. The more you care, the greater the motivator behind the purpose. As a leader, this is one of the most potent strengths you can bring to your role. If you care enough, you may transcend adequate leadership and enter greatness. And there are no schools to teach you to care, although they may illuminate and educate. Caring is something you draw from within yourself by reflecting.

For a purpose to crystallize and not slip back into the abstract, it must potentially belong in the real world. It must, somehow, be achievable. The word *somehow* is important here, because we must have a sense of possibility, and it need not yet be grounded in hard evidence. We don't need likelihood or probability, because it is still early in our journey, but merely a possibility. At this point we must know that it is worthy enough to care about and that it is not impossible. The sense of feeling that it is not impossible is faith. We all express it differently within ourselves, but we hear the language of faith all the time. *If we can put astronauts on the moon, surely we can solve this problem. There must be some way we can do that. If anyone can crack it, you can.* Leaders who have this faith – unfounded by methodologies and facts and figures – break through the *if* barrier. They are not constrained by doubt; they are confident that an outcome is possible. They are simply not yet sure *how*.

At this point, leadership creates followership. People provide the how when their leaders are driven by purpose and are unshakeable in their faith that the purpose can be achieved. This is the phase where leadership earns its value. People rally around a common purpose and direct their energies in a common direction, seeking a way to bring the purpose to life. This is the difference between management and leadership – the former the skill of directing something already preconceived more smoothly and efficiently, the latter the art of bringing something from the realm of imagining to the world of engaged action.

Transforming, for example, an existing fleet of transportation into low carbon emission systems is, we know, theoretically achievable. Yet it might be held back by a number of factors. Such a transformation is not technologically out of reach, but there is wholesale reluctance to do it. There is capital expenditure, requiring reserves to be spent. And while operating expenditures may reduce, the net present value of the enterprise is not attractive. Payback periods might be too long. There may be operational reconfiguration challenges. There might be a desire to see the assets live out their service lives rather than retire them early. These are issues of motivation and not physical. It is not that it cannot be done but that there is an apathy or unwillingness to do it.

In circumstances like these, a leader's greatest ability is to rally people around a purpose. It is to change minds, then actions. And it starts with the leader's mind being unassailably changed. That is ground zero. If your mind has not locked onto the faith that organizational change is entirely possible, you are on a different playing field to the one that hosts the big game. But if your purpose is sound and your commitment full, you build a geometric progression of engagement. You convert one person to your faith, then together you convert another two and together you convert another four and all together another eight. And as you build a groundswell of support and engagement around faith, you seek a more detailed how – a means of making it a reality.

Every leader, every innovator has had that moment of belief, of a breakthrough. It is that moment when the faith that has fuelled their enterprise is replaced by tangible knowledge of how to achieve their purpose. The moment when the burden shifts from leadership's shoulders as it carries the *if* to the organization's collective shoulders as it engages on the *how*. The organization changes from being driven by a leader's faith to believing in the plausibility of an outcome. We see this in organizations all the time, a powerful gear change that heralds plans, schedules, actions and a rapid upswing in the level of activity associated with the purpose.

That upswing is the doing. It is the perspiration. The detail. The systematic actions and continuous improvement. The alignment and realignment of the organization to move as effectively and efficiently as possible up the steepest part of the S-curve.

When the doing is done, there is reflection. Is it indeed the outcome that foreshadowed? What is the proof? How is performance measured? Are adjustments required?

Mindfully completed journeys of achievement tend to pass through these phases because the way we progress along difficult and sometimes hidden or invisible pathways (as most in the future are) is through an actualizing process. We also move from the abstract to the specific, because outcomes are tangibly felt only in their specifics.

A leader must own the genesis of this path, sculpting carefully the first two phases and then gradually ceding ownership to others in the organization while remaining – at the very least – present, engaged and visible throughout the journey.

These phases are expanded upon in the next sections. It is, however, useful at this stage to map them to the S-curve of change (Figure 12.2).

Compare this to Figure 11.2 from the previous chapter, which charted the process of organizational change. Note, in particular, how much of

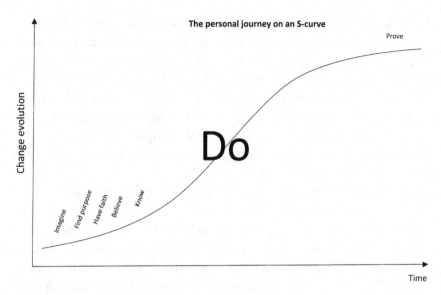

FIGURE 12.2
Staying in front: a leader's personal journey along the phases of organizational change.

a leader's own path of change must be traversed before the organization builds momentum and thresholds of organizational change are broken. Indeed, a leader must know in her own mind that change is not only possible but highly likely before the organization begins to shift its own paradigms. A leader's own journey through imagination, finding purpose, having faith and believing is the fountain of organizational faith and purpose.

The leader's actions, during which the talk is walked through the organization, is the fuel required to accelerate and change the pace of progress, to settle into the organization's transformed state and to embed the new paradigms of work so that they become the new norm. Those actions prove commitment. They include setting budgets to facilitate change, resourcing at the right levels to drive change, requiring and taking an active interest in the process of change and the indicators that change is happening, calling for accountability when the change does not meet the leader's imagination and belief, and celebrating as the milestones of change are met. They include resisting the temptation, often visited by employees who have been in the organization for a long time, to slide back to the preceding ways of doing business. Change is not a one-step phenomenon. It requires nurturing the new state to ensure it becomes a habit and, eventually, a way of doing business for tomorrow.

13

Imagine

In the first part of this book, many observations were made about the world in which we live, the role of business and organizations in our more recent evolution, and the role that they might play in the future. Retrospective reasons were proposed for the observations of the past, and rationales were offered for possibilities in the future. It is a useful process through which leaders explore the unknown. It uses some broad pathways of logic, as opposed to unfettered imagination, with which to explore possibilities. In this way, imagination is couched in what we know or infer. And while this is, indeed, a self-imposed limitation on how far or free our imaginations run, in the world of organizations there is an expectation that the tether to today's reality is tangible. Future states are planned in 10-, 20- or 30-year horizons for a number of reasons. Thirty years is roughly one generation; infrastructure generally needs significant technological, structural or utility facelifts within that timeframe; the time value of money makes future cash flows at today's quanta much less valuable than today's cash flows at the same quanta; and so on.

Those limitations aside, imagination is the start of all great things. The ability to imagine a better tomorrow and ask, *why not?* is one of the most powerful generators of developmental momentum we have. Its leverage is astonishing. It takes relatively little sweat to imagine. It takes almost no resources. It can be done anywhere. The conjuring of imagination takes just one person. Yet, once articulated, it can infect the imagination of countless others. It can spark others, billions of imaginations, furthering its vision deeper and broader into the universe of imaginings. It can excite, enthuse and engage billions. Imagined enough times by enough people, it can become a near-certainty, simply waiting for the right combination of technology and cost to turn into reality.

Yet it can also dissipate as quickly as it materializes. We can kill the fruit of our imaginings with trivial ease. Powerful as it is, it is nonetheless fragile. We can rein in our own imaginings with a simple flick of our minds. Labels like 'fanciful', 'impractical', 'unrealistic' and 'science fiction' can vaporize the things that are imagined. We can lose them, in milliseconds, forever. Great ideas can flicker for an instant and die, our minds careless with their disposal, disinterested in their retention or recollection because, well, there are plenty more flickers of imagination where that came from.

Albert Einstein, widely regarded in our time as one of the great minds of science and the universe, said two poignant things about imagination. One of them is a testament to its staggering power. *Imagination is more important than knowledge. For knowledge is limited whereas imagination embraces the entire world, stimulating progress, giving birth to evolution.* The other is a lesson that sounds as unlikely on first reading as it does ring true after contemplation. *If you want your children to be intelligent, read them fairy tales. If you want them to be more intelligent, read them more fairy tales.*

As leaders, some of our deepest ponderings ought to be about harnessing this universal power and growing this universal strength within our organizations. We should lead by example, encouraging our own imaginings rather than equating leadership with the bureaucratic arbitration of others' imaginings. Leadership could exhibit curiosity in the imaginings of others, and further the engaging and collaborative question, *why not?* with more enthusiasm than the authoritarian shackling of the burden of proof that accompanies the question, *why?* There is plenty of time and opportunity, as we shall see later, to pursue proof. Capturing and nurturing a spark of imagination, until it blossoms into a flame we can explore, should be a higher priority than quashing it in the rush hours of our working life.

All too often, we excuse the behaviour that accompanies the dismissal of imaginings, or the curiosity that we are reluctant to engage with, by blaming the lack of time for such indulgences. Surely there is no time to spend on imaginings when there are customers to attract, capital investors to appease and laws to comply with.

Leadership has long been praised for its ability to focus on the issues that should attract focus and to hold distractions at bay. During the twentieth century, as we attempted to hone this skill further and further until efficiency became our highest mantra, we built dismissive patterns into our accepted leadership paradigms. We embraced alpha-male-isms and pooh-poohed contemplative curiosity. We rewarded action over wisdom, short-termism over long-termism, tactical skills over strategic insights and, ultimately, practicality over imagination.

It was not until the early twenty-first century that we began to collectively (and even then only in the fringes of organizational leadership) become concerned at the loss of creative energy. We began to see that our leadership methods were pursuing safe, incremental gains rather than bold, transformational outcomes. Our leadership disciplines became more steeped in proving-before-doing (a justification model) rather than trying-before-validating (an innovative model). The phrase *what's your business case for that?* became a paralyzing roadblock for millions of employees in organizations who were trying to use their imaginations.

As the pace of technological change began to take off early in the twenty-first century, business models sought to methodically break some of the shackles forged through many years of textbook leadership and management styles. Terms such as *imagineering* supplanted engineering, and fast-fail models of innovation began to materialize. Steady and logical was augmented by nimble and empathetic. Leaders were being asked, more and more frequently, to access both left and right brain activity. In effect, leaders were being asked more insistently to lead rather than manage.

The distinction is vitally important because the very nature of leading requires a specific type of courage. It requires the willingness and ability to step into the unknown. It requires the conceiving of new scapes and new boundaries, of imagining beyond a small delta from today. It requires tremendous courage because the answer to the unknown could be right, or it could be wrong. After all, it is why it is in the unknown.

For leaders, this was (and still is) a sticking point. Textbook leadership has taught us, over several hundred years, that leading to failure is a cardinal sin. It is career limiting. Following into failure, on the other hand, is somewhat forgivable. It is a commonplace for a leader to fail, and for one of her or his executives to take the reins. Leading into failure is punished, but following into failure can be rewarded. The culture that is built around this underlying paradigm can be innocently toxic. It reinforces the view that too much courage is dangerous. Even where courage is celebrated publicly, it is a backhanded compliment, because it is punished for not being cautious enough with the reins.

The average leader must wrestle with the conundrum of how and where courage is acceptable. For the average leader, this internal battle – one that is rarely seen by others – is hardly a fierce one. Capitulation, and taking the safe road, has been rewarded in organizational politics for generations. Cautious extrapolation, rather than imagination, is often asked of leaders. It is asked by shareholders of boards, by boards of their CEOs, and by CEOs of their executives. So the courage to dare is a rare commodity in leadership.

This is not by definition a bad thing, because the very nature of taking calculated risks is based on cautious extrapolation. If we are committing the capital of others to an enterprise, it is reasonable – indeed, preferable – that left-brain structured caution is prioritized to a great degree. We may exercise imagination, but we are riding its accelerator and the brake of caution at the same time. This behavioural DNA can become the default setting, a second-guessing that keeps imagination tethered in the realms of a reality we fabricate around it to remain risk averse.

We rationalize this behavioural DNA easily enough. It's better to be safe than sorry.

In public sector organizations, the culture can be excruciatingly evident. It leads to observations that little gets done (or little gets done efficiently), that good ideas are choked in bureaucracy and that progress is slow. In the private sector, we formulate differential rewards to encourage certain types of risk-taking behaviour, some of which turn out to be regretful but many of which turn out to be useful catalysts to the imagination. Leadership norms have become progressively less imaginative, to the extent that we have to invoke catalysts of cash bonuses, equity bonuses and share options to stimulate our leadership out of that learned lethargy.

Little wonder, then, that if there are no catalysts made available for ethical business practices, that leadership is not compelled to become imaginative in achieving ethical business outcomes. In this learned culture, if the predominant response is to penalize unethical practices, our leadership imagination is stimulated in the direction of policing and auditing. We shift from seeking to be ethical, to seeking to not be unethical. These are not the same as each other, much like the cultural difference between seeking to win and seeking not to lose. In some cases, leadership imagination is stimulated in the direction of not being exposed. And so, inordinate amounts of time and organizational energy are invested into systematically more defensive strategies of problem-solving, rather than imaginative paradigm-breakers.

For the courageous leader, the path is even more convoluted. Among peer ranks, imagination is readily neutralized by the peer pressure of cynicism. Too much effervescent and imaginative leadership frays pre-existing bonds of caution and defensiveness. There is too ready a chorus of *what about this?* and *what about that?* of raised eyebrows and, most of all, the silent threat of loss of confidence within leadership teams. And leadership without invoking confidence is no leadership at all. A lone Messianic voice in an organization all too quickly becomes a lone Messianic voice outside of the organization. Ejection is a predictable by-product of the loss of confidence.

And so the triple threat to imagination in leadership plays out as follows. In imagining great (as opposed to incrementally better) outcomes, there is the risk of failure, which in turn is heavily penalized for – if nothing else – a wasted effort. In exercising imagination, we swim against a tide of normative behaviour, which is to embrace cautious extrapolation and move ahead in small, predictable increments. And finally, in exercising imagination, team cohesion is risked if the underlying culture of the organization is not already primed for this type of journey.

The key to unlocking a culture of imagination is held firmly within a board's collective hands. It is in these hands that permission is afforded, denied or – most confusing of all (equating to a kind of vexed denial) – held in ambiguity. It is a theme that echoes throughout this book; where a board exists, the board's ability to set culture is far more powerful than any other collective of leadership personalities in the organization. If the board is not demonstrating its courage in imagining, it is setting the tone for all executive leadership below that stratum to act in a similar way. And while it is certainly feasible that the imagination for businesses to add much greater value to society might be sparked within leadership teams despite ambiguous or contrary signals from the board, such an occurrence would be against the grain, and therefore the exception to the expected norm.

Why don't boards more readily ignite the DNA of imagination from their uncontested apex of governance and culture? There are plenty of examples of boards that have brought acute innovative mindsets to organizations; it is not that they are inherently unimaginative. The answer might lie, at least to a moderate and perhaps even a significant degree, in a historical trend of boards that are not particularly diverse. Boards that are not particularly diverse, in perspective and thought, tend to agree on similar things most of the time. This is both a bureaucratic strength and a strategic weakness.

Board diversity began gathering a lot of attention in the last two decades of the twentieth century. Symptomatically, boards looked a little bit male dominated; and in organizational history, this overtly sexist outcome was the flashpoint of change. Upon closer examination, it was apparent that board members were primarily male, were generally of advanced age and typically fell within a narrow bandwidth of socio-economic privilege. It did not matter if one looked in the United States or Denmark or China. Older, middle-to-upper-middle-class males were more in evidence than any other demographic slice of society on boards. Turning the microscope up a notch, more monocultural detail could be discerned. Board members might, in the main, be drawn from legal and financial disciplines, as well as senior executive familiarity with the type of business being governed.

It would be trite to ascribe this coincidence to an Old Boys' Club effect, although again, there is evidence of this effect if board recruitment practices are scrutinized across a wide enough sample. The triteness is there because boards do not, as a rule, race out to achieve such monochromatic membership outcomes with gleaming-eyed intent. But there are a number of prerogatives that predispose outcomes, and understanding these helps in seeing why such trends evolve.

A key prerogative is that board members must bring valued skills to a board. Historically, the three chief skills to draw upon were knowledge of the business (preferred), financial acumen (unavoidable) and legal knowledge (again, largely unavoidable or at the very least, risky to ignore). Given that each of these skill sets contain a great deal of variables, a heady mix of objectivity and subjectivity and, consequently, a very high likelihood that robust debate would arise in any of these three areas, it is prudent to have multiple people on a board that can usefully discuss each area with authority. In this way, better decisions are seeded and fertilized. However, the number of board members rises as we attempt to engineer this type of board strength. There is a practical limit to the number of dissenting collaborators that can be built into a group because the board must be able to make decisions. Boards that argue perennially are a recipe for disaster. So there is a mix of collegiate tension that needs to be fostered, a willingness to debate strongly but still honour the mandate that decisions must be made in a timely manner so that the organization can function.

At this point, the shape of the board begins to normalize. There is a predictable way of ensuring that decisions will get made, with an appropriate amount of preceding debate. It is common practice to ensure the board composition does not include wild cards, although Devil's Advocates (cousins of sorts) are commonplace. If it is ensured that the set of principles held by the individuals is compatible – within reason – with each other, collegiate decisions are more likely to be made. There will be a healthy and somewhat predictable bandwidth of views, but for the most part they can be rationalized through debate to achieve least-regret decisions.

This is somewhat easier to achieve in discipline-based skills such as finance, law, risk, audit, people and culture, digital technologies or business sector acumen than it is to achieve in, say, social values. As every Chairperson knows, the introduction of a left-leaning board member into a mid- to right-positioned board risks highly polarized, emotive debates on issues that can tie a board up in knots, decimate collegiality and undermine the ability of a board to collectively govern.

Board selection decisions have, historically, tended to adopt diversity inclusions judiciously. In fact, gender diversity challenges are, in and of themselves, generally not plagued by the spectre of board division on a range of issues. Women are not necessarily predisposed to opposing views on discipline-based skills than men. And yet, despite the absence of this risk, boards still struggle with achieving a more equitable gender mix. If the adoption of more diverse board membership – simply from a gender viewpoint – does not, at face value, risk the collegiate decision-making ability of a board, why are incremental gains beyond twenty-five or thirty per cent female memberships so difficult to attain?

While accusing fingers are liable to point to a narrower and shorter pipeline of female executives who are adequately "experienced" to take board positions, there is a collective societal sense that this is too glib an answer to be entirely true. It is also likely that there is institutional inertia that slows the pace of increasing diversity on boards.

Firstly, there are incumbent board members – many of them male, of a certain age group and often within a similar socio-economic bracket to each other. To increase the percentage of females on boards, some of the males would need to move. Now, we have three reasons that, together, are reasonably likely to slow the pace of diversity. We have some board members that may think *I don't want to move on until I retire or am elected out by shareholders*. We have some board members who may think *I don't want things to be too different around here* – a combination of unconscious and conscious biases. While not being entirely helpful in a diversity debate, neither are particularly malicious and are easily recognizable as very human traits. And there is the third reason, which is *we need to be able to agree on decisions routinely.* Together, the three reasons interlock with each other to help hold a status quo, whether it is against gender diversity or against a broader diversity of thought and imagination.

The quandary for collective leadership is particularly intense. A key to unlocking imagination at the board – particularly in light of business's role in society – is a greater diversity of perspective, experience and thought. Organizational experience with achieving something as logically straightforward as gender diversity has been slow and reluctant; why should other aspects of diversity manifest any quicker? The three interlocking reasons are still present and perhaps even more potent when considering diversity aspects outside of gender.

While boards continue to struggle to land relatively easy-to-imagine aspects such as boardroom diversity, there is a risk that homogeneity in board representation and thinking will persist for a time. While it persists, boards are likely to struggle with even harder-to-imagine aspects such as catalyzing societal good. And if boards struggle, so will the organization. Institutional investors are bringing greater pressure to bear to realize a broader imagination and will within boards. And so, to bring the paradigm of societally-conscious imagination to an organization in an authentic way, the broadening of thought must be anchored in board governance, down through the executive, through management, and into the minds of all employees. We all should think, *why not*?

14

Find Purpose

In the first part of the book, we also sought to shed light on the *why bother* question for leadership. Why should an organizational leader concern herself or himself with the broader well-being of society in the context of the organization's purpose? While the perspectives offered in that section provide useful considerations for a leader, the process of anchoring to them must come from the person. While that is easy to assert, genuine anchoring by a leader to a business purpose that is informed by those perspectives, certainly outside the purview of non-governmental organizations or NGOs, has historically been rare. The harsh truth is threefold. One, as leaders, we have not been compelled (other than by law) to fulfil a broader societal need. Two, we have not been schooled in how to do so. And three, as a result, we can exercise a choice to play around the edges, if we choose to play at all.

What we know, as both leaders and followers, is that if anchoring to the why is weak, the leadership lacks sufficient strength of purpose. Consequently, leadership in broader societal values comes across as vague and listless. Let us assume we are among those leaders who, as human beings, have an innate sense that societal good is a noble pursuit, for most of us undoubtedly are. We perceive this as an uncomfortable feeling of disjointedness, a sense that we are less than what we could be. The acceptance of it further enhances our disjointed feeling, the same feeling of disappointing capitulation that we might experience when we willingly take a lower road. Over a period of time this creates a greater rift between the way we lead and our preferred self-image as a leader. The gap, as it widens, feels more and more like a lack of authenticity.

In self-aware leaders, this manifests as a deeper disappointment and even, in time, a sense of burnout. We see examples of leaders who, at semi-retirement or retirement, turn with surprising alacrity to philanthropic efforts. They often exhibit a common thread, a nagging sense of holistic under-accomplishment during their careers. They may have met and exceeded shareholder expectations for many years and fashioned a comfortable retirement for themselves and their families, but their self-reflected value to society feels undercooked. From the perch of a comfortable retirement nest and with the absence of shareholder demands, they find the means to add some value to society. What they often lack, and what they once had, is an army of followers whose energy they might unleash in a cohesive strategy to contribute to society.

The solution is not entirely as simple as embracing a broader societal good within our organizational role as leaders, because we may fear the magnitude of difficulty involved in steering towards it. Many leaders would publicly scoff at this notion, for challenge is theoretically the elixir of leadership life. How many departing executives have we heard enthusing about looking forward to new challenges? But, as we will explore in the next part of this narrative, in private, as leaders, the existence of a problem without a presentable solution is generally vexing to leaders. It is the source of considerable intellectual and emotional burden in business. And for many – perhaps a vast majority – the antidote to this is to distance from the problem, a particularly attractive proposition if the problem is not business critical. It is to do the opposite of anchoring to imagination and faith. That society generally tolerates us doing so is sufficient excuse for doing exactly that.

If that sounds like leadership lacking in courage, that is because it is exactly what it is. But, as we will explore in the rest of this section there are pathways to solutions, and they provide some elements of courage.

Let us turn to a more important perspective than that from the top, for the leader's own perspective of his or her leadership can be manufactured easily enough in his or her mind. Let us look at the perspective of followers when they observe a leader. It is worth holding in mind that a leader needs followers in order to fulfil their roles well, but the reverse is not necessarily true. A follower might need the *job* more than the leader needs that particular follower in that particular job, but followers as a rule are not terribly dependent on good leaders to be able to conduct their roles adequately. Appropriate working conditions are generally both necessary and sufficient to achieve this. These have historically been provided by management and administrative functions, and now with rapidly increasing proficiency by artificial intelligence and logistical systems.

All economies, of course, recognize this relationship. Leaders are hired and rewarded for their ability to generate outcomes, not just for their ability to administer employees. Outcomes are generated by fashioning a culture that invites performance, by removing barriers to achieving that performance and by igniting clarity of purpose that fuels performance. The rest, as they say, is just logistics.

Imagine that you have hired 100 employees to manufacture electric vehicles. They all walk into their place of employment, each with a set of values. These sets of values are essential to their being, their self-realization. Every person will have a different set, with different levels of importance assigned to different values – the marvel of diversity. Your job is to focus them on a set of values that are relevant to the safe, effective and efficient production of electric vehicles. Some may have produced electric vehicles before, while others may not have. Some may have done so to different specifications, quality and safety expectations and user interfaces. Your job is to provide clarity and commonality of purpose, to ensure that you eliminate barriers to achieve this purpose and to conjure up a common will to perform at the highest, most competitive, outcome-focused levels of performance in achieving this.

Despite their diversity, they arrive with a set of common values. They walk into their place of employment with a set of values that you can bankably predict, with a high degree of confidence, across the majority of the 100 people. This set of values is grounded in the well-being of our society, in clean air and water, in socio-economic equity and low crime, in a stable climate, in access to natural resources, in their safety and the safety of their families, in education and health and in work–life balance, among many others. An employer's purpose that includes these is immediately engaging. How can it not be? It may even be expected to some degree or be disengaging if not present in the ethics of the organization. Common purposes need not start from scratch between employer and employees. They are already self-evident. The more of these that are embraced by leaders, the denser the fabric of common purpose becomes. And the denser this fabric, the easier it becomes to forge a common culture and to construct a workplace ethic that forms the bedrock of alignment. This is, for leaders, a gold mine.

There is a simple reason that these common purposes have not been readily embraced and used to forge workplace cultures. Their degree of difficulty is high. It is high because a great many factors, internal and external to an organization, are intrinsic to meaningful commitments in many of the things that matter to us as a society. And because of that degree of difficulty, it becomes a potentially poison chalice for the uncommitted leader, filled with uncertainties that carry with them the prospect of failure. Failure that we, as leaders, fear because it undermines the confidence we seek to inspire in our employees.

Since the late twentieth century, some low-hanging fruit in these common purposes have been harvested, and to good effect. This arguably began with employee safety, because of its significant effect on morale (which underlies the ability to forge a common purpose). It continued strongly because of increasing investor interest, not necessarily entirely because of its humanistic nature and the promulgation of laws and regulations around safety but also because investors argued that if leaders could not manage something as fundamental as the safety of their employees, it boded poorly for other, less visible non-financial risks. As organizations grew into the twenty-first century, leadership investment in work–life balance, anti-discrimination and anti-bullying grew. Like employee safety issues, these were largely affected by internal forces, and solutions could be marshalled using, largely, internal resources and stakeholders. Leaders began exercising muscles in aspects of life that were important to their employees, and not just important to shareholders or customers. It began, logically enough, with the issues that could be solved using, largely, internal resources. It spread to other forms of diversity than gender, including cultural diversity and LGBTIQ+. We are, and have been, increasingly brave with our application of an ethical lens to societal issues. This courage, buttressed with the knowledge gained from making positive changes to some of these socially relevant aspects of our employees' lives, bodes well for the future. But the tougher aspects – the ones with strong external forces – have yet to be meaningfully tackled at scale in the business world and the world of governmental organizations. Why this has not happened is all to do with leadership. And it is because the vast majority of organizational leaders – boards, CEOs and senior executives – are yet to find faith that they can (or should) do it while governing an organization that is not explicitly charged with such a task. Or perhaps they are yet to have faith it can be done at all – at least by them.

15

Have Faith

Faith is not a word that is used much in business. It is too spiritual. It finds its utility in religions and otherworldly pursuits, and sometimes in sports. It is hard to define. It is too vague. In the world of ethics, faith is often referred to as 'irrational belief', one that is unburdened by facts. The use of the word in the business world is more likely to arch eyebrows than it is to evoke any kind of fervour.

Yet the greatest leaders in history have inspired exactly this trait in their followers. Faith has moved people towards a singular goal with more power than any other of the seven characteristics that are discussed in this section, more so than purpose, which brings a rationality – the 'why' – to the goal. Purpose might provide the lasting 'aha' moment, but faith converts it into energy. Energy revolutionizes intent.

Faith, or irrational belief, energizes like no other leadership fuel. Think about an inspiring leader. What did you feel about that leader that caused you to act enthusiastically without knowing all the facts? What caused you to strive, when following that leader's directions was the only thing expected of you? We often refer to inspirational leaders, and we can almost certainly define some, or many, characteristics that contributed towards that inspiration. It may have been the way that leader engaged with people or how she/he made them feel. It may have been the strength of vision. It may have been their commitment to the vision or their acute sense of strategy in achieving that vision or the camaraderie they built around that vision or the clarity of purpose they brought to that vision or any number of things. But what did that inspirational leader spark in you, that you were energized to strive towards the thing that was exhorted?

The irrationality of faith, powerful though it is, is difficult to conjure as a leader using your traditional business management methods. And that is simply because you cannot teach faith. You can only infect others with it, which in turn means that as a leader, you have to have it first. So let's look at finding faith.

Humankind's greatest feats have begun with a pivotal realization. The realization might have been fleeting. It may have been momentary, or it may have lasted months, but in all likelihood it was not a permanent state of affairs, as we shall see in the next section. And that is because faith – irrational belief – can only sustain itself while we suspend our deeper need for proof, or it is buttressed by other correlations (including other people that hold the same faith). This latter observation is a very important one. The energy of faith can sustain itself for longer if there are many people holding the same faith who continuously help overcome the inevitable doubts that befall their neighbours. We will come back to this.

So our minds must first move from wishing or imagining, to having some kind of faith. The possibility, however small initially, must be grasped. It is not a difficult step, especially in our rapidly evolving technological era. We, as a society, are less and less inclined to dismiss something as impossible with every passing decade. Our recent history, the very few generations since the industrial revolution, has seen humans turn the impossible into the everyday occurrence at a frenetic rate. That is no accident. Our society is filled with billions of people who, fuelled by the heady euphoria of achieving the barely possible and the impossible, continue to strive to push back the envelope that distinguishes the possible from the impossible. Albert Einstein's exhortations to use our imaginations to see beyond what is in front of us have been adopted en masse by the people of our small blue planet. We make this first step with relative ease. Yes, there is a possibility that cancer can be cured. Yes, there is a possibility that we can eradicate poverty in this world. Yes, there is a possibility that we can sustain human populations with the finite resources of this planet. Yes, there is a possibility that we can colonize another life-bearing planet. The amount of energy that humankind generates around possibility is astounding. There is an unmeasured, deep well of this energy latent in our society, a well that expands with our growing population, our greater intellectual and economic connectivity and our increasing boldness to push back the envelope of possibility. Leaders who recognize and are able to harness this energy are able to direct it powerfully towards a purpose.

For now, let us focus on a leadership task. You are the leader seeking to transform your organization or your own part of the organization. You have a good idea of what the transformed organization might look and feel like. You need to enlist the willing help of many in order to effect this transformation. Your MBA playbook tells you how. Perhaps you break the task into bite-sized pieces. You create purpose around both the task and its component pieces. You assign the bite-sized pieces to individuals or sub-groups. You inspire innovative thought, encourage diversity of thought, you move through both divergent and convergent phases and conceive of the transformation path. You are on your way.

Here, you have set up a process and controlled it, directing it towards a solution. You do not know precisely what the solution looks like, but the parts of the process are configured to self-determine the appropriate solution, or solutions, as you go.

We have all led in this way, and so there is nothing new here. The process is almost mechanical. Machine learning (or artificial intelligence) could do this today and probably do a very good job.

Now consider the same task in which you envision a somewhat preposterous transformation. It is not merely materially incremental in the way that transformations often are, but it represents a paradigm shift of monumental proportions. In fact, you almost discarded the thought initially, because it felt irrational. But as you examined why – preposterous though it is – you might have considered it, you realized its purpose was substantive, perhaps even mould-breaking in its potential value.

Yet even in your own current mindset, your vision is well to the left of possible. It is even slightly to the left of plausible. It is borderline irrational.

It is at this juncture that great things happen. You sit with it. You ponder it. You turn it over and over in your mind. As you do your envisioning gets clearer and in its own internal resonance, the idea grows merit. Its purpose, its 'why', becomes more profound. With every rotation in your mind, it becomes clearer and more purposeful. You have no clear idea of how to achieve it, and that aspect gets no clearer perhaps, but the vision and purpose grow. There is a sense of excitement that builds in you. Some people report a 'buzz'. All of this is internal. There is little visible indication of this growing energy. Others may sense that you are distracted or preoccupied. But this immense energy, the one that is conceiving great things from nothing, remains invisibly within. And you dare not speak of it, because it is still irrational, still to the left of plausible.

The world-changing actions of countless individuals over the millennia have started in this silent, lonely space. Some have sat in this space for hours or days before action ignited. Others have sat in this space for years, decades or a lifetime. Yet others have not emerged from this space but instead passed on these thoughts in their notebooks and memoirs, and others have picked them up to continue.

When we emerge from this space – when the irrational, left-of-plausible thought has emboldened itself sufficiently to externalize in a meaningful way – we do so on faith. We do so because there is enough collateral, built between the envisioning and the purpose, to put ourselves out there and float the irrational belief. It is personally risky and requires conviction born of faith to externalize it, not certainty, or even probabilistic leaning. It may be tinged with implausibility because the how is shrouded in uncertainty, but it is outweighed by the strength of the vision and the heft of its purpose. And this balance, in the one person's mind, has crystallized sufficiently to imbue the individual with faith. This is the launching pad of leadership that achieves great things. It is the moment in which you can say to yourself and others, 'This is worth doing, I don't exactly know how, but I know it can be done'.

What is important to note here is that if, as the leader, you cannot find this space in you, then you cannot leverage the power of faith in your organization. It is also important to note that finding this space may take anywhere between a few hours and several decades. And finally, it is critical to understand that finding this space is achieved in the lonely inner expanse of the mind, and only if enough inner attention is devoted to it.

What that means for leaders is time to think, and to think deeply. Since, as a species, we are not given to thinking too deeply about things that we do not care about, it presupposes that such deep thinking is applied to things that matter to us individually. In the world of organizations, things can be made to matter even if they do not really matter to all individuals. We make good use of roles specifications and remuneration to make things matter, but they are no substitute for really caring. This was discussed previously, when employee sentiments were considered. Most people have an innate human preference for a safe, equitable, harmonious society and a clean, healthy environment. However, we have been schooled to separate our work from such innate human needs for many decades. Subsequently, the innate care factor has been trained to park itself out of sight and suspend operations in our parallel working world. But it is there, and it is perennially accessible.

What do great leaders do when faith crystallizes in their minds? They infect others with it. The beauty of leadership positions in organizations is that it bestows on an individual a certain influential advantage. Many schools of thought correctly point out that influential advantage is not reliant on organizational position alone. But the converse is also true, that leadership positions come with their own weightiness in debate. We pause and listen to them because of their station. Consequently, leaders are uniquely positioned to infect others with their own faith.

There are only two ingredients required for infection. The vision is one, and the purpose is the other. As we noted above, once the combined resonance of the two outweighs the gaps in the 'how', it is in the realm of faith. The rest is merely the vectors of infection and its aggressiveness. Getting faith to spread is about spreading yourself as a leader and leading with enthusiasm. The first is easy enough if you believe in that currency labelled 'visible, felt leadership'. You get around. Much of it is necessary and becomes timetabled in for you, and some of it requires you to mindfully extend to your stakeholders. The second – leading with enthusiasm – rarely needs mindful development if you have faith in something you care about. This is the magnetism that changes cultures, spreads visions, amplifies purpose and forms futures.

What does infecting look like? For a start, it is real, authentic. You cannot infect others with faith if your own is not authentic. In an organizational culture where posturing has historically been given great importance, authenticity can be hard to spot, embrace or anchor to. The old adage 'Fake it till you make it' is the enemy of faith. As a leader, your personal responsibility in this area is clear. If you wish to lead with faith, you must first be authentic.

From there, infection takes the form of communication, both in words and in the spirit with which they are delivered. Communication of the vision and the why, admission of the missing how's, and your visible, felt commitment to the mantra 'this is worth doing, I don't exactly know how, but I know it can be done' are all necessary. The communication must be frequent and consistent, because mantras become meaningful only when repeated with feeling, over and over. Faith is easy to infect because it grows in potency with numbers. People infect and reinfect each other, provided the faith virus is constantly in the air. And this can be achieved by making the issue a perennial conversation and a core purpose of an organization. It creates a buzz.

Of the many successes that true leaders may contemplate achieving in their lifetimes, a legacy of transforming a society for the better through their own infectious leadership is perhaps the highest. As human beings, we are highly susceptible to feeding our innate desire for a better society, a better environment and a better life. We are therefore barely resistant to infection. We become resistant only when faced with binaries such as 'the sole purpose of business is to make profits for its shareholders' or 'it is not business's role to make society a better place' or 'doing good takes away from the bottom line'. These manufactured antibodies are strong, their prevalence wide, and their impact has been evident in our economy for well over a century. Take away those binaries and the potential for inspired, inspirational leadership grows exponentially.

This liberated – and liberating – leadership is crucial if we want our organizations to meaningfully contribute to the societal ecosystem. It is not reserved for just our boards and CEOs but should be the norm for all levels of management in an organization. The likelihood of reflecting leadership that uses the power of faith to harness human ingenuity and industriousness is vastly increased down through the organization if boards and CEOs model such leadership strengths. In doing so, we model not just faith in the existence of solutions to our greatest problems, but also faith in our people to help find those solutions.

16

Believe

If faith was a form of *irrational* belief, the next progression is a more *rational* belief. Rational belief needs some evolving or accrued proof that an outcome can be achieved. It is underpinned by some evidence that the hoped-for outcome is gradually less reliant on faith and more reliant on progress towards that outcome. Faith without evolving proof can be sustained for a little while through people or groups that self-reinforce the energy, but in the world of business, patience is less readily available as time progresses.

When organizations achieve great things over a long period of time, it is because they build a system of belief that sustains effort. Imagine that a pharmaceutical organization had faith that it could make basic vaccinations affordable and available to everyone in the world. This is a big call – bold and audacious, and certainly lacking in a detailed 'how'. But let's say it begins with faith. *We don't know how, exactly, but we know it can be done.* If it has been done before with, for example, smallpox vaccines, then despite not knowing exactly how it can be done, we can shift from faith to belief.

You may wonder that this seems obvious. Yet often, within organizations, we become insular. We sometimes forget that every day, other organizations take implausibly innovative steps forward in all manner of applications, from health to technology to art and more. In tackling the world's ethical, economic, social and environmental challenges, one organization is hardly alone. Others have achieved surprising outcomes. And in the business world, there is no shortage of ego. If another business can achieve something significant, most worthy leaders would back themselves to do much the same, or better. And if you, personally, have that sense, you move very quickly from faith to belief. There is no evidence so compelling that something can be achieved if it has been achieved to some extent before. So if your vision is progressive but relatively modest (for example, achieving fifty per cent female senior leadership, carbon-neutral energy use or flexible working arrangements), the chances are good that someone else has achieved highly creditable outcomes in these spaces. In those cases, shifting from faith to belief is generally straightforward.

But what if the vision has not been achieved before? What if its newness, boldness and audaciousness are one-off propositions? Or, somewhat dishearteningly, they are propositions that have been attempted before and failed. Clearly, shifting from faith to belief is less trivial. The belief rarely appears in a flash of clarity, like a miraculous realization. Much more often, especially in an organizational context, belief is pondered into existence. A great deal of organizational effort is required to shift from faith to belief.

This requires us to have a sense of the how. How will the thing we think is possible actually become possible? It is in this step that the pondering happens, and innovation is teased. Great leaders spend a great deal of time encouraging the pondering. Bridging the gap from faith to belief creates the funnel with which to harness ongoing amounts of organizational energy. Time may pass, and progress may be slow, or even occasionally stagnant. It may have taken 20 or 30 years for organizations to develop a wonder-drug or a next-generation technological component in a smartphone. Yet incremental progress fuelled efforts even as successive leaders came and went. Progress is a more powerful driver of human behaviour than a charismatic leader is, and great leaders understand this well. If we take just one step then the next step and the one after that seem increasingly possible.

Much of this final third of the book is devoted to providing fodder for that possibility of progress. It is meant to encourage the pondering, to nurture it and to help bridge the gaps that cause leaders to sometimes falter.

The step from faith to belief is the step that allows us to progress from leadership that inspires to leadership that delivers. Faith often needs little more than collective optimism to build its power. Belief needs a route, a pathway and a line of sight to the destination. But it also needs commitment.

It is not rare to meet board directors, CEOs and executive leaders who have plenty of belief that the worst effects of contemporary issues such as climate change, poverty, child labour and infant mortality can be averted.

These same leaders may even deny that true failure has occurred in respect of these issues to date, pointing out that the issue is not failure *per se* but the lack of concentrated effort. In other words, we have not tried hard enough, or long enough, or with enough conviction or resilience for setbacks.

This definition is knitted deep within the fabric of corporate thinking, and it goes something like this: *If I haven't tried yet, then I have neither succeeded nor failed. I have simply not tried.* This thinking quite effectively preserves the faith that the task can be successfully undertaken, without adopting a more holistic view of failure, which is that the absence of the will to try is in itself a failure of personal or organizational leadership.

Symptoms of failure are rationalized in a more obvious but no less effective way. Failure might have occurred because cost-effective technologies are not yet available. It might have occurred because the appropriate economic policy platforms do not yet exist. Failure might be experienced because success factors were not clearly identified. These rationalizations allow us to avoid the consideration of failure as an absolute and instead allow us to identify the gaps to failure. This type of thinking preserves faith because it permits the dream to stay alive in a partially passive way. It allows us to more easily rationalize failure, permitting a second and third chance to be bought, over and over, for as long as we can maintain faith. Once again, it is powerful because it has a sense of positivity to it. It has a cheerful acknowledgement of an opportunity to improve in its lexicon, which builds hope and which in turn preserves faith.

It is important to reaffirm here, from the previous chapter, that the currency of faith within an organization is a good thing. Without faith, purpose languishes and perhaps does not grow beyond the boundaries of abstract imagination. Without faith, our mind is preoccupied by *I wonder*, whereas with faith, there is the excitement of *this could really be*. Without invoking our employees' faith, at the very least, we cannot spark the first bursts of engagement. For leaders, the ability to infuse with faith those who follow us is a coveted skill.

But faith has a dark side. While intoxicating, it is a lazy motivator. It is prone to abdication. *Someone else will surely do it.* It is too easily seduced by excuses. *It's ok; we'll do better next time.* In the face of facts and figures, faith too easily succumbs to organizational fracturing, the very opposite of the cohesion that is needed for leaders to achieve inspirational outcomes.

Belief is a firming factor in organizational leadership. Belief is the exciting spark of faith turned into a flame fuelled by strategy, tactics, facts and calculated risks. Belief is faith buttressed with the benefit of, at the very least, theorems and circumstantial evidence. It is a pathway that may not be entirely visible as it winds through to its destination, but we can glimpse the general arc of its trajectory to the destination. It may not be clear, in detail, exactly which sections of the path are asphalt, cobbled or bare earth, but at least it is known that the footing is not entirely treacherous all the way along.

Leaders must first trace this pathway in their minds before their own faith is turned to belief. They must retrace this pathway in their minds, over and over, until the deviations from iteration to iteration become minor and the details slowly crystallize. The pathway need not be complete by any means, but it must become firmer over time until the faith that was once there has become belief. This is the essence of strategic leadership.

17

Know

Just as progress along the route of faith morphs into belief, so too does the route of belief crystallize into knowledge. We see it when we get close to commissioning a project, debottlenecking a process or otherwise reducing the number of unknowns between ourselves and a successful outcome. We move from believing that we can achieve an outcome to knowing that we will achieve it. This is not the finish line. This is the point at which we typically select the scale of effort and the scale of engagement needed to complete the journey.

In investment circles, it is where the greatest confidence can be mined. As unknowns dwindle, interest in the initiative rises. At this point, the number of supporters can be increased. Fence-sitters can be swayed, and detractors can be encouraged to reconsider their position.

As leaders, we make precious little of this transition. We might make it a 'phew' moment of relief. We might make it a temporary waypoint for some quiet high-fives while we get on with the work of actually implementing the initiative. After all, we need to implement the visionary, purposeful initiative, count the key performance indicators and make sure kudos are well earned, instead of celebrating too early. While that cautious optimism might be appropriate in some cases, we risk missing a pivotal engagement phase.

Silence, at this juncture, is a potent cure for organizational momentum. And it is a cure we do not need. In order to move from believing in success to knowing that success is within reach, we need to reinforce purpose by communicating and passing on this surge in confidence to our people.

Let us recap the journey so far. We have envisioned change. It is a change that will, if successful, make our organization more valuable in the societal ecosystem. We have been brave, in leadership and in collective commitment. We have shown faith in bold, audacious change that speaks to the authenticity of what we are trying to achieve. And we have talked about it, bringing as many people along on the journey as we can. Organizational resources have been dispatched to take us from faith to belief, and we have travelled a path of decreasing unknowns progressively, until we are now very confident that we will deliver on material parts, if not all, of the envisioned change.

During this journey, as engaging as our leadership style might have been, we have not converted all of our staff, suppliers and contractors. We have engaged excitement and anticipation in perhaps a small percentage of staff actively engaged in the initiative, and maybe sparked curiosity among others – perhaps ten or twenty per cent of our stakeholders if we are lucky.

Our job as leaders is not merely to take visionary initiatives to their successful conclusions. It is, additionally, to supercharge the culture of the organization so that it actively seeks more initiatives and drives them to their own successful conclusions. In order to do that, the cadence of envisioning, faith, belief and knowing should be continuous. Because in those first four phases of success lie the closest energy source that we have to a perpetual motion machine. Closing the loop between envisioning and knowing creates a spring of optimism, innovation and enthusiasm for more. At 'knowing', we see landfall in our voyage, and can call on others in our armada to begin their own journey. At 'knowing', a new neural pathway is mapped between the highly prospective ideas bank and the investment in action. As leaders we want this way of thinking to move from project- and initiative-based incubators to continuous business innovations.

But there is more value at this phase. We can swell the ranks of supporters among our staff and stakeholders, building more buy-in for the current initiative as well as future ones. We can make informed decisions about pilot programmes or upscaled implementation plans. We can engage collaborative partnerships with business partners and with other organizations to redouble our own efforts. In other words, we can leverage to create resonances.

Let us look more deeply at leveraging the support and why it is important.

Currently, most of the barriers to organizations making a genuine societal difference fall under two main headings. One is the long-held belief, among leadership, that businesses are here to add value to investors, shareholders and customers – and that anything else is a bit of a distraction. While there are highly visible examples of business leadership that does not think like this, the fact remains that the overwhelmingly vast majority remain in that thought paradigm. The second heading is broadscale apathy. Decades, and perhaps centuries, of workplace conditioning have conspired to create the illusion that doing good for society is the responsibility of a few people whose roles are inextricably tied to making the organization look good. Doing good for society is not a part of the core business and therefore is not a priority for engagement.

This second heading is particularly insidious in our organizational cultures. Most people in organizations have some level of care about good societal outcomes – not just because they are good for everyone (although that is certainly a compelling reason) but also because our lives are largely lived in the sphere of existence that is connected to good societal outcomes. It is the default setting within which our value system is created, long before we enter the workforce. We have simply learned to separate it from our work because that has been the norm. It is one of the primary reasons we have a 'work life' and a 'home life'. We seek to find some sort of personal balance between these two all the time. We know that there is a strong correlation between our work life and our home life that is largely triggered by our work life. If we work long hours, we have less leisure time, and potentially a less fulfilling home life. The same is true of stressful work or work conditions that make us unhappy. At the same time – and only at scale since the start of the twenty-first century – it has been recognized that working conditions that improve non-working lives increase the engagement of employees at work. The specific co-dependence factors of work life and home lives are still being understood, but the existence of the co-dependence is increasingly given attention to by leaders. Yet we are only at the start of that phase of organizational evolution. The term 'flexible working arrangements' is giving way to concepts of integrated work. We are conjoining these two spheres of life.

As work life and home life become more integrated with each other, societal values and work values will almost certainly become more intermingled. What is important to society is likely to become increasingly more important to organizations and their stakeholders, more so than today and more so in ten years than in five years and so on. However, the expected speed of such intermingling is likely to suffer from historical and demographic inertia. Do we rationally expect the Generation X or Millennial vice president, foreperson or manager to seamlessly transition from their 15 or 20 years of maintaining work life and home life separation, and toward an integrated view? And, if not, then do we risk harbouring a legion of people managers who fail to adequately and authentically champion an integration of values that the next generation of graduates, cadets and employees expects? Do we rely merely on an array of people and culture processes to retrain our more senior ranks to think and live integration paradigms? Or are there more 'live' cultural levers that organizational leaders can use to shift internal paradigms in a way that adds broader value? We know, from our experiences with gender diversity and safety, for example, that training creates awareness, but behaviours create cultural changes.

In the 'know' phase, we have huge resonant behavioural energy to access. By acknowledging and celebrating internally the journey from envisioning to knowing, we can as leaders create a groundswell of change to perspectives within, and outside, our organization. Not just for the sake of change but also because it allows us to access the fence-sitters and the detractors and shift their own paradigms. It allows us to demonstrate through lived experience the potential for integration of organizational values and social values and dismantle some of the work/life barriers across which we previously had to find 'balance'. We can replace the concept of balance between work and society with the act of integration of these worlds.

18

Do

The journey of achievement culminates in the phase of doing. We put into action the thing we once imagined to be possible. We test the things that were once theoretical for us, and these things become part of our new norm. Our mindset shifts from *can do* to *are doing*. A future state is reached.

This phase is rightly celebrated because it crystallizes imagination, achieves purpose, rewards faith, supports belief and actualizes knowing. There is relief because effort pays off. For investors, there is a change in the tide of funding, from an outgoing tide to an incoming stream. We move into a phase of debottlenecking and optimization. We tweak and improve. The journey has not ended, but where we once marched forcefully with eyes forward, we now look down to the ground at the finer detail there as we fan out. There is a great deal of iteration in doing because once we think that something is working, we find out that it's not quite right, and our knowing is questioned. When trying to align business activities with societal expectations, expect this phase of doing to be visited and re-visited by doubt. Be prepared for doubt to creep in. And this is because understanding stakeholders' expectations takes a while, especially when those expectations are in a constant state of development. It feels like the goalposts are being moved.

Do not throw up your hands in frustration and give up. Organizational thinking has taught us to give up too quickly. If something does not work (for example, an advertising campaign), we are inclined to ditch it. There is a ruthlessness to our business approach which, while it might be appropriate for many organizational targets, does not work as readily with creating social value. Giving up on the doing, in these contexts, only makes an organization look fickle. Stakeholders lose faith and trust is eroded because the 'fast fail' tactics of organizational efficiency simply do not resonate in the same way in the social world. In society, enduring commitment is prized higher than Tinder-like fast-fail processes.

We reaffirm purpose and calibrate whether the thing we imagined is truly delivering on its purpose. When we conceive of new products, or services, we check that they have the utility that we thought they would.

We do these things well in the marketplace, and less well when it comes to societal benefits. There is a reason for this. Let's call it the freebie effect. It works something like this. Imagine, for example, if the organization decides to reduce its water footprint. That is, it decides to reduce the amount of freshwater it takes from the natural environment in undertaking its operations. What, precisely, is the purpose of that? A core purpose might be the recognition, in an area, of the scarcity of freshwater resources. Those resources might be used by other industries and communities in the area. Rainfall patterns may not be adequately replenishing these resources in the face of extraction, whether they are in dams or in underground aquifers. So the core purpose of the activity might be to ensure that there are enough freshwater resources to go around. Let us say the organization embarks on a water saving programme. Some process design is reconfigured, recycling loops are grown and strengthened, and the water use of the organization in delivering one unit of its output is reduced. Water efficiency is achieved. We put in a tick in the box, target achieved.

If that is all we do, we have not displayed enough leadership curiosity. But that is precisely what we often do. Water use reduction at target rates has been achieved, and our job is done. If we were project managers charged with reducing said rates, our job would have been done. But the core purpose was to ensure there were enough freshwater resources to go around. Our leadership curiosity might embolden us to ask if this had indeed occurred.

We often stop when we reach outcome or output and fail to check whether a purpose has been met. Dusting off our hands in satisfaction of a job well done, we bank the outcome or output and move on to the next thing. And while admittedly the outcome or output has been decidedly positive, the leadership failing all too often seen in organizations is a shortfall in the holistic view.

Consider this another way. If the primary purpose was to ensure there were enough freshwater resources to go around, have we tested – in this doing phase – if the purpose is being met? Perhaps not. If we are testing whether our water use has been reduced in our overall process, we can certainly tick that box. That is not the box we set off to tick. But we generally accept that our work here is done and celebrate ticking it.

Scratch below the surface of why we are so satisfied with that outcome, and we find two common perspectives in organizations that set out to add value to society. The first is mild indignation that the success is questioned. After all, without the water saving initiative, things would have been worse. An improvement has been achieved. As leaders, we often support this rationale, which is a close relative of the argument that we should not look a gift horse in the mouth. The second perspective is often positioned as a second line of defence behind the first. We assert that ensuring there is sufficient water to go around was not our job in the first place (unless we happen to be the water allocation regulators).

As organizations, the paraphrase of these two perspectives is this. *It's not our job to achieve that outcome, and now we've done our fair share in helping out.*

Both perspectives are fair and valid. But are they leadership perspectives? Are we leading, or merely filling an expectation?

It is an interesting phenomenon, world over, that businesses claim leadership when outcomes are achieved, yet little connection is made to the underlying purpose. Consider, for example, philanthropy. The most-quoted output or outcome of the philanthropic activity is the amount of money put towards a cause. We regularly hear about the amount of money that is being put into healthcare, education or poverty. Sometimes we are furnished with ancillary 'scale' details such as the number of patients assisted, or the number of children supported in education, or the number of lives improved. It is much rarer that we hear of outcomes relative to purpose. For example, if poverty alleviation is defined as the number of households whose income is raised about $2 a day, we are rarely presented with information about how many households are lifted above this threshold. Yet the quantity of money put in is frequently headlined.

We have become used to accepting quoted outputs and outcomes without questioning the purposeful impact that has been achieved. And while these outputs and outcomes are possibly reasonable sound bites for the uninformed observer to hear, we should be more curious as leaders. This is particularly true of leaders who marshal and deploy business resources towards societal improvement. What is the improvement that has been achieved, relative to the purpose conceived? As leaders, we levy this question with our products and services. The societal value we attempt to create should not be immune to our leadership curiosity and rigour.

The issue is critical to the central theme of achievement. It is powerfully engaging to envision and to create purpose. It is infectious to spark faith, and it is empowering to build belief. There is a crescendo in knowing that all of these are creating a new outcome. But all of these can be deeply undermined by actions that are less than what they could have been, relative to purpose. The undermining can worsen if shortfalls are not bravely acknowledged. They worsen further if outputs are celebrated in a wave of PR that feels poorly linked to purpose, overblown or hollow. Cycle through this a few times, and it is inevitable, perhaps, that the next new envisioning will be met with a level of cynicism. Excitement is traded in for pragmatic pre-judgement. Positive currency, once lost in that exchange, is difficult to regain.

For any leader, that direction of stakeholder engagement is diametrically opposite to the ideal. We want engagement to increase, not wane into cynicism. And the impact of what we do is the key to accessing cycles of increasing engagement. It is the key to changing cultures for the better.

We want to connect what we do to the purposeful impact of doing it, rather than the headline output of what is created. That means, as a leader, we cannot lose sight of the purpose of what we do. We cannot let ourselves, and others, succumb to output-accounting at the expense of delivering to purpose.

Why then does it happen as often as it does? What can we do to change it? As leaders, we need to stay in the game beyond the first few steps. We need to be engaged as the doing begins, to ask the right questions. How do our actions relate to the original purpose? Is the purpose still reasonably holistic, or has it become more self-serving? Have we traded in aspirations for PR value? What are we measuring as we move to the 'do' phase? Much of the depreciation of intent occurs because, as leaders, we lose interest and move on. The heady excitement of envisioning, purposefulness and the engagement of faith often tails off when the hard, detailed work commences. By the time we get to 'doing', the initiative has been delegated sufficiently that unless leadership stays engaged, ownership of delivery would be transferred far away from its source. Vision and purpose may have been lost in translation. The higher value, once measured by its purpose, may now be measured by reputational currencies that are prone to inflation with PR. The vision shrinks.

As leaders, when this happens, it can seem that we are placed in a lose–lose position. We lose if we do not address the shrunk vision. But we also lose the remnants of pride that might be salvaged from completing the doing, even with its lesser impact. By this stage, time, effort and resources have been spent. Commitments have been made. Often, it is easier to let the vision shrink than to invigorate it. After all, we rationalize that we can always build on the shrunk vision.

Pushing ahead with doing in these circumstances appears to save face. It saves face precisely because the majority agrees that it does. It is a game of perception, and it pays little heed to authenticity or to a commitment to clarity of purpose. This willingness to depreciate purpose can be found in many of the actions that many organizations have taken to address societal concerns. Time after time, we have seen it in the slow winding back of initial aspirations, as so-called reality takes effect. We point to issues of practicality and of factors conspiring against us to justify the regression. And we slowly but surely settle for a lesser vision. We are served better in the long run and in our leadership culture by taking a step back. There is better value in discipline. We can question, at the 'know' stage, our own authenticity. If we were to move to doing, would we fulfil the purpose we defined earlier? Or are we incrementally depreciating our vision?

19

Prove

Over many decades, the claims of organizations have been dogged by stakeholder cynicism. Publish your profits, and analysts will pore carefully over those numbers, seeking signs of creative accounting. Publicize your performance indicators, and the public will ask questions of their definition, their measurement, their consistency. Talk about your achievements and have them deconstructed in search of flaws and shortcomings. The cynicism has grown to such proportions now that claims made by business organizations appear to reflexively ignite veiled suspicion and underlying disbelief.

Some of it is healthy. Science, after all, questions evidence robustly, and we do not characterize science as a cynical discipline. But below the healthy fact-finding is a deeply compromised level of trust in businesses, organizations and corporations that has managed to find its way into every aspect of society.

There are two ways in which organizations typically respond to this, neither of which takes society off the well-worn path of compounding mistrust. One is greater exhortations and advertising. We double down on public relations, fighting each wave of mistrust with a stronger wave of communication. Social media is cranked up, our logos appear more frequently attached to good news stories, we sponsor sports stars and sports events and the CEO and board get out more. We do everything but kiss babies for photo opportunities. It does not seem to make a lot of sustainable difference. It may hold back some of the tides of mistrust, but the levels rise regardless.

The second response is less visible and darker. Organizations are less motivated to become societal leaders if that privilege is constantly eroded through mistrust. We start to bother less with such aspirations. What would be the point in doing good unless either there was an economic windfall associated with it or it had some useful public relations value? We feed society's cynicism in ourselves with some of our own self-cynicism. Our employees imbibe this self-cynicism readily, because they are, first, foremost and always, members of society. No amount of internal communications can remove the shadow cast by our individual and collective internalization of public cynicism. We can tell ourselves that we are a wonderful and caring organization through the most inspired of internal communications, but every employee suspects that there is some hollowness to the claim. Even the smallest margin of dissonance, between what we tell ourselves and what we feel, contributes to an organizational culture of inauthenticity. In turn, this feeds our internal apathy about the place of business in society and creates a further separation within the business ecosystem.

It is little wonder that the place of businesses in society has been slowly but surely displaced from its throne of socio-economic saviourship. We have become necessary but not necessarily wanted. We are hardly embraced.

This veil of cynicism plays out in even-increasing calls for transparency, which is a request to neither explicitly lie nor lie by omission. Year after year, corporations are asked to disclose their affairs. The underlying commentary behind this request is that society is not given the truth, or the whole truth, on issues that are of rising importance to the planet and its people. Whether it is climate change, labour conditions in supply chains, environmental stewardship, water access for all, pollution of air, land and water, bribery and corruption, dealings with government and political parties or taxes paid, there is an increasing clamour for more. And when that information is disclosed, there is a further request to have that information assured, endorsed by an independent third party. Proof is demanded, and boards are made increasingly accountable for the validity of that proof.

This momentum is hardly likely to abate until trust is restored. As we all know, trust must be earned. And trust, when lost, costs more to earn back. The road back is long for organizations right across the world. It is lined with good intentions, the fulfilment of those intentions and proof of outcomes. If organizations claim to pay fair taxes, audited financial records are required to confirm that claim. If organizations claim to reduce their carbon footprint, proof is required using standardized means of accounting for such claims. If organizations claim to preserve human rights, proof is required of the grievances that arise, the nature of them and how they are dealt with. The road back is long and is prone to slippages of two steps forward and one back. Positive achievements in one area can be undermined by failings in another area. Momentous changes in the management of child labour in supply chains can be neutralized by a single sexual discrimination incident.

Organizations, unlike scientific laboratories, are not particularly enamoured with proof. We tend to use other indicators. For example, if a mobile device manufacturer wishes to gain 'proof' that consumers love its brand of device, it looks to sales. If sales peak, the assumption is that consumers love the device. It may simply be better than alternative brands of devices (i.e. the least worst option). It may be that it is Christmas time and sales are up. But organizations will tend to settle on this metric as sufficient proof, and celebrate accordingly. Meanwhile, the consumer is ambivalent about the product, and observes our celebrations with bemusement. Similarly, with bringing benefits to society, we look to selective feedback. If the public does not complain, we assume a reasonable job has been done. Objective measurements can be hard to find and to gather at scale. It is important that as leaders we are mindful about gathering proof and maintain a curious attitude to what we hear as feedback. Those who report to us are eager to tell us what we wish to hear, and that is certainly not proof. Be prepared to look for proof that what you are doing to deliver benefits to society does, indeed, deliver those benefits. And if not, look to what you think you know about what stakeholders expect and how you will genuinely meet those expectations. Be prepared to go back a little bit, to regress. This is not failure; it is a process of adjustment and optimization. Finally, as a leader, cast cold eyes on the difference between what you first imagined and what proof of outcomes tells you. Be prepared to reject ineffective outcomes, but also be prepared to accept gaps, albeit grudgingly. Communicate both your proof and your conclusions to stakeholders. There is a great deal of trust to be earned in this phase. And while it may feel like it comes at the cost of good PR (who would rather not claim glory than to acknowledge imperfect outcomes?), it has far more long-term value than faking it.

Take a look at your own annual report or read the corporate reports of others. Does it feel like we are pushing good news? Or are we being truthful, factual and acknowledging failures? Are we addressing those failures by telling our stakeholders, with honesty, how we will adjust our process and outcomes? Are we following through on those promises? It does not feel like a glorious path (compared to dressing up sub-optimal outcomes and celebrating in a wave of PR), but it is far more effective in authentically progressing our relationships with stakeholders.

Corporate reputations teeter on a cliff, and there is collective societal willingness to push those reputations over a precipice. While seemingly unfair when viewed in the moment, it is nevertheless the culmination of over a century of repetitive and compounding failure of organizational leadership and culture. And it needs to be removed. It is similar to a carried-forward loss that must be whittled away annually by accumulated profit. It is a liability that can only be removed by consistent positive action, proof of that action, the absence of negative action and the proof of that too. It is a hard reality, but as leaders, we are used to hard realities. We simply need to get on with the job of proving the detractors wrong.

20

The Board

For many organizations, nowhere does individual and collective leadership become more important than at the board. The board occupies a unique position at the vanguard of an organization. Theoretically, it brings together people of different experiences and perspectives to form well-rounded wisdom and direction for a company. It owns all success and failures, both in fiscal terms and in ethical terms. It has power – not necessarily to command and control but to shape and direct an organization, including its culture, along lines that best serve the organization and its stakeholders.

This position applies with arguably its greatest meaning to those publicly listed organizations that carry a sizeable proportion of both the planet's financial resources and public shareholder interest. But it applies with considerable gravitas elsewhere, to privately held businesses, to government and to non-governmental organizations. It is a position of great accountability and responsibility, and therefore great trust is placed in it. But it is also one of relatively little depth of exposure to the organization's inner workings. This paucity of deep exposure occurs because of the board's relatively high vantage point, which is of course necessary to effect both a broad external perspective and a strategic internal perspective for the benefit of the organization. It also occurs because of the board's relatively sparse day-to-day interaction with the organisation. Further, it occurs because senior executives become adept at managing upwards, and nowhere is this attribute more finely honed than at the interface between executive and non-executive aspects of leadership. The board by virtue of its deliberately removed and theoretically less-fettered vantage point, and the propensity of senior management to 'manage' the board, inherits a mantle of great accountability that comes with the danger of insufficient granular insight.

Different boards manage this interface differently. A combination of soft and hard touches is employed, often perceived by executive leaders as spectrum opposites of amicable going-along and frustrating intrusiveness, respectively. The combination varies between situations within an organization, from business phase to business phase, and between market dynamics.

A relatively great deal of effort is expended on financial health, and on governance and audit. History has shown, relentlessly, that accidental or deliberate financial mismanagement has contributed to a high proportion of organizational death blows and failures. Over the period of a century or more, the potential for crippling an organization's financial health has been studied and counter-studied; neutralized and back-burned; checked, double-checked and triple-checked. Because the permutations for financial mismanagement – both accidental and deliberate – are high, boards have invested in views and counter-views, employing multiple board members and external advisory bodies to ensure that financial matters are very carefully managed. There is no denying, given the frequency of financial mishaps witnessed around the world, that this discipline continues to be of particularly high importance. The stakes are high and can often be a matter of organizational survival. The focus on financial aspects is, appropriately, significant and dogmatic. For other, non-financial, elements, the focuses may wax and wane. Some organizational focuses may be in periods of wane for many years at a time. Historically, much like in executive ranks, boards have followed the money more diligently than they have followed the path of a greater good.

Increasingly, this accrued imbalance between financial and non-financial aspects of organizational governance has been questioned. Its wisdom is unclear to many, although its evolution is acknowledged. *Why* the imbalance has accrued has, historically, not been of great debate. An imbalance has been accepted for over a century. Reflexively, financial issues overshadow all else. The more debated subject is if the prevailing imbalance is appropriate. This consideration that has led to incremental shifts in that balance over time. While there has been visible progressive evolution in board considerations of business in society (beyond philanthropic efforts), there has not, to date, been a sea change in board governance. As a result, the news continues to be awash with reports of unethical or quasi-ethical board governance relating to non-financial aspects such as customer stewardship, human rights, sexual harassment and others.

The board's role is multidimensional, compounding a great many facets, viewed both at 30,000 metres and with microscopic-level magnification as required. In its highest gear it sets direction, endorses and drives strategy, and mindfully shapes the culture on an organization. Within a business ecosystem, for many of the reasons discussed previously, the cues for direction, strategy and a culture that will support the successful achievement of these come from outside the organization. These are the cues that we read from customers, from investors, from our current and future employees, and from the society that surrounds us. These are the stakeholders who are constantly forming, re-forming and supporting our business purpose.

Whereas the board's engagement on financial matters has occurred at a frenetic pace since the first stock exchanges came into being, the board's historical involvement in non-financial issues has developed pace in a more modest fashion. Some observers would classify the pace as leisurely, or even lethargic, between the start of the industrial revolution and the so-called Industry 4.0 in the second decade of the twenty-first century. The observation is not without merit. The format and composition of boards themselves had hardly changed in nearly a century, resisting diversity in gender, culture, identity and age, and forming a resultant impression of monoculturalism. Progressive paradigms were notably slow to shift. Issues like digitization and social media were grasped at the turn of the century with, as institutional investors noted, frustrating slowness. Boards were in danger of inheriting a dinosaur-like stigma associated with the public sense of an inability to move with the times. Financial acumen, the business ecosystem was signalling, was important, but so too was an increasing array of non-financial considerations.

Aspects like employee health and safety arose as board-relevant issues early in this evolution. As employment laws became more mindful of employee rights, issues such as non-discrimination, anti-harassment, inclusivity and other elements of social equity became prominent. This employee well-being and greater psychological focus brought with it a tide of knowledge regarding employee engagement. The benefits of engagement were quick to be grasped, for they unlocked doorways to effectiveness, efficiency and innovation, representing the higher-order strategic leanings that boards were expected to leverage. From safety and health, which represented diligence and hygiene factors that were protected by law and covenants of ethics, to employee engagement, the involvement of boards in these areas grew strongly.

It is useful to reflect on such trajectories, because they represent a parallel arc to the ones that might be taken with other societal virtues. In the early twentieth century, employee safety and health were not mainstream concerns. People were fortunate to have jobs and were considered individually stupid, careless or unlucky if they suffered an injury at work. Policies and laws came into place, protecting the safety and health of workers as the industrial revolution accumulated pace after World War 2. There was employee unrest after fatalities and, in particular, multiple fatalities. Union representation within organizations allowed unrest to be marshalled and focused. While these predictably became issues of executive management to address, they nevertheless impacted on the reputations of organizations, the collective board and individual board members. This impact was promulgated by an insightful (for its time) investor question.

It ran the query that if organizations could not carry out something as basic as their core business without hurting or killing people, what did that say about other, potentially more difficult, management challenges? What did it say about the locus of control of the organization, its discipline, the alignment of its leaders to a reasonably universal expectation and its ability to deliver on such a thing? These latter questions are clear board considerations.

The psyche of board members evolved. There was obviously a tremendous career stigma in being associated with an organization that had exhibited poor financial governance. A board member's attractiveness to other boards was diminished if he (and at the time, male board members were by far the most prominent of the species) had been on a board that had failed its organization. While the stigma once was confined to financial matters, it began spreading to employee safety, because it reflected, at a sufficiently high level of accountability, competence at running a business. In the same way that we might doubt a short-order cook's competence if the omelette was passably tasty but a great deal of time had been spent by the customer removing broken eggshells from the palate, the messiness of adequate business delivery accompanied by a poor safety record carried negative connotations.

Global board self-reflection has not been uniform, nor has it been of Renaissance proportions. European countries were among the first to begin to overcome, at scale, some of the inertia that had been baked in over time. Important shifts were initiated late in the twentieth century and mostly continued with visibly increased momentum into the twenty-first century. Governance around financial aspects received greater attention in policies and laws. Board diversity was addressed with more vigour, focusing on the diversification of representation in gender and depth of sector knowledge. Other aspects, such as multiculturalism (coinciding with a more global economy) and age diversification (reflecting younger stakeholders), progressed less quickly.

Board diversity was pursued because of the recognition of the strength that is forged when different perspectives and opinions are brought together. Naturally, because decisions are required to be made by the board, the richness that diversity brings must eventually be distilled to points of agreement, and convergence reached. The process of including diverse inputs instils in decision-making a broader set of considerations, and the broader thinking ignites more expansive and multi-faceted processing.

However, the strength of diversity was not always recognized in boards. Not long into the first industrial revolution, it was obvious that boards were often comprised of like-minded people. They were mostly older men, often from similar educational backgrounds and not-dissimilar socio-economic settings. Board members were generally chosen for attributes such as intelligence, financial acumen and an understanding of the business environment, all of which are distinct assets. They were often recruited through personal networks. These similarities bring with them a tendency to think similarly on a variety of issues outside of financial and business aspects.

The search for diversity in boards began with the acknowledgement that monocultural thinking was often a precursor to dangerous groupthink, which in turn risked narrowing a board's field of vision. They manifest as blinkered views, prone to blind spots and limited perspective. They are a weakness in boards. The drive to diversity occurred not necessarily because it was an equitable thing to do but because narrow-band thinking at the board had proven, time and time again, to be precursors of organizational failure, particularly in an expansive world. As businesses evolve further, this narrower thinking is likely to become unaffordable.

When organizations deal increasingly with a rapidly growing selection of external factors, boards are exposed to challenges that were potentially not a regular part of the curriculum of learning – both academic and professional – that executives engaged in over the last few decades. The

Fourth Industrial Revolution, this current phase of business evolution that is often referred to as the world forges its way through the twenty-first century, is characterized by many parallel changes.

There are many types of businesses that did not exist a mere decade or two ago, and more new types of businesses continue to form as the world goes through a historically unique phase of connecting and disconnecting globally, and disrupting locally. At the same time, many of the older types of businesses have become extinct. The way business is done has revolutionized. There is greater business-to-business connectivity, greater business-to-customer connectivity, and even much greater business-to-investor and business-to-shareholder connectivity than ever before. Additionally, it is highly unlikely that this connectivity will plateau any time soon. Greater integration is all but inevitable, mostly because the digital era continues to provide us with more and more adept means to do so.

On top of this, the environment in which business is carried out is transforming. Once, businesses dictated terms. Products and services were provided to enable society, and society – in the main – accepted these gratefully. Since the 1970s, there has been a growing questioning of the terms that were once dictated. Whether, as a board member, one agrees or disagrees with the questioning is largely irrelevant. It is unavoidable that, at some point, the questioning must be faced and answered. Boards are faced with a new dilemma. New skills must be developed, together with a new mindset, to deal with the greater questioning and scrutiny applied from a multitude of sources within the ecosystem that a business functions. Where once questions that were deemed irrelevant could be conveniently ignored, each passing decade leaves less room for avoidance.

Now, boards must adopt a more challenging paradigm. Where once like-minded individuals on a board could confidently make leadership decisions while somewhat insulated from a staggeringly wide range of external societal factors, that era – and that insulation – is all but gone. Boards are increasingly being compelled to expand their curriculum, and at a much faster rate than ever before in industrial history. There is greater pressure to increase the number of subjects that they must authentically engage in. This requires harnessing a greater diversity of thought and opinion than ever before. With this broader subject range and greater diversity of input, groupthink is hardly an option. Board dynamics are likely to experience greater debate and challenge. This will come with no diminishment of the need to juxtapose multiple perspectives and to resolve them with appropriate and timely business decisions.

While the diversity of thought and perspective is a powerful and increasingly necessary ingredient across a broader sphere of considerations that boards must engage in, this power must also be harnessed. The magnitude of this challenge is partly the reason why board change occurred slowly. Boards must be able to debate, argue and agree in a collegiate manner. This dynamic is created slowly, with a deliberate selection of board members that can bring robust and constructive challenge-and-agree strengths to a board. Once this delicate balance is painstakingly achieved, there is a natural reluctance to change abruptly. Yet change is inevitable.

This bodes for a more complex future for boards. As the apex of governance, charged with not just day-to-day dependability but also with forming and choosing the right strategic trajectories in a rapidly transforming business ecosystem, new and better functional modes will be called for. Board members will need to, individually and collectively, understand more about a greater breadth of social, socio-economic, ethical and environmental issues as society becomes more empowered to question these dimensions.

While this has been known for quite some time, the cagey dance that occurs between business, politics and society has allowed a kind of status quo to exist. Despite many well-chronicled failures of governance in boards across the globe since the middle of the twentieth century, the momentum for change has been sluggish. Those failures have, in the main, delivered significant blows to shareholders. In some cases, board failures have damaged communities and customers. Here, restitution and recompense have been the dominant form of response, with a systematic improvement of governance forced painstakingly through legal and political channels. Yet these channels are activated only when the frequency or magnitude of such occurrences breaches thresholds of collective pain. What is becoming evident now is that the collective is growing in magnitude and the thresholds of pain are lowering. It is of no practical use to estimate and argue the rates of growth in magnitude or the rates of lowering of pain thresholds. These are not mathematically assessable, nor can they be extrapolated with any kind of sensibility to tell us when to act or how much to respond by. The era of incremental change at boards may be at an end, and there is mounting pressure for better modes of governance.

The business ecosystem surrounding organizations is complex. Sometimes its tides change swiftly and other times languidly. As actors in this ecosystem, we are prone to alarm when the tides change so swiftly that disaster looms but are otherwise generally content to hope (and even prefer) that leisurely change is sufficient. We are eternal optimists or confirmed denialists. Boards and board members are not immune to the same failings of blinkered thinking, denialism, unfounded optimism and even passive disinterest to things that do not matter to them personally. When enough of these characteristics congregate at the board level, they begin to form corporate culture. And so a wide range of perspectives, some of which will almost certainly be inherently conflicting, should be harnessed within the board.

A casual observer can be forgiven for thinking that there is considerable inbred reluctance, at the board level, to do this. Culture is formed at the board, and nowhere is it likely to be more set than in a boardroom of between 7 and 12 individuals. This collection of individuals is formed to collectively determine and spearhead what the organization focuses on, and how it is governed. These individuals are selected for the skills that they bring to the highest platform of governance in the organization. They are selected for the accrual of board value they can represent and, importantly, for their ability in decision-making diplomacy, which is to debate, disagree and reach an agreement. They may not have executive powers, but when it comes to organizational culture, the buck stops with the board. Studies of corporate failures reaching back into the 1970s and peppering organizational history for over half a century, industry reviews, senate committees, parliamentary investigations and royal commissions alike have landed on that very same conclusion.

Historically, boards were formed of the largest shareholders, a type of control exerted by the most significant original investors in a business. As publicly listed companies became more prevalent, this means of selection of board members faded, although it still remains practised surprisingly frequently, particularly in privately held companies. Here, an underlying historical truth becomes evident – that boards originally existed to exert control, ostensibly for the welfare of the shareholders.

Early cultures formed by boards had a strong profit-and-dividend focus, a logical focus to include. An organization cannot be commercially sustainable if it does not hold this focus quite high on its agenda. Additionally, this focus represents primary value to shareholders, particularly if those shareholders are relatively few, and substantially invested in the company. The democratization of shareholders, through the introduction of public trading of securities, diluted this proposition. Rather than managing the financial interests of a relatively few, relatively significant, and often relatively interconnected, investors, the last century has witnessed the rise of a majority of relatively smaller shareholders. This majority has been somewhat disconnected from each other, except via mechanisms afforded by the organization, such as annual general meetings or annual reports. These mechanisms are notable for two characteristics. One is their relative infrequency, often dictated by minimum standards imposed by the securities exchange. The other is their relative control by the organization, who sets the agenda and content. As a result of these two characteristics, while perturbations may be exerted by shareholders in these forums, they have (so far) often been experienced as fringe concerns.

The internet of things continues to change this setting, and at an astonishingly fast pace. Many organizations have developed informative and useful outward-facing communications using digital platforms and a range of social media avenues. Some have asked for, and engaged with, expressions of concern from their stakeholders using these platforms. This has permitted useful insights that boards can access to help maintain a contemporary view of stakeholder concerns.

However, these commendable connections are small compared to the rapidly increasing ability of shareholders to communicate with each other, more often in groups related to specific societal issues. They are able to compare views, compare the dialogues offered to them by the companies they are invested in, contrast these to a wide variety of other perspectives, and be part of a more collaborative matrix of influence upon each other. In mere numbers, this outweighs the outreach of individual businesses or even coalitions of businesses. But there is more. The tone of such interaction is different too; it is less formal, more trustingly inquisitive and more collaborative than the modes of engagement through business-delivered channels. Information and misinformation are exchanged, debates are carried out and opinions are formed in a dynamic and fluid manner. This represents an existential change in the way boards are able to discern what is important to the shareholders (and indeed other stakeholders) of the company compared to the last 100 years or more. This existential change has only commenced in the early part of the twenty-first century.

What this means to boards is that the danger of being out of touch is escalating. Under those circumstances, clinging doggedly to old paradigms is – of all possible ways of addressing the danger – quite possibly the least effective.

The absence of diversity of thought and opinion in a board, particularly in relation to the societal issues that are elevating in the communal psyche of stakeholders, is deeply problematic. Yet it cannot be solved simply by diversifying the composition of boards to encompass facets of these issues. It requires a board composition that is more than just representative of agendas and areas of knowledge but has the individual and collective desire and mandate to be genuinely connected to societal issues. At the nexus of this desire, or alternatively the lack of desire, is the one-word question, *why?* It is demonstrably true, for the vast majority of companies, that there is no doomsday around the corner – if we measure the distance to the 'corner' by the tenure of the existing board. Indeed, if a significant measure of a board's success is its evasion of disaster, then simply by virtue of timescales, most boards are likely to be deemed successful during their tenures (or at least not a failure) in respect of societal issues. This tenure – in practical terms, some 10 years between full board rejuvenation cycles – promotes stewardship over leadership in relatively slow-moving societal issues. This often-unspoken bind accounts for a great deal of passive inertia in boards that are witnessed in respect of environmental, social and other non-financial governance aspects.

There is no evidence that simply adding to the diversity of board members will break this bind, although it is self-evident that low diversity of thought will not result in appreciable change. Therefore, in addition to bringing a diversity of thought and opinion to a board (which in turn will probably include gender, cultural, socio-economic and other aspects of diversity), another ingredient is required. It would be obvious to nominate something like greater governance around societal issues, and indeed this has been implemented with varying degrees of uptake in securities exchanges around the world. It is also fair to expect that these governance issues will become more and more important over time, and also to expect that more and more securities exchanges will adopt such themes. Once again, this pace of change is likely to be gradual, and in all probability even generally reactive to increasing public concern. This is not a widely admired leadership paradigm and is akin to the coercion of leadership to act on issues that it otherwise does so with some reluctance.

The energy for quicker, more reactive and ultimately more proactive change lies in the leadership offered by board members, both individually and collectively. For this energy to be generated and accessed, boards and their members must cultivate a genuine and contemporary concern for broader societal issues. This concern should supersede outmoded philanthropic considerations, in which one 'does one's part' by contributing to a worthy cause. The concern should not *replace* philanthropy, because the contributions to worthy causes do good, and the removal of good is by its very definition a retrograde step. Rather, the concern could take the form of societal leadership that is enacted through the lens of business responsibility for that same society.

The chair and the board members have different leverages in precipitating this mindset. The chair is more able to elevate such issues to formal consideration than individual board members can, although coalitions of board members and occasionally individuals can agitate to create the momentum for such elevation. Both mechanisms are successful in board governance, although not necessarily equally. Conversely, chairs do have the authority to de-select issues nominated for elevation, and so there is a genuine power vested here. The power is particularly potent in this context because, as pointed out previously, it is rare that societal considerations present a clear and present danger in the context of the board's tenure. Therefore, on the principle that what is important and urgent will (and should) generally supersede that which is important and non-urgent, board agendas typically only infrequently engage societal issues that do not pose material impending or strategically devastating negative effects to the company, or with a lighter touch. Often both the low frequency and the lighter touch are evident, effectively and in pragmatic terms relegating these societal leadership considerations to a lower rung on the ladder of board priorities.

A counterpoint often posed at the board level is that the unfettered addition of agenda issues leads to one or more of three things. There could be (a) a dilution of the board's focus by virtue of spending time on ancillary issues, (b) insufficient time left over to deal adequately with the important and urgent issues and (c) too much board time (and therefore potentially shareholder cost) added to corporate governance to account for these issues. While these are all valid arguments, they highlight a point of leadership that, under current governance mechanisms, only boards themselves can usefully address. This is because two are perspective-based prioritization constraints and one is a point of effort versus remuneration.

The notion of diluting a board's focus assumes that there is a hierarchy of priorities that the board accurately calibrates. Yet concerns in society, expressed increasingly stringently since the late twentieth century – among customers, investors and governments in particular – suggests that the calibration is not particularly accurate, at least from the perspectives of most other stakeholders other than corporate leadership. This view is strongly expressed by an increasing percentage of the world's largest institutional investors. Even retail shareholders, the most humble of the investor groups, express similar concerns. Further, boards operate with established committees to address focal areas of concern. Aspects like risk, audit, health, safety, environment and remuneration are very often afforded extra effort via such committees. Such committees focus substantively on complying with laws and standards, and, as is well known, laws are predominantly a lagging indicator of societal needs. They come into effect well after the need for such laws has been established, playing a continuous game of catch-up with society. Laws and regulations hardly capture the definition of the term 'proactive'.

The notion of insufficient time is, in some respects, an artifice. Boards, particularly those with a high percentage of non-executive directors, are not in a full-time role. There may be 10 board meetings per year, plus reading time for the admittedly voluminous material that is often prepared for these meetings, plus committee meetings and other attendances and engagements. In that context, there is often ample elasticity during a fiscal year for broader societal considerations to receive attention. In the second decade of the twenty-first-century committees with labels such as 'Sustainability' were developed to promote this focus by a small handful of listed companies around the world. This embryonic step signalled, at least at the margins of the business world, that prioritization was being afforded to broader societal needs. Yet the symbolic addition of a board committee to focus on an aspect of its governance, while commendable, should not necessarily be considered a paradigm shift. History is littered with examples of organizations that failed in fiscal governance despite a functioning audit committee or failed in risk management despite a long-established risk committee. There is more to effective leadership, as this narrative will explore shortly.

Finally, the expectation for boards to do more, and for shareholders to therefore foot the bill for the extra effort, is a remuneration question. There is a certain common sense to expecting higher remuneration for more work but only if the original work, its expected outcomes and its remuneration were all satisfactory. Again, investor sentiments indicate otherwise. By any socio-economic measure, a board position, for the amount and calibre of work required, is well remunerated, especially in the top 100 to 300 companies of any securities exchange. The question arising is not whether more of the amount and calibre of board input should be requested for more remuneration, but whether the existing remuneration is done justice by the true diversity of board input accessed.

These are contentious points, and raising them causes consternation within a board. At its core is an unappetizing message; that more is required of boards to bring organizations into line with, and preferably leading solutions to, the concerns that plague society. It implies an unsavoury conclusion that boards are at risk of failing society. It is not an easy concept to listen to, let alone acknowledge and rectify. Given the pre-eminent status of boards, and despite their formal subservience to the shareholders, the key to addressing this gap rests firmly with the ability of boards to self-reflect honestly and authentically, and then to take the bold steps that are needed to effect a different, perhaps societally enhanced style of leadership.

For now, individual board members and, collectively, organizational boards, have a leadership paradigm shift to navigate. And these shifts are predicated on the answers to a few questions that frame leadership capacity in this area.

It is valid to ask of a board and its individual members whether the business's place in society requires that it assumes a leadership degree of stewardship for societal welfare. The answers typically vary, but the most common answer is underpinned by a 'yes but' in its punctuation. The hedge offered is steeped in the long-held notion that business success and societal welfare are mutually independent ideals. In political words, one cannot be capitalist and socialist concurrently. Boards have historically acknowledged that the business has a *responsibility* to support the welfare of society, but that it is not the actor with *accountability* for that welfare. Because of this, a threshold of performance is identified. For a business, the bare minimum threshold, defining the term 'responsibility', is abiding by the law. Discretionary performance is defined by philanthropic activities. For most organizations, the preferred state comprises meeting the law and undertaking a certain amount of philanthropic support to a cause that has some resonance with stakeholders. This package usually constitutes sufficient 'responsibility', and the vast majority of boards do not subscribe to doing any more or taking any more accountability for society. It is not uncommon to hear, in boards, a firm view that further societal accountability beyond legal requirements sits with the government.

By 2020, this was shifting, but only at the very margins, and inconsistently so. Climate change had hit the radar of many listed-company boards as multiple stakeholder groups began querying the role of corporations in, firstly, contributing to global warming and secondly in responding to the concerns raised as a result of the observed shifting weather patterns around the world. With discernible reluctance, boards were beginning to look at the issue with greater governance rigour. The narrative heard in boardrooms was of the form *'we should ...'*, *'we should be seen to ...'* and *'we have to respond ...'*. These are not ordinarily associated with leadership stances. They are grudging responses to diplomatically coercive forces. In 2019, when the first school climate strikes began across the world, an estimated 5,000 businesses around the world (predominantly the United States, Europe and Australia) gave their employees permission to take time off to attend these strikes. While this was a creditable number, in context it was only a very small proportion of the number of businesses in the world. The vast majority of top listed companies were notably absent from the list, indicating that the overt support was confined to the smaller end of the business world. Several business CEOs made dour public statements, citing business priorities, that employees were free to attend, provided they took formal annual leave or a vacation day. The culture presented by such stances – which are at face value objectively rational – is more administratively dogmatic and less engaging leadership.

And so the first step in the paradigm shift is for boards to pivot away from being the victims of stakeholder coercion to drivers of the agenda for societal well-being. It requires putting away the notion that businesses are purely for business and taking on a leadership mantle of stewardship of societal well-being. There is no doubt that this constitutes a voluntary adoption of a more complex role. The will to do so typically emanates from the belief that the role of businesses in making the world a better place is a worthy one. In this belief, the term 'Captains of Industry' has a more holistic meaning than its traditional application to balance sheets, profit statements and cash flow and to politically astute posturing on issues of the day.

This pivot in a board's mindset is necessary but not sufficient to change culture. Enthusiasm without means rapidly declines into showmanship. The culture quickly becomes one of making small successes appear large or masking failures with rhetoric. Therefore, simply having a will at the board to take leadership in enabling good societal outcomes is insufficient. Boards must become more curious and knowledgeable about societal issues and not merely be aware of the balance of debate among stakeholders.

To further this direction of development, the professional diversity of board members must be combined with other aspects of diversity such as the gender, cultural and socio-economic domains. Boards were once substantially selected from four major pools of talent: legal, financial, knowledge of the type of business that the organization practised and the business interests of major shareholders, where relevant. In a typical board of 7 to 12 people, it was normal to find that the vast majority of board members (6 to 10) would be drawn from these four areas of expertise and interest. While there were certainly exceptions to the norm through most of the twentieth century, it was not until the late twentieth century that boards began to show systemic investment in other areas that underpinned organizational success. Aspects of business such as people and culture, information technology, customer and retail insights, branding and others were increasingly evident in board memberships. However, well into the twenty-first century, the classical financial and legal skill sets still dominate boards, often in duplicate or triplicate strengths, at the expense of broader skill sets.

Board skills matrices became increasingly used since the late twentieth century to bring diversity of skills and knowledge to a board in a systematic fashion. They have been useful in identifying and filling gaps as board members' tenures are rotated. They are a useful tool if used with clear intent. However, the clarity of intent is often missing, because the dominant question *should we be leaders in enabling societal welfare?* remains unanswered, or answered in the negative. As a result, board skills matrices can operate much like a risk matrix, in that the boxes appear ticked but the depth and strategy beneath that may be wanting. Once again, generating that insightful depth requires the board to meaningfully grapple with what is, at its heart, an existentialist question of purpose.

Through that collective engagement, a culture of societal stewardship can be nurtured, one that is much more than compliant with laws, one that has an enlightened societal focus. With this foundation, strong opinions can be formed at the board level. These opinions are important because they set the tone for CEO direction and executive action, two critical aspects that will be examined next.

21

The Executive

If an organization was a band of musicians, the CEO would be the lead singer. No other role is given the spotlight as much as the chief executive gets. Read through the business pages of any newspaper in any country and mentions of the CEO outnumber all other roles 10-to-1. The role sits at the top of the executive ranks. It can be transformational for an organization, or it can be responsible for its untimely demise. It is an iconic role, and it defines a great deal of the organization's character. History has celebrated the hero CEO time and time again, and so its position in the organizational hierarchy is easily the most prominent, both internally and publicly. Its power and influence often eclipse all other roles, including the board's. Yet for all its impact, its effectiveness in a well-governed structure relies substantially on board endorsement and board support.

The interface between board and CEO is a delicate one. The board must tread a thin line between empowering a CEO and holding the CEO accountable, and must be highly collaborative as well. Too little empowerment and the CEO's ability to get things done becomes curtailed. Too little accountability and the CEO's performance is left dangerously in his or her hands. Too little collaboration and the CEO may take the company in directions that the board eventually disagrees with.

Structurally, the CEO reports to the board, of which the chair is considered the first among equals and generally orchestrates and controls the board's functions. In a practical setting, the relationship between the CEO and chair is generally the nexus of the exchange between the board and the CEO. It functions like a spinal cord in that it is essential, but it is highly dependent on broader board machinations. A high-functioning board and a disciplined chair together form the most desirable governance setting for a CEO.

The choice of CEO is one of the most inspected aspects of business decisions by investors, of both the institutional kind and the retail kind. Confidence is key. If investors do not have confidence in CEOs, the tenure is unsustainable. Because of the high importance placed on confidence, many CEOs are selected based on either past CEO tenures or their proven senior executive abilities. Both are historical attributes. Recruitment processes are typically quite focused on the past as a predictor of the future, at least in distilling from a wider pool of applicants the final shortlist. There is also a repetitive trend in the most desirable attributes sought from these applicants. Among the top attributes reported by CEO recruitment specialists, an understanding of the business and financial acumen have for over a century ranked at the very apex. Certainly, there are many other attributes that are considered, but candidates without these two characteristics rarely progress beyond the first cut of CEO applicants.

If this feels like a conservative model, that is because it is. In selecting CEOs, risk-taking is rarely exhibited. While many CEO appointments may be surprising in that the most-expected candidate may not be chosen, a cursory glance below the surface often shows that the classic CEO formula – a solid past, an understanding of the business and financial acumen – dominates the makeup. For many decades, this cyclic model of forming and selecting CEOs has been the norm. Templates have not, in the main, varied. There is a classically defined core of desirable CEO attributes that has thrived in the DNA of business ecosystems for well over a century. This is not to say that CEO typologies have not evolved over time. They have. Most notably, they have transitioned from managerial to leadership roles as they accrue the sets of skills and the associated stakeholder confidence in leading over managing.

Except for certain types of organizations (non-governmental organizations or specific types of consulting firms), business does not, in general, look for CEOs with a proven record in societal issues. This is not to imply, of course, that CEOs with societal skills are rejected, but it is typically not an attribute that is actively sought. It goes without saying that CEO candidates with anti-societal tendencies would have odds against them to make it through a selection process, although there is sufficient evidence to show that many have beaten those odds and, collectively, given CEOs a bad name. There is no organizational subject more widely discussed in the media than the CEO who must go. Scandals involving CEOs outnumber all other executive team members by orders of magnitude.

In recent decades, with the emergence of greater expectations around workplace culture, physical and psychological safety, anti-discrimination and inclusivity, as well as engagement-inspired productivity, there has been a notable expansion of the desirable attributes of CEOs. A more empathetic, strategic, empowering individual is generally foreseen for CEO roles, in addition to the aforementioned core business acumen attributes. It is a complex role, and the narrative in this book is not intended to be exhaustive about the subject. Rather, the intent is to draw some broad considerations around the current mould of the CEO and focus on what kind of emergent leadership characteristics might be more attuned to our ever-changing world at this, and a slightly further, point in our societal evolution.

In CEO searches, core attributes are quite carefully specified. Core attributes often include a deep business acumen. For example, we tend, although not always, to hire CEOs to lead an aircraft manufacturing firm if they have acumen about that industry. A CEO's ability to understand and manage finances is often also highly desirable. Selecting, shaping other attributes, such as the ability to take feedback constructively or the ability to form and empower teams and so on, are key aspects alongside these. We stick to a formula and rarely deviate from it.

The engine room of an organization and its control system are formed by executive leadership. These are the people who report directly to, or perhaps are one step removed from, the CEO. We recognize them as the inner sanctum of leaders. Individually, their power to shape organizations might generally be less than that of the board or the CEO, but collectively they form the template of the organization's culture.

How many times have we seen talented, purpose-driven CEOs fail in their visionary endeavours? There are countless examples in which those failures manifest from executive leadership as a collective. A CEO is one person, and although the position's footprint across the organization is both substantial and easily recognizable, the executive leaderships' collective footprint is often far greater. It is not unduly unkind to observe that both positive cultures and toxic cultures are grown organically in executive leadership. In its less attractive form, corporate politics live and breathe at executive management levels. Unhealthy internal competition is often born here, as is selfless collaboration. Executive leadership is the crucible in which corporate culture is moulded.

The fact does not go unrecognized, but it is less mindfully considered than most people would imagine. This is not unsurprising, if considered deeper. The CEO's job is often a lonely one. Sandwiched between the board and the executive leadership, the role must act as a powerful pivot that turns will into outcome. The key to manifesting outcomes is the executive leadership. Yet executive leadership is often a collective of talented and wilful people. We do not hire executive leaders because they are yes-men and yes-women, and if we do, there is a deeper issue afoot. If a CEO does the recruitment job right, the executive leadership is a diverse group of challenging, independent-thinking peers. Energizing and directing this group in an appropriate way for the business, finding the sweet spot between maintaining control and giving this team its head, is often a CEO's greatest challenge.

How is this done? Unsurprisingly, we often default to a textbook mechanism. We anchor around a business purpose, and we rely on tangible and intangible rewards. The business purpose may be an envisioned outcome. In a capitalist, market-driven setting the outcome might be vested in financial outcomes and share value, underpinned by consumer alignment. In a government setting the outcome might be vested in visible milestones within society. Rewards might be remuneration, bonuses, career advancement, keeping your job and the like. While every organization is different, we – perfectly logically – link vision to outcomes to rewards in some way. But organisational DNA is broadly similar, in that we think, act and reward our employees within the microcosm of the organization's boundaries.

Executive leadership sets a tone, and a tempo, for the organization's culture. It is internally viral. Collectively, this stratum has a greater power to shape an organization than any other incumbent stratum. We lose sight of this power because, as we all know, the board can fire the CEO and the CEO can fire every one of the executive leadership. We often equate this single ability with organizational power, whereas the truth is much more multi-faceted and, therefore, vastly different. The board operates as an influential, heads-out-of-the-weeds coach; the CEO chooses priorities, and the executive leadership makes those priorities happen. The rubber hits the road right here. If we wish to change the way businesses work for the greater benefit of society (or, at the very least, the determined avoidance of dis-benefit to society), a different set of priorities must happen at the executive leadership level.

The highly prized CEO strategy of allowing his or her people to excel while remaining their organizational servant is well known. Serving CEOs provide the support for their executive leadership, and indeed all employees and contractors, to excel in the direction chosen by the organization. This direction may be distilled from the board, synthesized in executive leadership and endorsed by the board; it may bubble up from the humblest valleys of the organization or manifest as a combination of some or all of the above. Once adopted, a CEO's genius is in allowing others to excel at delivering.

Who are these executive leadership types? They, too, spend most of their lives with family, friends and pursuits outside of the organizational context. Indeed, the most-talented executive leaders are more prone to poaching by other organizations than talented CEOs. Some may spend their careers in one organization or two, but the vast majority float from one place of work to the other, because they are in demand. They are – particularly since the last decade of the twentieth century – highly mobile creatures. Their world view is shaped by events and experiences outside of the organization, from within the stakeholder-centric world in which we all live.

Yet the tenure of the average senior executive in an organization may be several years longer than the tenure of the average CEO. Add to this the fact that, by definition, there are far more senior executives in an organization than the sole CEO and we might conclude that the culture of an organization might have more collateral in boards and the executive leadership than in CEOs. Why then are executive team members so much less visible in culture than CEOs? Much like the band and the lead singer, we the stakeholders invest in the presence of the chief vocalist, the front person. We are more likely to remember Mick Jagger than we are the drummer, bassist or songwriter. Yet any CEO worth their mettle will tell you, unequivocally, that they can do nothing without their executive leadership team, while the same might not be said of most rock bands! We, as stakeholders, and especially investors, would do well to heed the words of those CEOs.

The sheer weight of numbers will mean that for every aspiring CEO who makes it to that role by virtue of marginally more talent (relative to the needs of the organization for that time), there will be 10 to 15 aspiring CEOs that become a member of an executive leadership team. The pool of talent that congregates into that team has 10 to 15 times as much inherent firepower as the one person who ascends to the CEO role. In organizations, there is not enough weight given to this equation. In reshaping organizational culture towards a better balance of business performance and concurrent societal value, it is – in terms of available cultural leverage – preferable to work with an executive leadership cohort (including the CEO) than a single CEO. But also given the option of working towards reshaping the organizational culture with the CEO alone, or with the executive leadership minus the CEO, there is more value in taking the latter proposition and 'catching up' the CEO at a later date. Assuming each member of the executive leadership works 50 hours a week – with apologies to those who clock in 60 or 80 hours – the combined team has some 10 times more engagement time and possibly 10 to 100 times more engagement touch-points within an organization than the average CEO. There is simply more latent cultural leverage there. It is a learned behaviour that we think otherwise and look to the CEO, almost exclusively, for transformative outcomes. We forget that without the band, it is just average karaoke.

22

The Organization

When leaders refer to organizational culture, there is frequently a sense of mystery to its form. The vocabulary used to explain culture can often be vague, conveying a sense of intangibility. Yet culture is perceived quite tangibly by those immersed in it. We surmise a great deal about organizational culture from what happens around us, and what does not happen around us. We can compare and contrast the cultures of different organizations, and we can quickly form reasonably accurate, high-level views of prevalent culture without much mindful effort. The reality is that culture has definite shapes, colours and textures, and they can be described. The sense of mystery associated with culture relates more to its ability to change, seemingly effortlessly, like a chameleon among its surrounds. It is the same sense of mystery that is associated with, for example, the shape of a rock in a stream. It has been worn to a shape by the stream flowing around it. Science can quite readily predict the shape that the rock would take if furnished with a few details such as the flow dynamics of the stream and the materials that the rock is made of. The mystery of the rock in the stream can be explained by simply breaking down the forces that have shaped it. In that way culture, while clearly more ethereal than rocks and water, is not that different.

The concept of culture has been around for a very long time. It means many things to many people, as it should. We may like or dislike a culture, or we may be neutral, or something in between, or our feelings may vary from issue to issue. Each person may have a different sense of energy from culture; it may feel empowering to one person and disempowering to another. Some cultures work for some people and not for others. There is no 'right' culture, but there are plenty of unethical, unhelpful or unhealthy attributes that can culminate in a bad overall culture. How can leaders better process the characteristics of the culture they wish to include, and those that they wish to exclude, from the way their organization works?

Setting culture in an organization requires mindfulness. There is a great deal that must be done in both talking and walking a culture. But before that, culture must be crafted. It requires an architecture within which governance can work effectively. The shapes, colours and textures of culture can, and should, be created with strategic intent. During the latter part of the twentieth century and into the twenty-first century, the spectacular failures of governance in organizations were attributed, more and more, to culture. The role of leadership in building and protecting a culture has been increasingly highlighted in policy, governance and regulatory reviews of organizations. Terms like 'toxic culture' have been used to describe organizations that have shown systemic and alarming failures of ethics and duty of care. We have moved on from thinking of culture as a happy (or unhappy) coincidence of environmental factors that were simply present. Now, we have come to recognize that culture is something that, despite the vast number of factors that push and pull at its shape, can be deliberately designed and built. It can be shaped, deconstructed, rebuilt, nuanced and emphasized in places. Culture can change the people that work within its environs and vice versa. It is co-created by the very people that work within it, formed from the values, beliefs, behaviours and interactions that are within, around and between those people. Those people, in turn, spend most of their time living their lives outside of that culture, in a world where they are among the 7 billion and counting stakeholders, each with their own needs, wants and agendas.

In a stakeholder-centric world, an organizational culture that adapts to, meets and keeps pace with its stakeholder priorities is, by definition, the one that serves its stakeholders best. Within a societal ecosystem, this ability bodes well for the long-term sustainability of the organization; its likelihood of surviving and thriving as society evolves is much greater than an organization that does not have that ability.

This elasticity of culture is important because, for leadership, the task of developing a culture is immense. But as times change, so does the requisite culture. It is time- and energy-consuming (and wasteful) to re-set culture periodically. The ability for culture to shift in tune with societal values and expectations can, to a large extent, diminish the angst associated with 'changing the culture' as times change. Culture, therefore, is at its best when it is both the right one for the time and has the inbuilt DNA to change at or greater than an evolutionary pace with its external environment.

This ability begins with a willingness to listen, and empathize, with stakeholder concerns. It is essential when considering the needs of the time, and when considering the changing needs with time. Many organizations mindfully do the first and leave the second until the gap between the culture that is in place and the culture that is needed becomes large enough to spend the time and effort upon. This creates a 'catch up' culture, which is much less nimble than an 'anticipate' culture and accesses less of the strategic value that the latter brings. This strategic value coalesces around innovative behaviours, first-mover advantages and reputational currency. However, it should be recognized that 'fast follower' cultures – the ones that nip on the heels of the leaders – access much of the value of 'anticipate' cultures, with perhaps exposure to less of the risk.

'Catch up' cultures can slip backwards quickly if they are not nimble enough. Cultures that are sluggish or strong-but-rigid carry with them the risk of being the opposite of listening cultures. Their rigidity makes them less stakeholder-centric, which in turn effectively stamps a use-by date into their DNA.

There are several characteristics that, when evident in the governance of culture, go a long way towards aligning the people in an organization. People in an organization are, as the term implies, organized into groups in at least two dimensions – functional or delivery lines and the amount of accountability they carry. The first has much to do with the flow of activities that converge to a specific delivery of the organizational purpose. The second cedes greater accountability to fewer people, is synonymous with pyramid structures of power and influence and is the concept that we generally equate with leadership strata. In general, the higher the leadership stratum, the greater the breadth of accountability.

When referring to people in an organizational context, it is often useful to consider leadership in its own specific light, as well as the organization as a whole. How leadership is defined is specific to the organization and the context in which it operates. The 1 to 2 per cent of people in an organization or department that collectively leverages the remainder in meeting the organizational or departmental purpose makes for a reasonable first approximation of what is meant by 'leadership' in a structural sense. Placing leadership under its own microscope is important because the culture of an entire organization has very little chance of working as designed if the leadership of an organization does not, individually, collectively and consistently, exhibit the hallmarks of the culture. The majority of the success factors for organizational culture rest in this stratum, comprising the board, the CEO, executive leadership and the next one or two layers of operational leadership.

Three aspects of architecture that ground an organizational culture in broad societal relevance are a set of values that define internal good and bad, an internal way of making decisions that consistently navigate areas of grey and an authentic connection of these to external stakeholders. Let us refer to them as values, decisions and connections, and consider them one at a time.

Most organizations have a set of values that are formalized into a code of ethics or company charter. They are chosen from a vast array of values that could be selected. Their choice and their wording are at their most powerful when they capture two things: internal authenticity and stakeholder expectations. The set of values is rarely exhaustive. A few are chosen. The values are, much more often than not, positive outwardly expressed narrations of the negative characteristics we would like to avoid in an organizational context. They are seldom uplifting, even if they are positive. Often, they signal the darker corners of human work behaviours that are best avoided for the health and sustainability of the organization. For example, the value of treating everyone with respect is a positive expression of the toxic organizational traits that are wished to be avoided – disrespect, harassment and bullying, for example. The value of embracing diversity is a positive expression that captures the blights of discrimination, whether in the form of unconscious biases, conscious discriminative behaviour or systemic disadvantage.

A useful way of thinking about values is a bit like a uniform. Consider an industrial uniform, perhaps some steel-capped boots, dark pants with reflective stripes, a blue fire-retardant shirt, safety helmet, safety goggles and hearing protection. They capture a sense of belonging and some minimum aspects of safety, but they are not, in and of themselves, informative about how we do our work. We might recognize a fellow employee from the uniform but not necessarily know or understand what they do in the organization, how they fulfil their purpose or how they contribute to the integrity and prosperity of the organization. They do, however, convey a sense of belonging.

Values are more than a uniform, of course, but their reach should not be overstated. They are important, even essential, to building culture, but they are very much a simple, foundational aspect of culture. Values are binary. We either espouse them or we do not. We cannot aspire to be slightly discriminatory under the values-based construct; we are either discriminating against others or not. We cannot only slightly bully and harass; we either tolerate it or do not. Greyness in values is an ethically dangerous concept because the elasticity of boundaries can be both high and insidious in nature, causing foundational organizational characteristics to change fundamentally.

As a result, values are usually set to be non-negotiable and non-hierarchical. For example, if values are set around safety, human rights, bribery and bullying, they are all assumed to be equally valid. If they were not all equally valid, then it could be assumed that trade-offs can be made between values, which in turn would then undermine the effectiveness of these values.

Depth of culture is found in decisions. How we navigate the complexities of decisions in an organization is a much more potent indicator of culture because it involves many trade-offs. Decisions involve conundrums; if they did not, decision-making would be both easy and obvious. The way we formulate and validate trade-offs is a deep and insightful perspective on organizational culture. If values form a boundary around our permissible behaviours, decisions describe how we function within those boundaries.

Ethical expectations by most stakeholders would be that organizational decisions are made that are both good and right. The concept of good and right is a classical ethical construct, describing beneficial outcomes of an action as well as morally obligatory actions. However, stakeholders are neither clear nor particularly vocal in their emphasis on good and right. Stakeholders are generally unified in expectations that organizational decisions are not *bad* and *wrong*, somewhat disapproving of organizational decisions that are either bad and right or good and wrong and somewhat ambiguous around what is good and right. The grey area is huge.

The quandary this presents is significant. As we strive for a greater diversity of thought and perspective in the organization's pursuit of creativity and innovation, decision-making and trade-offs are destined to encompass a wider universe of possibility. This is a good thing because it is a trademark of wiser and more holistic decisions, but it also stretches the envelope within which trade-offs are made. Decisions that might have previously embraced 10 possible outcomes may now corral 100 combinations of trade-offs. As this universe expands, organizations seeking to juggle these permutations and arrive at outcomes that are both good and right are likely to be increasingly challenged by the sheer ambiguity of it all.

While paddling in this vast pool of ambiguity in how decisions are arrived at, it is presumptuous of leadership to assume that there is a clear culture at play. In order to empower a workforce to make decisions that are aligned with a mindful culture, it is necessary for a hierarchy of principles to be applied. Principles that – through both their content and hierarchy – provide signposts to good and right decisions go a long way towards filling cultural voids. Principles in the English language, such as 'i before e, except after c' solve the majority of spelling conundrums that appear. Mathematical principles such as 'the order of operations' that are taught in junior school allow us to navigate all of the arithmetical problems we are ever likely to encounter in our lives, even though we cannot foresee all of the *specific* arithmetical problems we might come across.

It would be optimistic to assume that any such set of hierarchical principles would work for all decisions that are required to be made by people in the organization. However, principles that help people make decisions go a long way towards providing the DNA of culture. It is not trivial to code such principles into an organization's DNA – the process can take months or years – but it is a powerful touchstone for culture.

There is sometimes a deep reluctance to commit to such a hierarchy of principles. The preference of leadership in many organisations is to keep its options open, so that decisions maximise their ability to be fit for purpose at the time they are needed.

Lastly there is connection. It is impossible to form boundaries around values and constrain decisions to principles in the real world because there are simply too many permutations and combinations. Our cultural rulebook would need to resemble some complex computer code, specifying every variance and sub-variance of circumstances, and the list would be endless. And even using the most complex of computer code, the world changes every day; and so new circumstances will arise. Circumstances that did not exist yesterday – such as autonomous vehicles – will exist tomorrow. We would have to update our rulebook every day.

And to we turn to connection to give us consistency. We try to apply the principles of decision to different aspects of our organization, using the collaboration of people to constantly update our understanding and application of those principles. We create an open dialogue in how we use the principles of decision; we challenge each other and offer different perspectives. We bring together this melting pot of thought to help co-create our culture. In order to do this well, of course, we need to tear down walls in our organization, or better yet, stop them from being built. But of course, in the real world, just like our history of keeping business and society apart, we have probably built walls over time. They have shaped, and reshaped, with the influence of various leaders, and they have changed texture and colour with the influx and turnover of staff from other organizations.

Of the three, values are used the most frequently in organizations around the world. They can be readily found on websites and in annual reports. How decisions are made is generally less structured. There are presumed benefits to maintaining optionality. If external circumstances change, it feels operationally advantageous to change how decisions are made – although the folly of doing so is clear. And connection is even more rarely used because comparing notes on ethical decisions can make us feel both vulnerable and confronted. More so because rarely, in ethical decision-making, is there one single 'right' answer, although there are very often many wrong answers.

To form and evolve culture in an organization, particularly one in which there is a desire to balance, in a stakeholder-centric way, business performance with social performance, the three attributes – values that support that balance, a decision-making framework that allows societal needs to be factored in appropriately, and connections across the business that support organizational growth and maturity in such decision-making – must be present. Importantly, they must be lived in the ranks of leadership – the board, executive leadership and below – consistently, courageously and visibly.

23

Language

Each of us knows at least a handful of jokes about corporate-speak and buzzword bingo. Organizations thrive on a certain type of language that others in society find bewildering, and sometimes comical. The true masters of the acronyms are probably the armed forces, which create, use and dispose of acronyms at such a rate that your tenure in service can be accurately defined by which ones you are familiar with. Corporations and businesses use them prolifically. Through the use of language, organizations communicate quickly and efficiently about the common parameters of organizational process and success. Perhaps the language also serves to impress upon themselves, and others, that there is serious business afoot. Three-letter-acronyms, or (ironically) TLAs, are used as a rapid-fire shorthand. If you know them, you're probably a proper corporate player. If you don't, then you're a novice or an outsider. We use them to define who's who: the CEO, the CFO, the CIO, the CSO, the CRO, the CMO and the COO. We use them to define key parameters: the KRA, the KPI, the ROI, the NPV, the IRR and many others. We use them to define relationships: B2B, B2C, C2C, B2G and so on. We use them to define processes: FID, COD, IPO, BPC and EPC. And of course there are two-letter, four-letter and five-letter acronyms galore in the organizational dictionary.

Over the decades, organizations have built their own lexicon with which to convey concepts, ideas, activities, facts and results. It is a normal cultural evolution – this search for language that binds common purposes, common ideals and a common way of thinking and behaving. It is notable that few, if any, of our commonly used organizational acronyms refer to societal impacts or welfare. It is true that some have been created – EIA, SIA, RAP, BAP and SDG, for example – but they are more often used in specialist fringes of the corporations and organizations that contribute to economic activity and progress, and less often known by the majority of organizational employees.

Language, we know, is important. It can be used to include, and exclude, people from social processes and from organizational processes. It is code. Not necessarily in a secretive way but in an intentionally meaningful way. Paying special attention to language brings a range of insights that we would otherwise miss, despite their overwhelming prevalence in our day-to-day activities. Observing and responding as a leader to the organizational language that is commonly used is a powerful way to make changes in subtle but enduring ways.

The leader that uses KPI far more frequently than SIA (for those who are unsure, these are Key Performance Indicator and Social Impact Assessment, respectively) is, whether she likes it or not, sending a powerful subliminal signal. Of course, that leader's role might (classically) have leaned towards KPIs more often and with more focus than SIAs, but the use of language can extend or truncate our organisational voice. Language is powerful because of its power to both include and exclude. It is tempting to consider only its inclusive properties, but its exclusion effects can be equally potent. Consider the simple use of pronouns and the subtle but powerful undercurrents they can create in the context of gender. The use of 'he' or 'she' can deliver both intended and unintended messages. Within the corporate world, this basic use of language has changed, and continues to change, to signal both conscious and unconscious intents around inclusion and the avoidance of exclusion.

If we wish to shift organizations from the myopia of their narrower focuses to wider, more inclusive considerations, language is important. Note that we are talking about organizations and not just leaders. We do not want the second prize of leaders who drive their organizations in a better direction. We want the first prize for organizations that are innately wired to go in those directions. We want the power of one hundred, one thousand, ten thousand or a hundred thousand employees thinking, seeking, innovating, doing and succeeding in a more self-energized form.

But let's start with you. What is the language you display every day? What signals do you send to those that look to you for cues? They are looking for a broadband of cues, from the specific to the general, from the polarities to the balances, from the consistencies to the inconsistencies. How does your language map to the broadband? It starts in your own head, in the non-verbal language that you use to process your thoughts. What are your focuses and your defaults? Do you think of profits and margins, or do you think of purpose and impact? Do you think of them both concurrently, and if you do, which thoughts are louder? Why? Do you respond in your inner language to current external stimuli (like shareholders on the phone demanding returns) or to your historical experiences, and what is the balance of effect that they each have on you?

My working life, probably much like yours, has included exposures to many leaders. Some exposures were in the context of my role as a follower of their leadership, others as observers of their leadership, others in peer relationships and others reporting to me but taking accountability for their own arena of leadership. Cast your mind through the many dozens you may have developed some insight to. Which ones did you feel were 'faking it' in matters of social welfare? Which ones did you feel were disengaged and not even bothering to fake it? Which ones did you genuinely feel were authentically invested? The chances are that you, like me, can tell one type of leader from the other. You may not have a dossier of proof, but your instinct is powerful enough to enlighten you. Agreed, it may occasionally be wrong too, but you may find – as I do – that it tends to be right.

The reason is, of course, that if a person's actions do not begin with an authentic thought, the resulting dissonances are eventually sensed by others holds true. 'Eventually', in this context, is a function of the frequency and intensity of personal interaction. The more frequent and intense personal interactions are, the quicker 'eventually' becomes. Between a CEO and her executive team, for example, frequency and intensity are both typically high. Between a CEO and her customer service representative at the call centre, frequency and intensity are low. Thus dissonances pass from CEO to the executive team readily, where they are individually processed. If the processing results in a pass-through of dissonances ('she says she wants to squash all human rights infractions in our supply chain but means something less'), they progress through from the executive team member to senior management, from senior management to middle management and so on. None of this is, of course, new information, but it is astonishing how easily we forget its potency.

Some leaders may be more adept than others at internally running one line of thinking and externally miming another, but such skill rarely passes the tests of time and performance. We eventually sense it, and the organization becomes tainted with that sense.

So as a leader, being aware of your internal thought processes and your values is vital to the journey you might wish to take your organization on. We would be naïve if we thought that all leaders who espoused the safety of their employees had thoughts firmly anchored in the sanctity of human life, health and welfare, but it would be marvellous if we could. If indeed organizations were able to make such recruitments as a matter of course, we would not need so many laws and regulations governing a CEO's and the board's duty of care around employee safety. So, too, we are all aware of leaders who demonstrate misogynistic traits but champion gender diversity and equality in the workplace. The advent of the sexual-harassment Me Too movement, which sparked to life as early as 2006 but then took off in 2017, sent shockwaves through the organizational world. More tellingly, it caused a palpable undercurrent of discomfort throughout the working world, because there was an underlying self-acknowledgement among many (predominantly male) executives that their thoughts, subtle deeds and not-so-subtle deeds could be exposed in the glaring light of public inspection. In our carbon-conscious world, we are aware of leaders who stand up vigorously for climate action but possess two or more fossil-fuelled vehicles. It is a fact of life that corporate pantomimes are played out every day, but it need not be a fact of life that we bury our own heads in the sand and ignore that something is amiss.

In acknowledging this, the intention in this narrative is not to call foul but rather to call our very human shortfalls and, more productively, to encourage a quiet and private addressing of them. Our thoughts are our own, can remain safely internalized and – in the magical power of our own consciousness – can be influenced by ourselves. But that will to influence will not begin until we acknowledge the dissonance to ourselves.

The call to action starts here. It begins in the quiet of one's own mind, with clarifying our private narrative. At the beginning of this book, stakeholders and trends were considered. These factors, and others like them, drawn from a diversity of opinions from around the world, should enhance the fertility of our own minds. Some of those factors may not resonate with our lived experiences, while others may. We may find ourselves drawn to issues of gender diversity but lukewarm on issues of water security. But in the quiet of our own minds, in the organizational language that has its roots in our thoughts, we ought to seek our own clarity. The call to action encourages consideration of the United Nations' Sustainable Development Goals, a useful list that catalogues the areas of most impact for humanity as a whole. Some of these areas may sit closely to our organizational activities; others may not. The point is there are many areas of personal and organizational endeavour that contribute to a better society, and most people are likely to find their care factor vested in a couple of those areas. There is no correct list to develop in your mind; there is rather a grounded sense of care for some of the aspects of humanity, with the grounding strong enough to reject any dissonance between thought and action in your organizational leadership.

Encourage this mindset because it grows. Care factors beget care factors. Passion for linking organizational success to societal well-being grows. The compounding effect is powerful when it manifests in leaders of organizations. You may start with modern slavery, move on to climate change and then address education for young girls in developing economies; whatever your pathway, it is a progressive one because it grows in scope for society.

Cultivate this mindset because it is far more powerful and engaging leadership style than picking the issue of the hour simply because it is topical, or because it would be unseemly not to, or because it has PR weightiness to it. As a leader, look for the things that matter to you, because you will grow the power of authentic passion and that, in turn, will ignite organizations. Then your language will be compelling. You will use terms and acronyms associated with your chosen passion, and they will spread in your organization because you make them popular by uttering them frequently. Whether you are on the board, the CEO, in the executive leadership group, a senior or mid-level manager, a supervisor, a graduate or an apprentice, your language will be compelling. And of course, the more your leadership is legitimized in the organizational structure (for example, because you are the CEO, the CFO, the company secretary or indeed, a role-bearer of significance to others), the more status your compelling language carries and the more viral that language becomes. The less you will require speaking notes from the communication team, the more you will say what you mean and the more impact that will create in your organization.

Choosing powerful language will engage the organization behind your vision if your authenticity is not in question. As with all employee engagement, the why is key. As discussed in previous chapters, few employees would be fundamentally against the ideal of a better society – one with a less compromised natural environment, more equitable outcomes in communities, greater safety and security, and a more predictable future for children. Platitudes such as 'it's the right thing' have been used so often and for so long that they have become clichéd. The why should be related to recognizable values. 'Right' is too subjective (and it is a coverall word) to resonate.

While the why behind addressing climate change, or poverty, or water security is broadly understandable, it is also important to capture in the language of the company why *this* organization is engaging in *this* issue, as distinct from the many other issues that have similar merit. Relevance allows the lexicon of the organization to grow, and for the language to enrich and spread. Context allows a deeper and more engaging interpretation of intent and of the value of the effort being applied, which in turn energizes thought and innovation rather than merely following directions.

For many years, companies struggled to acknowledge and act on climate change (and many still do). Part of the reason may well have been that there were too many climate sceptics to allow a groundswell of support to build within many organizations. However, it was more likely that leadership on the issue did not resonate. Firstly, corporate leaders may have been addressing climate change mainly because investors were requiring some attention to it. The same corporate leaders were silent on fossil fuel use, used recycled language on the dangers of climate change, behaved no differently in their consumption practices to climate sceptics and were fuzzy on why *this* organization would engage in *this* issue. Even if they were clear on the latter, the conviction displayed did not match the gravity of the why portrayed. In the one breath, leaders would forewarn of incredible shocks to the planet's ecosystem from the effects of climate change and commit to tepidly incremental 5 per cent changes. In the same strategy leaders would use accounting techniques to improve their carbon abatement numbers, a tactic that fatally wounded any authenticity that had gone before. It is hardly surprising that nearly two decades of this leadership language – compelling though it sounded in bite-sized pieces – failed to energize organizations to innovate and change at scale. It failed to ignite passions in others. How many of the hundreds of millions of employees across the globe working under leaders taking the helm against climate change altered their own consumer habits to transform the world beyond the boundaries of their own organization? The answer is, of course, very few – an indictment of middling, rather than transformative, leadership. Despite a widespread leadership focus applied to an issue that had global significance and planetary-level impacts, we – individually and collectively – pursued small gains within the boundaries of our own organizations. The language of leaders was insufficient to ignite enthusiasm beyond our 9-to-5 responsibilities despite addressing a problem that transcended the workplace and affected the very fabric of our lives, and those of our children.

Such missed opportunities must be learned from because we cannot perennially miss them. We cannot squander second, third and fourth chances because the number of chances available to us as a society on many of our challenges is finite. In many cases, we have already run out of chances.

The calibre of leadership applied in the corporate world to the societal challenges of today must be lifted to a level where leaders believe in what they are doing. That authentic belief must be forged into language that engages and avoids dissonance. Authentic and resonant language, backed by visible commitment, has a much greater chance of engaging employees to passionately tackle the issue placed in the frame by leaders.

But language, powerful though it is when founded on authentic drivers, is not by itself sufficient to create change in the way organizations think about, and act on, their ability to enhance society. More tangible things are needed.

24

Habits

If language helps communicate culture, habits help form it. Consider, for example, industrial safety. At a time when industrial safety was becoming increasingly problematic for organizations around the world, it was recognized that something was missing – an ingredient without which all the words and all the industrial safety processes in place would not bridge the gap that was needed. This was a safety culture. In its practical form, it was merely the habit of paying attention to safety risks before engaging with tasks that involved those risks. Human behaviour needed a kind of muscle memory to switch on the act of proactively paying attention to safety risks.

In the early part of the twenty-first century – some decades after industrial safety had been elevated to board-level concerns – safety psychologists identified that a simple habit, once cultivated, helped put safety concerns at the front of peoples' minds before they engaged in tasks. Different organizations coined different names for this – 'toolbox talks', 'Take 5' and 'safety moments' all tried to activate this habit of pausing to talk about safety issues. In pursuing this safety culture in an organization, this habit was cultivated by everyone, everywhere within the businesses. Whether you operated heavy machinery or ran spreadsheets, meetings to discuss the work at hand began with these habit-forming sessions.

There was considerable sheepishness when the process began in organizations. While it made perfect sense to many for forklift operators and power line inspectors to discuss the hazards they might face during their shift, it felt trite to many for accountants and call centre operators (for example) to discuss hazards before their relatively hazard-free shifts. Safety psychologists disagreed that it was trite, for three reasons. One, they reasoned, it was fundamentally oxymoronic to address the safety culture of an organization by only addressing it in part of an organization.

Secondly, and more compellingly, to do so created two systems of awareness and, subsequently, two divisively different safety cultures within an organization – one for personnel that faced more risk and one for personnel that faced less risk. Three, and much more pragmatically, they pointed out that the safety of the forklift operators (for example) depended to some extent on the safety awareness of the accountants (for example). Why? Because, as an example, some forklift operator accidents may be caused by inadequate preventative maintenance schedules or the ordering of substandard (read 'cheaper') parts, which may be managed by accountants. Connectivity and culture formed a resonant force.

It was pointed out that it was probably a large and somewhat unproductive task to track all of the interrelationships between departments in the organization and identify those departments that had absolutely no bearing on safety risk, and then excise them from the process. The unproductive task would only need to be repeated each time there was an organizational shuffle.

In short, implementing a safety culture relied on participation. The more participation, the more organizational DNA was created.

And so, groups of accountants would start meetings with a safety moment. They would bring up a safety issue at work if possible. But if not (and in a hazard-benign environment one might often struggle to identify a bonafide safety issue), they might talk about a safety issue at home, or on the way to work, or one they had heard about. In fact, anything went.

Did it make accountants safer? No one knows, and no one felt compelled to find out, because that was not the intention at all. The intention was to shift safety culture uniformly in a certain direction. That shift was to apply to everyone because of the organizational connectedness.

The lesson, adopted far and wide around the globe, was consistent in its message. If you wanted to influence culture, introduce habits for everyone.

Shared responsibility and accountability then underpinned homogeneous shifts in safety culture. In the years to come, organizations followed this up with safety incentives such as bonuses for everyone. These bonuses could be lost by everyone if one person, or one department, incurred safety incidents that caused the organization to breach its safety target. Why was this done? It was to give everyone a piece of ownership for everyone's safety.

The habit cultivated in this example was hardly earth-shattering. It was merely a habit to practise mindfulness about safety. Nor was it fool proof.

In a meeting of ten people, one person could talk about a safety issue at home, two people could listen, and seven could be daydreaming about last night's reality TV show cliffhanger. But of course, it was not intended to be fool proof, or even to remotely approach such an ideal. It was purported that an organization that did not have such a habit would likely make more errors of safety judgement than an organization that had such a habit in place. There were no control samples with which to test this hypothesis, no controlled experiments to validate whether such an action did indeed result in fewer safety incidents. We all know that the more mindfully we do something, the less prone to accidents we are.

A parallel question could be applied to the concept of fulfilling the organization's purpose – let us say it is to manufacture screens for cell phones – while preserving value for society (or adding value to society) by considering social and environmental factors. What habits can be cultivated to increase the level of mindfulness to progressing or achieving this balance?

In 2014, one of the largest mining companies in the world was exploring and developing mineral opportunities in some remote parts of the world. In many of their sites, they were encountering vulnerable indigenous tribes. The vulnerabilities of some indigenous groups were numerous, from susceptibility to new infectious diseases to introduced alcoholism, to physical and economic displacement. There were significant existing gaps too in education, in sanitation, in water supply and in health. The mining company typically deployed exploration and advance engineering crews to these sites for months or years at a time. As prospects improved and it appeared that the mineral reserves had economic value, these forays into these remote areas would convert to large operating mine sites, accompanied by significant infrastructure works.

The board of the organization recognized that the vulnerability of indigenous people to this kind of activity was high. It was relatively easy for employees and contractors to carelessly or irresponsibly infringe on the basic human rights of the indigenous groups. Many of these countries had poor regulatory controls to prevent such infringements, so that line of defence did not always exist or was not always enforced to appropriate standards. The board insisted that the culture of the company be shaped to pay attention to risks of infringing on basic human rights.

Executive management responded with a strategy to increase mindfulness via a simple habit. Before each exploration operation or mineral sampling operation, a mandatory review of human rights vulnerabilities was to be undertaken. Focused questions were to be asked. What damage could be caused inadvertently? How might that be mitigated? Was the mitigation sufficient in the eyes of project teams? What could be done better? This habit was to be practised prior to mobilizing crews into an area.

Within two years, this habit had become more sophisticated and had embedded itself in the organization. People no longer had to be reminded that it was mandatory. It had become part of a reflexive process, a habit. It became second nature to drilling operatives who had, a mere 24 months ago, scoffed at the idea of such mollycoddling ways. Not only were human rights infringements considered and consistent efforts applied to avert them, but the culture had expanded to seeking, and implementing, initiatives to improve health, education, water supply and sanitation. What was particularly notable was that the scope of the habit spread without interference from the head office. A second nature of caring about the welfare of indigenous people had been forged from an initial project to habitually think about it before sending large dozers in.

Yet while culture shifts the normal distribution of an organization's thinking, it does not insulate against outlier thinking among its ranks, and it does not supersede leadership discipline to hold the line. In 2020, another global mining company purporting to have exactly the same culture and habits in place destroyed an area of foundational indigenous significance, causing investors and employees to express global shock and outrage and governments to review the company's and its leaders' social license to operate.

Leaders who seed good habits within the organization may be surprised at the life these habits take for themselves. And yet, it is hardly surprising that this would occur, if we assume for a moment that a good proportion of human beings are predisposed to being decent. As leaders, we should seek ways in which to bring this out. A good purpose (for example, protect the welfare of indigenous people) does not need much over-selling. Provided there is an authentic leadership desire to achieve that good purpose, permission granted to spend time and energy on it, and encouragement applied to support the forming of good organizational habits that help achieve that purpose, there is little impediment to progressive action. People are not torn because the message is unequivocal – in this case, protect the welfare of indigenous people. There are no mixed messages, either overtly or covertly, that such welfare considerations should only be carried out if budgets permitted, or if time permitted. The commitment is as close to absolute as is practical.

It is at this nexus that leaders can offer permission to excel through encouraging good habits. If the first phase – the use of authenticity and language – is to signal a passion for, and commitment to, societal welfare, this second phase – creating good habits of mindfulness – empowers employees to fearlessly explore delivering on such commitments and amplifying such passions.

As we noted in the example of the safety moments, such habits may not come naturally to everyone. In a group of 10 people mindfully considering societal welfare associated with an organizational activity, some may be engaged and others may be passive riders. But the aim of this strategy is not to achieve some kind of percentage compliance of mindfulness. It is to encourage a habit that can take hold and grow in an organization, and develop a life of its own, morphing into new cultural attributes for the organization. In this petri dish for organisational culture, we are not necessarily seeking 100 per cent transformation on Day One. We are merely seeking growth and spread in culture, an increasing tide of willingness to engage in the leadership passion you have seeded.

It is important to note that in this phase we are attempting to convert passion into culture, and will into habit. We are not yet trying to solve issues. We are still in the phase of creating and harnessing energy for the ideal of doing business in a way that improves societal welfare. It is not a rules-based approach (other than mandating habits). Nor is it delivering on any particular key performance indicators. Remember, in the safety example, there was nothing expected from the habit of safety moments other than to be mindfully present in considering safety. Similarly, with the human rights example, there was nothing expected beyond the mindful consideration of the welfare of indigenous people.

Seeding these habits of mindfulness, by mandating them if necessary, is a powerful way for leaders to signal that they are looking to their employees to engage in something that is important to the organization. It is not coercive; there is no expected outcome beyond the act of engaging. These habits are an invitation to participate in your vision (even if they are mandatory). Their message is strongly 'please consider' rather than 'please perform', and because of this they are a gentle way of building a groundswell of engagement.

Of course, simply being mindful does not necessarily resolve anything. If we were to rely on mindfulness alone, consistent performance would be highly elusive. Our cultural engine might be switched on, but its steering may not operate yet. We would simply be having our employees engaging on the problem with good intent and not necessarily solving it consistently. And so we need to take habits and forge them into something more potent and bankable in achieving our aims of protecting and enhancing societal welfare.

25

Disciplines

Not that long ago – and it continues to persist in many organizations this far into the twenty-first century – we gave the responsibility of societal value-creating work (to support Millennium Development Goals, Sustainable Development Goals and philanthropy) to whomever had the time and enthusiasm for it. We did not particularly invest in growing skills in this area, or on developing organizational capacity in this area. It was not unusual for a CEO or a board member to nominate a spouse or a personal assistant with little education or training in the area to do much of the heavy lifting on societally relevant initiatives.

The observation is made not to belittle such efforts or to undermine the value of personal assistants. It is to point out that, not so long ago (and in many pockets of the business world today), organizational cultures dealt with such efforts as though they were hobbies. The weight afforded to such initiatives – in terms of capability sought – was considerably less than the consideration we might give to the selection of, say, a financial analyst, or an engineer, or legal counsel. Yet, as you might have gathered in the narrative so far, the societal problems of the world are easily on a par, in terms of complexity and degree of difficulty, with structured finance models, construction specifications or contract administration.

After the turn of the century, organizations witnessed a growth in formal roles, created specifically to address issues of corporate responsibility. More and more gravitas was afforded these activities, boards became more involved, and it became more commonplace to see board subcommittees devoted to this area of endeavour. In the 2020s, between 3 and 5 per cent of listed organizations have a specific board subcommittee (often termed a Sustainability Committee or a Corporate Responsibility Committee) that brings top leadership focus to bear. The percentage is growing steadily.

So we see resources and focuses being elevated to help businesses become a more broadly useful part of society than the wares that they sell. There are ways that leaders can lead endeavours of societal welfare better and more authentically, and use language and mindful habits to re-integrate their organizations into mainstream society. But how are these characteristics put to good use?

It is important for any organization that its reason for existence remain at the centre of its activities. How, from the many Sustainable Development Goals and their sub-targets, do organizations best choose how and where to apply their focus? How do they approach such focuses with an appropriate discipline that maintains a strong sense of relevance to the organization's stakeholders and goals?

The language and discipline of risk management has been used effectively for many years, predominantly in financial and operational arenas. Standards have evolved, the sophistication of analysis has improved and investors are increasingly relying on their view of risk to evaluate prospects. Organizations develop their own risk appetite. When their risk appetites have formed and matured, balancing the needs of their stakeholders in a way that is most appropriate for themselves, they form their own distinct risk signature. It is now reasonably easy to compare and contrast two different organizations, even operating in different areas of the market, and characterize the similarities and differences in their risk appetites. In the mid-2010s, there was an upswing in the use of risk practices to better characterize non-financial risks, and several stock exchanges began to require listed companies to use risk frameworks to inform their stakeholders (notably, investors and shareholders) of the risks they needed to manage and how they were managing such risks.

The mature processes that exist in mainstream business functions to capture, characterize and where necessary ameliorate risks to meet a company's risk appetite culminate in Board Risk Committees or Board Risk and Audit Committees. Here, at the apex of corporate accountability, there is a strong regulatory onus on a disciplined and well-informed approach to managing risk. Increasingly, shareholders are looking to risk disclosures in order to be able to make well-informed decisions about investment. So too are lenders and government regulators.

One of the more impactful ways of focusing organizational effort on the optimum selection of arenas of corporate responsibility is to map the organization's risk profile – and, in the case of SDGs, the opportunity profile – against the external setting, the internal setting and the footprint of the business. The structure of risk management is useful in directing our efforts to achieve what we want (desired outcomes) and to avoid what we don't want (material risk impacts). It is also logical and pragmatic and operates to a simple formula of progressively reducing risks by exerting controls and influences where they can be effective. Most of all, it brings discipline to how organizations can progressively improve their positive contribution to society and simultaneously reduce the risks that they pose to society.

Risk-based processes, and their outcomes, are continually subject to organizational review. This skill has been honed now for two or three decades in business and has become more sophisticated and bankable over time. There are still spectacular failures of risk management, often for a number of reasons that have little to do with the maturity of risk management processes generally and more to do with failures of governance, judgement and leadership. The tools are not blunted; the fault lies with the artisans.

For organizations looking to take more seriously the nexus between business success and societal benefit, risk management offers structure, discipline and transparency to decision-making. These are not merely decisions regarding which SDGs to back, but ones on how to set desirable outcomes and progressively achieve them in complex settings. Risk management is able to operationalize the business of contributing to society in much the same way as it has operationalized financial management, logistics management, technical and technological management and – in more recent times – industrial safety management.

Because the language of risk reminds us constantly of two aspects, why something is important (consequence) and how that something important might come undone (likelihood), organizational culture can form around a higher level of cognizance that complements and supersedes procedural and rules-based thinking. It stimulates curiosity around how our actions or inactions can contribute to failure and allows us to access a mindset of continuous development rather than a mindset of blindly complying with a process or standard. For the things that matter in society – such as our safety, well-being and economic security – this is a more engaging way to systematically and mindfully improve our organizational contribution.

Compellingly, for leaders and architects of organizational effectiveness, the task of preserving and adding value to the business ecosystem needs no new modes of operation. The language and discipline of risk are well entrenched in many organizations and continues to gain popularity across the world. This represents a streamlined means of introducing a broader definition of organizational success, without creating new methods of underpinning performance in those areas.

Also compellingly, for boards, the elevation of this intent can fall into well-used mechanisms of governance. In the same way that emerging risks around cyber security, machine learning, blockchain and other technological trends are being addressed, these emerging focuses can be incorporated into similar governance styles. They can be presented, to stakeholders, with the same transparency afforded to other – financial, market, logistical, et cetera – risks. An established process to being a societally responsible corporation, as well as to bringing greater value to society, can be used at the apex of organizational accountability.

Compellingly too, for investors, the broad range of risk issues such as climate change, labour standards in the supply chain, water access and pollution can be seen and understood in a format and language that liquidity, capital, commodity price and other risks also use. The broader aspects of risk and success that are derived from considering societal welfare more generally can be framed and communicated similarly to other, more classical risks. Investors can map these risks to the risk appetite of the organization and inform themselves more readily. Aspects such as climate change were, approaching 2020, already using risk-based foundations to further inform investors and discharge the organization's duty of care to remain transparent.

Also compellingly, for governments and regulators, the binary test – whether organizations are compliant or non-compliant with laws – can continue to be tested in regulatory processes. But it is well known that laws lag behind societal expectations, which in turn are based on acceptable and unacceptable risks. So governments and regulators can build their own confidence in the organization's approach towards changing societal norms, by considering the organization's own assessment of their risks and how they proactively approach them.

Using the discipline of risk to ensure that organizations address something as important as maintaining and enhancing their relevance to society is a logical approach. Nevertheless, there is a tendency to apply 'common sense' principles and standards-based criteria for such significant and complex issues. The concept of businesses working authentically in society's ecosystem is still caught in limbo between hobbyist approaches, on the one hand, and untrusting compliance-based rules, on the other. Neither is appropriate; one risks being too blasé and the other risks being a blunt instrument.

Risk-based approaches can help direct the habits of mindfulness about business's place in society's challenges to thoughtfully modulated and more consistently effective strategies to address them. And the more that this planet's diverse organizations apply such common and easily-understood disciplines, the more transparency can be encouraged between organizations and stakeholders. Then more strategic and far-sighted collaboration can occur. For if organizations are to make a dent in society's challenges, they will not do so individually but together, in a connected and aligned way.

26

Courage

I have been a part of, and observed, many businesses in many parts of the world grapple with balancing organizational success against societal responsibility. Experiences vary, but two characteristics are common. One is that the transition is not easy. The goalposts move, history and inherited cultures weigh heavily and create great inertia, and leadership exhibits various degrees of engagement, disengagement and even feigned engagement. The second is that the journey requires an inordinate amount of courage to begin and to stay a course.

In closing this narrative, I felt it important to focus on courage.

Courage needs a foundation of conviction. Conviction, in turn, has foundations in passion. I encourage aspiring and existing leaders to look within themselves and search their passions for society. From the many areas that society needs greater efforts from us, I encourage them to find some that move and motivate them. You are a part of this planet and its people, and a part of humanity. You are a privileged part of it, because you lead people, in organizations. Even if you do not yet have formal leadership roles, you can be a leader of thought and aspiration. You have the opportunity to harness the power of organizations – all of which have learned to apply diverse efforts to a common purpose – during your time in your profession. Before you take your own leadership roles, you can be more curious about the world and your organization's more holistically useful place in it. You can gravitate to leaders and organizations that want to make positive changes and you can throw your weight behind their efforts. As you grow into leadership roles, you can bring your greater influence to bear on people and on the organization you serve, connecting both into the business ecosystem. You can preserve the things that make our society beautiful and improve the things that would reduce risk and suffering in humanity. You can practise a new form of leadership and be the reason that relationships, that businesses, corporations and other organizations have with society transform. Your influence, over the decades of your careers and beyond, can be a part of the force that brings businesses back from societal estrangement and mistrust.

It will not be easy. But it will get easier as more aspiring leaders and existing leaders engage on a larger and more purposeful professional journey. Have the courage to speak up in your own organization about how it can be a more valuable part of society. Challenge the artificial barriers that have been built over time, separating the business world from the rest of the world. Question the partitioning of roles between government and corporations, and ask, *are we not all in this together? Might I not today work for a private business, tomorrow for a government department, and experience the same environment, education, health and climate effects no matter where I am?*

As you grow your leadership skills and apply them, have the courage to seek and lead collaboration. While every contribution is valuable, bringing positive changes to society at scale takes co-ordinated contributions. Use some of your time as a leader of your own organization to inspire leaders of other organizations to join with you. Collaborate regionally, collaborate around important societal themes, but above all, just collaborate. Share the vision, share the effort and share the societal improvements. Have the courage to share the PR and better yet eschew it completely. Ego gets in the way of greater outcomes.

Recognize both the value and the limits of philanthropy and have the courage to move beyond it. Challenge your board to evolve and progress to greater, and admittedly more difficult, aspirations. Acknowledge that writing a cheque is a simple task, that connecting your organization and its talent to society can be much more challenging and impactful; choose the path that offers a more true test of leadership.

Have the courage to think beyond budgets and to seek value. Avoid partitioning some profit aside for corporate social responsibility and merely checking in on appropriate spending patterns. Instead, seek outcomes, then apply resources to achieving them. Have the courage to be clear on what the organization should be achieving in society and the determination to consistently anchor that clarity in the top few layers of your priority list.

Find in yourself the courage to talk authentically about your passions for society and to compare notes with other leaders. It does not devalue your standing as a business warrior. On the contrary, it adds to it; it enhances your appeal as a leader and it helps propagate a greater leadership narrative.

Challenge your fellow board members, knowing that their views may have been forged by decades of classical business wisdom and knowing that your board's value lies in critically challenging yesterday's groupthink. Ask *why not* more often, and be the leader in the boardroom that society – perhaps your children and grandchildren – would wish you to be.

Above all, have the courage to think for yourself. Listen to the wisdom of those who have led before you and then question it. Question if it can be improved upon. Look around you today, look to tomorrow, and ask what kind of leader you should be. Ask what your leadership legacy should be. Ask what sort of leaders you would mentor, by your own thoughts and actions. And then move purposefully in that direction.

Index

Printed in the United States
By Bookmasters